Progress in Gestural Interaction

Springer
London
Berlin
Heidelberg
New York
Barcelona
Budapest
Hong Kong
Milan
Paris
Santa Clara
Singapore
Tokyo

Philip A. Harling and Alistair D.N. Edwards (Eds)

Progress in Gestural Interaction

Proceedings of Gesture Workshop '96, March 19th 1996, University of York, UK

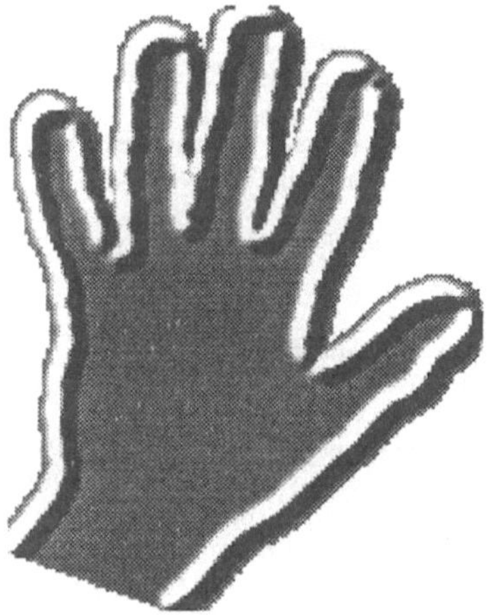

Springer

Philip A. Harling and Alistair D.N. Edwards
Department of Computer Science
University of York, York YO1 5DD, UK

ISBN-13:978-3-540-76094-8 Springer-Verlag Berlin Heidelberg New York

British Library Cataloguing in Publication Data
Progress in gestural interaction : proceedings of Gesture
Workshop '96
1.Gesture - Congresses 2.Sign Language - Congresses
I.Harling, Philip A. II.Edwards, Alistair D. N.
302.2'22
ISBN-13:978-3-540-76094-8 e-ISBN-13:978-1-4471-0943-3
DOI: 10.1007/978-1-4471-0943-3

Library of Congress Cataloging-in-Publication Data
A catalog record for this book is available from the Library of Congress

Typesetting: camera ready by editors

34/3830-543210 Printed on acid-free paper

Contents

Introduction

We would like to welcome you to the proceedings of the first Gesture Workshop. We have been surprised at the need for this workshop and have been completely overwhelmed by the number of people who have wished to take part. Originally, we thought that we would only get about 10 papers and so planned the workshop around one day. In the end, we have received 23 papers in total with 45 participants taking part.

The purpose of the Gesture Workshop was to bring together researchers working on gesture-based interfaces and gestural interaction and to provide a forum for the presentation and exchange of ideas and research currently in progress. This workshop encompassed all aspects of gestural interaction, including:

- what are gestures?
- appropriateness of gestures used in interfaces
- interactional issues
- coarticulation and the segmentation problem
- the applicability of gesture-based interaction to interfaces and applications
- suitable applications
- sign-language recognition
- focus on the techniques and algorithms used in the recognition and segmentation of manual gestures

We would like to thank everyone for making the workshop possible: for taking part and submitting their papers (mostly) on time despite the short notice of the workshop (the original call for papers only went out in November 1996).

The workshop is to be run again in 1997 in Bielefeld, Germany (see `http://www.TechFak.Uni-Bielefeld.DE/GW97/`).

Philip Harling
August 1996, York.

Towards Appearance-Based Multi-Channel Gesture Recognition

G. J. Sweeney and A. C. Downton

Department of Electronic Systems Engineering, University of Essex,
Wivenhoe Park, Colchester C04 3SQ, UK

E-mail: {irnbru, acd}@essex.ac.uk
Telephone: +44 1206 872910 Fax: +44 1206 872900

Abstract

Sign Language is a rich and expressive means of communication used by profoundly deaf people as an alternative to speech. Computer recognition of sign language represents a demanding research objective analogous to recognising continuous speech, but has many more potential applications in areas such as human body motion tracking and analysis, surveillance, video telephony, and non-invasive interfacing with virtual reality applications. In this paper, we survey those aspects of human body motion which are relevant to sign language, and outline an overall system architecture for computer vision-based sign language recognition. We then discuss the initial stages of processing required, and show how recognition of static manual and facial gestures can be used to provide the low-level features from which an integrated multi-channel dynamic gesture recognition system can be constructed.

1 Introduction

Gesture recognition as a novel input or as an assistive technology presents a classic problem for pattern recognition - mimicking what a human does. The gestures which we wish to recognise belong to the domain of sign language and in particular British Sign Language (BSL). BSL is a multi-channel gesture language: elements can appear simultaneously in the face (non-manual channel) and and in the hand action (manual channel).

Our work is concerned with both these inputs. We shall discuss gestures in the form of static posture (shape) recognition and also in the form of dynamic gestures (motion and shape). In the case of the non-manual channel, this involves the tracking and analysis of facial expressions. Finally, we shall discuss the architecture and framework of a system to combine these multi-channel gestures.

2 Human Body Motion Analysis

Recognition of Human Body motion has recently been focussed on the recovery of 3D body posture [11, 6], however, initiatives in 2D appearance-based analyses have also begun to appear, for example Pfinder [3].

When trying to recognise human activity, articulated 3D models provide the most intuitive data (analogous to that recovered by invasive systems such as the VPL Data suit) and thus are suitable for feature recognition. Gavrila [4] has recently used a multi-view approach to demonstrate gesture recognition with this type of model for whole body tracking.

For the domain of sign language, these 3D model methods have been proposed for analysis and synthesis [7] and for transmission of sign language imagery [12]. Rehg [13] has used this approach to track a hand for whole hand interaction while Ahmad [1] and Heap [10] have used 2D imagery to infer 3D knowledge for a real-time vision handtracker.

For sign language recognition, Starner [14] has demonstrated a 40 word appearance-based Hidden Markov Model (HMM) American Sign Language (ASL) recogniser using cued segmentation. The inspiration for this approach is derived from the success of HMMs in handwriting and speech recognition and uses a strict grammar to recognise sign sequences. Sagawa [8] developed a sign language translator for Composite Japanese sign language to spoken Japanese using a lexicon of 17 signs and 25 sentences constrained using a sentence level grammar to produce a word detection rate of 97.3%. However, this used instrumented gloves to recover the finger flexion.

The approach described here follows that of Starner to use cued detection to ease the localisation of the hand features and obviate any problems of varying skin tone. However, we are interested in the multi-channel output of BSL and use a cued initialisation to locate the head in the image.

Our objective is to build a small (approx. 50 sign) multi-channel recogniser and also to investigate the underlying architecture necessary to achieve successful (and) real-time recognition.

3 Overview of British Sign Language Analysis

British Sign Language (BSL) is the primary language of communication for the deaf community within Britain. Though encompassing many dialects the language is heading steadily towards a recognised standard set of signs which has been aided by the publication of the BSL dictionary [2].

Our interest in sign language is twofold. First, we wish to recognise the signs produced by a signer in a way analogous to speech recognition. Secondly, there is an interest in sign language transmission for video telephone. In this paper we discuss a computer vision appearance-based approach targeted at recovering the multi-channel output of BSL.

Sign language contains many aspects which are inherently interesting to computer vision researchers. The presence of non-rigid objects (human beings) represents a very difficult vision task for identifying and locating body parts and for tracking objects with high degrees of freedom. The allowed range of movement results in varying views of the same object and reduced visibility when objects obscure one another eg hands contacting face.

For vision research, sign language can be broken down into separable research goals of facial information processing such as lip-reading and expression analysis and body tracking for whole body posture estimation which is applicable to gait analysis and hand gesture recognition which could remove the need for flexion-based sensing systems such as those found in "Virtual Reality" (VR). The combination of these inputs for multi-modal interaction is now one of the fastest growing areas of research in the vision and VR communities.

3.1 Tracking and Recognition of Dynamic Manual Gestures

To analyse the manual content of BSL we have to be able to locate the hands in the imagery and extract a representation suitable for analysis. Our subjects have varying skin tones and, rather than use a colour normalisation approach, we have followed Starner [14] and adorned our signers with coloured gloves and used a cued segmentation scheme.

For feature representation, Starner used a bounding ellipse to represent the handshape, however, this does not provide any finger-level detail. To get finger-level detail we use Fourier Descriptors (FDs) [9], which encode the boundary of the shape as sinusoidal waveforms. For positional representation, we use a body centred co-ordinate system rather than the image co-ordinate system of [14].

3.2 Tracking Face Motion and Recognition of Facial Expressions

BSL is a multi-channel communication language which generates information in manual (hand articulation) and non-manual (facial expression) channels. To analyse the non-manual channel, the head must be located at each image in a gesture sequence and a facial expression determined before presenting it in combination with the manual channel to the recogniser.

In multi-channel signs, interference occurs between channels (and within channels) when one channel visibly obscures the other. Thus for head tracking, the head must be tracked when it is both fully visible and when the hands obscure the view. Since cued segmentation is used to determine the hand position the merging of the hands and face is easily determined since no skin tone merging occurs. Thus, it can further be determined which facial features are visible and which are not. When the visibility of facial features has been resolved recognition of the whole facial expression can be attempted, or the individual features can be labelled and processed at a higher level.

3.3 Integrating Manual and Non-Manual Gestures

For a multi-channel recognition system we require to the integrate the two separate channels through one high level combinational classifier which can generate a unique gesture label. There are many approaches to achieve this classification, for example we can combine the separate channels into one complete feature vector and use this information as training data. Alternatively, we could generate separate recognition systems for each channel which will enable them to be used as single channel systems in other applications. Finally, we could subdivide the channels into a cheremic level and train separate recognisers for each cheremic component.

Our approach is to train each channel separately and then build into a higher level recogniser the recognition of both manual and non-manual combinations of signs. The non-manual content is synchronised to the manual content so that only the facial classifications during the recognition of the manual gestures are considered.

In integrating these two channels the resolution of one plays of the other. The manual channel can extend outwards from the body and a wide field of view is required. The facial component requires a narrow field of view to secure a higher resolution to locate the features and discriminate between expressions. Therefore we use two cameras to record the channels separately.

4 Implementation of Handshape Recognition and Tracking

4.1 Static Handshape Recognition

For isolated handshapes our initial objective has been to develop a classifier which can discriminate between handshapes using the contour of the hand represented by FDs. For static handshape recognition, a constrained view of the handshape against a neutral background is considered and segmentation of the hand from the forearm at the wrist joint is performed, Figure 1.

4.1.1 Hand/forearm segmentation

Detection of the forearm entry point, Figure 1a, is performed using edge detection on the image sides. Entry points are located and a binary threshold applied, Figure 1b. A morphological erosion is performed and the boundary extracted, Figure 1c. A polygon representation of the boundary is constructed, Figure 1d, and the wrist is located by parsing the change in thickness along the contour. When a step change in thickness is detected, this is assumed to be the wrist location. The remaining points now represent the hand, Figure 1e, and we can extract the original chain code representation for further processing.

4.1.2 Hand outline classification

Classification from the hand outline was performed based on features. Firstly, the contour is represented by the harmonics of a Fourier series. This can be viewed in essence as a vector quantisation process taking vector of length T and reducing it to at most a size N.

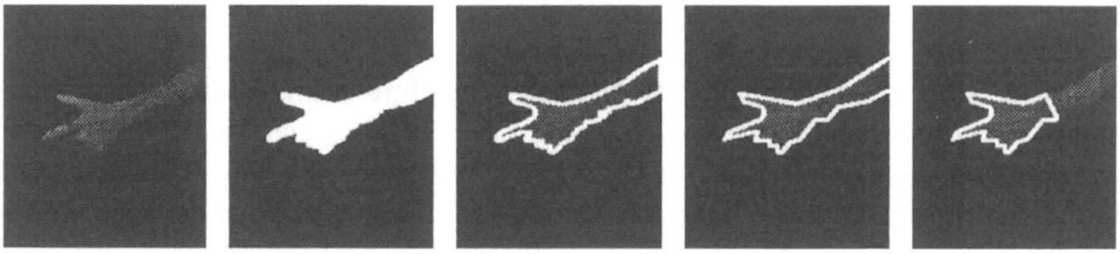

a. Original b. Binary c. Boundary d. Polygon e. Detected hand

Figure 1: Segmentation of the forearm from the hand

4.1.3 Fourier descriptor classification

The chain code is represented as a sequence of points (x_t, y_t). The x and y positions are considered separately as signals x(t) and y(t). Fourier descriptors based upon the first 25 were extracted for each x(t) and y(t) component of the boundary.

$$A_n = \frac{1}{T-1} \sum_{t-1}^{T-1} x(t) e^{jn\omega t} \tag{1}$$

$$B_n = \frac{1}{T-1} \sum_{t-1}^{T-1} y(t) e^{jn\omega t} \tag{2}$$

To achieve invariance to rotation, translation and scale, these descriptors require normalisation such that $A_n = A_n/A_1$ and $B_n = B_n/B_1$. For a singular feature vector $S_n = ((A_n)^2 + (B_n)^2)^{\frac{1}{2}}$.

The effect of harmonic expansion is shown in Figure 2.

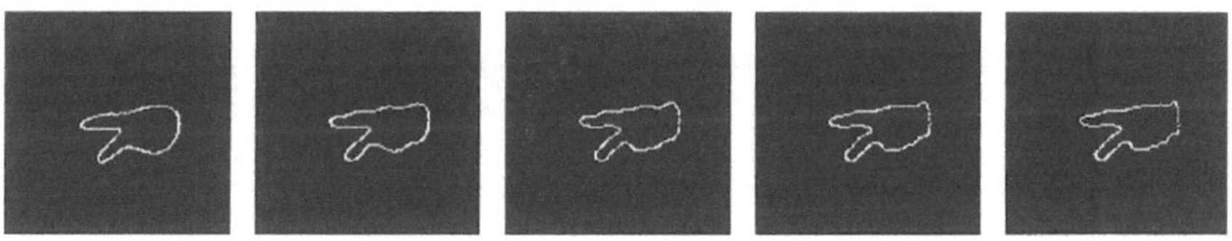

a. $n = 6$ b. $n = 12$ c. $n = 15$ d. $n = 20$ e. $n = 25$

Figure 2: Effect of harmonic expansion

4.2 Dynamic Gesture Recognition

The static case is a limited example of gesture recognition, however, the static techniques described above can be extended to handle recognition of the hand posture produced in dynamic gestures as encountered in real BSL.

4.2.1 *Feature Extraction*

Our need is for a signer-independent strategy. Therefore, *a priori* information is assumed about the capture system such as fixed camera parameters and distance from camera. This slightly constrains the appearance-based approach, but all features used in the experiments are two-dimensional in nature. It is assumed that the background is known and we thus make use of the difference image to identify the hand positions. The illumination throughout the capture period is assumed to be constant. To simplify the extraction of the hand from the background, in more general cases than those described in 4.1 we use coloured gloves [14, 5] to locate the hands and eliminate skin tone variation. Using a different coloured glove for each hand , feature extraction is performed as per Figure 3 and Figure 4.

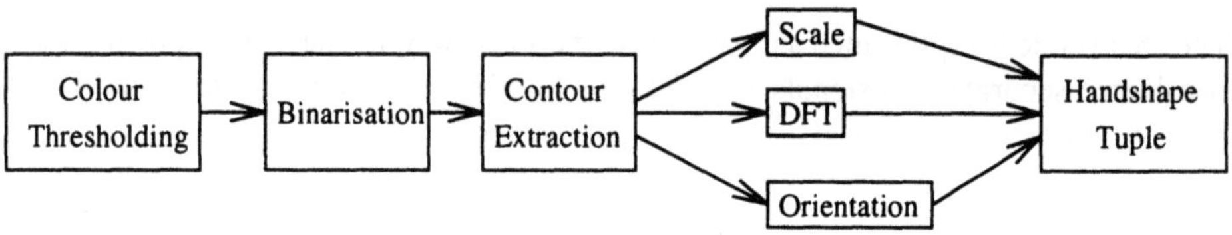

Figure 3: Feature extraction of handshape data

The handshape tuple comprises information on scale, orientation and shape. The location of the hand is represented by a body-centred co-ordinate system using the body-centre to hand-centre distance and the absolute orientation.

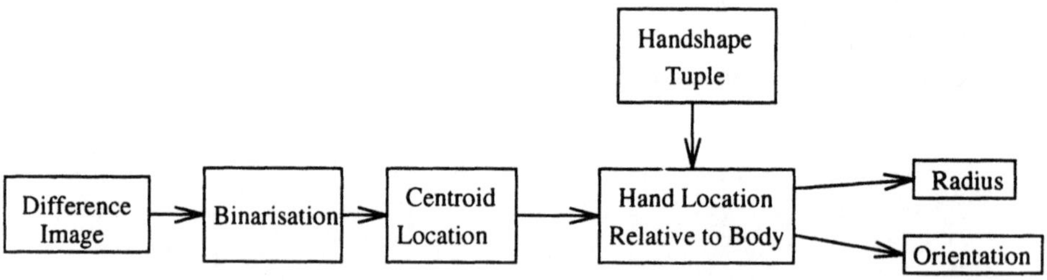

Figure 4: Feature extraction of handshape position

4.2.2 *Architecture*

Two architectures are being investigated for a small set of gestures, a general recurrent network architecture which accepts the input as a whole, i.e. the feature vector contains both hand posture and spatial movement, and a network-per-gesture system with a higher level network for which the input spans the outputs of all single-gesture networks.

4.2.3 *Continuous Recognition*

So far the architectures presented represent an isolated dynamic gesture recognition system. To recognise continuous gestures we must adopt a grammar or use contextual information. Starner [14] uses a sentence-level grammar to constrain the search to only a small domain of the lexicon. We are faced with a similar problem in that as the lexicon size grows we are required to calculate across a larger gesture base.

5 Non Manual Features

Extraction of the non-manual features produced in BSL using vision is inherently more difficult than tracking facial position and expression alone because occlusion can occur when a hand crosses the face. Analysis of the facial features has so far only been performed where occlusion has not been present. The objective is therefore to track the head under temporary and partial occlusion and determine the visibility of facial features before any analysis of these facial features can be attempted.

5.1 Head Tracking

We model the head as an ellipse so that the task of tracking is to deform the ellipse to match the size (scale) and orientation of the head. If the head is represented as a grey level function, the task is to match a template extracted from the previous image in a sequence to a single location in the new image. Therefore the task can be attempted in three ways

- Shape matching
- Grey level matching
- A hybrid of Shape matching and grey level matching

At present, the shape matching approach has been adopted, within which an image driven method allows an initial shape to distort to forces present in the image but constrained by simple rules relating the ratio of the major and minor axis.

6 Multi-channel Architecture

The combination of both manual and non-manual inputs can be considered as a hierarchical pyramid arrangement, each channel classifier feeding into a higher level combination classifier, which produces the final gesture classification.

6.1 Multi-channel feature location

The requirement for the user to wear coloured gloves should not present a continuous user with any discomfort, however, a similar solution for the location and tracking of the face would meet with user resentment for the system. Therefore, we make use of the difference image and an initialisation posture to determine the location of the head. The system is, therefore, not automatic in the initialisation phase.

To locate the head the user is requested to initialise the system by raising their hands above their head Figure 5b, the difference image is calculated from Figure 5a to leave the person Figure 5c[1]. The centre of the gloves are detected and a square box with the right hand as origin is extracted Figure 5d, the boundary is filled in to give a continuous contour Figure 5e. The chain closed chain at the topmost of the box is extracted Figure 5f and a polygon constructed Figure 5g. Parsing the angles in the polygon we select the longest running concave sequence. The pixels lying on the chain between the extreme polygon vertices are used to construct an ellipse surrounding the head Figure 5h.

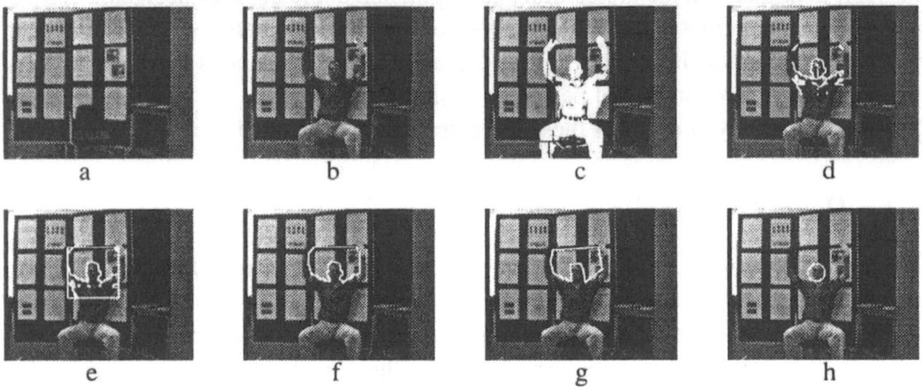

Figure 5: Semi-automatic head extraction

7 Results and Conclusions

Implementation effort has so far focussed upon bottom-up solutions to the static handshape recognition and facial expression recognition problems. Databases of handshapes and facial expressions have been collected and tested using several standard algorithms including MLP neural nets, Linear Vector Quantisation and the k-means algorithm.

For a set of 9 handshapes trained using 6 signers for each handshape, recognition rates of around 77% were achieved for signers from the training set and 72% for signers from the test set, who had not been seen before. The major limitation on recognition performance resulted from difficulties in segmenting the wrist accurately from the forearm. Similar work on recognising eye status (open or closed) from a training set of 51 eye images of 3 female subjects and a test set of 16 images from 2 male subjects, produced a correct classification rate of 62.5%.

Although these absolute recognition rates are indicative of low-level recognition performance, the overall architecture described above is intended to work not with hard

[1]Note that here the resultant difference is masked to show the relationship with the original image Figure 5b

classification results but with ranked lists of alternatives. Higher-level contextual constraints defined at each level of the architecture outlined above will then be used to improve overall performance. Work to integrate these higher-level contextual constraints is currently in progress.

References

[1] S. Ahmad. A usable real-time 3D hand tracker. In *28th Asilomar Conference on Signals, Systems and Computers*, pages 1257–1261. IEEE Computer Society Press, 1995.

[2] British Deaf Association. *Dictionary of British Sign Language/English.* Faber and Faber, 1992.

[3] C. R. Wren, A. Azarbayejani, T. Darrell, A. Pentland. Pfinder: Real-time tracking of the human body. Technical Report TR#353, Media Lab, MIT, 1995.

[4] D. M. Gavrilla and L. S. Davis. Towards 3-D model-based tracking and recognition of human movement: a multi-view approach. In *International Workshop on Automatic Face- and Gesture- Recognition*, pages 272–277, June 1995.

[5] B. Dorner. Chasing the colour glove: Visual hand tracking. Master's thesis, Simon Fraser University, June 1994.

[6] A. C. Downton and H. Drouet. Model-based image analysis for unconstrained upper-body motion. In *International Conference on Image Processing and its Applications*, pages 274–277. IEE, 1992.

[7] H. Drouet. Image analysis for model-based sign language coding. Master's thesis, Dept of ESE, University of Essex, June 1991.

[8] M. A. H. Sagawa, H. Sakou. Sign language translation using continuous DP matching. In *IAPR Workshop on Machine Vision Applications*, pages 7–9, December 1992.

[9] S. Hanlon and R. Boyle. Evaluating a Hidden Markov Model of Syntax in a text recognition system. In *BMVC*, pages 462–471, 1992.

[10] T. Heap. Robust real-time hand tracking and gesture recognition using smart snakes. Technical Report TR.95.1, Olivetti Research Limited, Cambridge, United Kingdom, February 1995.

[11] D. C. Hogg. *Interpreting images of a known moving object.* PhD thesis, University of Sussex, 1984.

[12] M. Kokuer. *Model-based Coding for Human Imagery.* PhD thesis, Dept of ESE, University of Essex, 1994.

[13] J. M. Rehg and T. Kanade. Digit eyes : Vision-based human hand tracking. Technical Report CMU-CS-93-220, School of Computer Science, Carnegie Mellon University, December 1993.

[14] T. Starner and A. Pentland. Visual recognition of American Sign Language using Hidden Markov Models. In *International Workshop on Automatic Face- and Gesture- Recognition*, June 1995.

ARGo: An Architecture for Sign Language Recognition and Interpretation

A. Braffort
LIMSI - CNRS, BP 133, 91 403 Orsay Cedex, France

E-mail: braffort@limsi.fr
Telephone: +33 1 69 85 81 21 Fax: +33 1 69 85 80 88

Abstract

This paper presents a recognition and interpretation architecture dedicated to Sign Language.

A sign is composed of several co-occurring parameters that allows several heterogeneous bits of information to be emitted simultaneously depending on the variation of one of these parameters. Sign languages vary from one country to another and each has a specific vocabulary. These signs are called conventional signs and can be listed in dictionaries. A second kind of signs is extremely frequent in sign language communications: the non-conventional signs. They are created during discourse, depending on need and context, and cannot be listed in dictionaries. Moreover, some conventional signs may have one or more variable parameters, depending on context. These signs are named Variable signs.

Sign language functioning is based on simultaneousness of information and spatial rules governing sign relationships, and the vocabulary is not completely known a priori. For these reasons, classical sequential treatments are not sufficient for sign recognition. Our architecture tries to take into account such a functioning. It is composed of recognition and interpretation modules. The first module is based on Hidden Markov Models and allows us to classify conventional, non-conventional and variable signs. In the interpretation module, a virtual scene allows to store context and to complete the meaning of variable and non-conventional signs.

Because of its ability to deal with non-conventional signs, this system can be used both for sign language and co-verbal gestures.

1 Introduction

In human communication, gesture is used to communicate information, in the same way as speech. A continuum exists in the capacity of expression, which begins with simple co-verbal gestures along with verbal speech, and ends with sign sequences, making up a sign language discourse.

Sign languages and oral languages differ a lot in their production and syntax. Hearing people have difficulty to learn sign languages and it is difficult for deaf people to learn oral languages. Design of a translation software remains a long term objective, particularly because of the technical problems in tracking all the body gestures. But presently, one can consider simpler applications such as educational software, gesture edition software, or other specific tools.

With this aim, we want to state the problem of gesture recognition and interpretation, and give a first proposal: a tool allowing to treat sign sentences.

In that follows, we present successively a brief description of Sign Language functioning, a brief review of sign recognition methods and our proposal based on two complementary modules: A HMM based Recognition module and an virtual scene based Interpretation module.

2 Sign Languages Functioning

In sign languages, syntactic and semantic levels are structured in such a way that, for the same content, the mean production duration is approximately the same in speech and in sign languages. This is done by means of syntactic spatialized relations, and frequent use of simultaneous information [4].

There are five parameters [8]: **configuration** (or hand shape), hand **location** and **orientation** with respect to the body, hand **movement**, and **face expression**. Several heterogeneous piece of information can be emitted simultaneously depending on the variation of one of these parameters.

Syntactic exploitation of these parameters takes into account the iconicity requirement of sign languages. Thus, the different parameters are specialised depending on their own nature. We present now their main functions.

2.1 Sign Language parameters

Among the five parameters, we will deal only with hand parameters, because we haven't any system to measure facial expression.

- Configuration is the hand shape. Its main role is to take up a part of the shape of the action object.

- Movement represents an action carried on or by the object. Moreover, movement dynamics allows to differentiate verb aspects.

- Orientation corresponds to hand orientation with respect to the body. It is given by the wrist configuration (rotation, flexion), the hand axis's and palm's directions. Orientation allows us to conjugate some verbs, or to precise object orientation in space.

  Depending on the kind of signs, the orientation parameter may have a semantic information or not. Thus, it has a different status than the two previous parameters, and for interpretation, its precise value is sometimes required, and sometimes not [1].

- Location parameter is hand location in space with respect to the signer. Its main function is to represent the place where action is carried, or a generic place. Moreover, location allows the signer to express spatial relations between persons and objects in the discourse.

  However, a lot of signs are performed in a neutral zone in front of the signer, and has no particular syntactic function or semantic value [1]. This parameter has a status quite similar to orientation.

2.2 Conventional, variable and non-conventional signs

Each sign language has a specific vocabulary, which depends on the country. These signs are called **conventional** signs. They can be listed in dictionaries.

But a second kind of signs is extremely frequent in sign language communications: the set of **non-conventional** signs. They are created during discourse, depending on need and context, and cannot be listed in dictionaries. They are based on physical features of objects, and thus, can be interpreted independently of country culture, and can be used during conversations between two deaf persons of different countries. They are also frequently used in ordinary conversation in everyday life.

An example of such a kind of sign is the **classificator**. It is a sign which describes and represents a whole class of objects having a similar shape, size or thickness [8]. They can be used in two kinds of syntactic functions: a descriptive function and a replacement function. They can be integrated into verbs as super-pronouns (pronouns showing the shape).

Classificators use are very frequent and their meaning completely depend on context. We have noticed that configurations used for the classificators are the same that the most frequent configurations used for the conventional signs [1]. They are those for which the shape is able to express a simple morphological feature of an object or a person.

Some other signs are defined as conventional, but are particular because one or more of their parameters are variables, depending on context. We call these signs **variable** signs.

An example of such a kind of signs is the **directional verb**. Directional verbs are conjugate in space. All the participants are located in a fictive scene placed in front of the signer. Then, movement direction and hand orientation establish the agent's role and the patient's role.

2.3 An example

To illustrate the spatial and parallel functioning of sign languages, we give now an example including conventional signs, classificator and directional verb (Figure 1).

- The first sign has, in the French Sign Language (LSF), the meaning "*garçon*" (boy). It is a conventional sign.

- The second sign is a classificator. It is used to indicate the boy location with regards to the signer's location. Standing person are generally represented by such a vertical classificator.

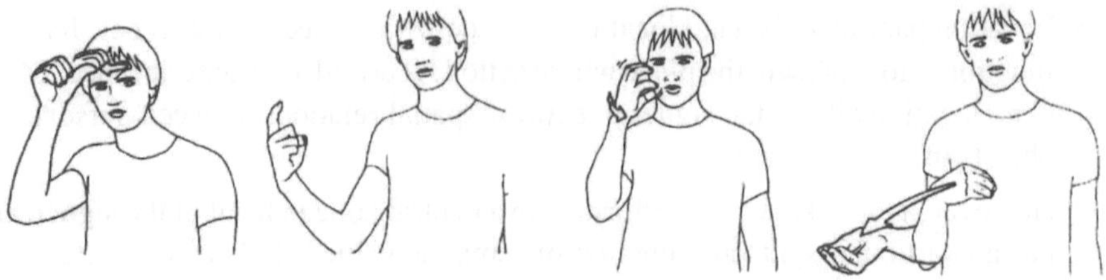

Figure 1: The sign "*garçon*" (boy), a "vertical" classificator, the sign "*pomme*" (apple), and the verb "*donner*" (to give).

At this step of the sign sentence, we know that there is a boy, located at the right of the signer.

- The third sign has, in LSF, the meaning "*pomme*" (apple). It is a conventional sign.
- The fourth sign is a directional verb and has, in LSF, the meaning "*donner*" (to give).

  Because the movement direction is from signer to a right location with regards to the signer's location, we can deduce that the signer gives something to the boy.

  Because an apple was signed before, we can deduce that the signer give an apple to the boy.

Thus, the complete sentence expressed by the signer has the following meaning: *"I give an apple to the boy at my right"*.

Sign language functioning is based on simultaneousness of information, and spatial rules governing sign relationships. Signer builds an image in three dimensions, in order to allow his interlocutor to "visualise" and understand the message. The first conclusion is that a classical recognition tool will not be sufficient to treat all kind of signs, and that we need to deal with the context to interpret plainly the message.

3 Sign Language Recognition

Gesture recognition is the set of techniques allowing the computers to interpret the events issued from physical captors. Recognition consists of a categorisation of the perceived phenomena: the continuous numerical representation must be transformed in a first step into a representation vector and then, after a decision step, into a discrete symbolic representation [11].

Recognition systems generally function on a defined vocabulary. This vocabulary can be previously learned by some particular systems during a learning step. For each unit of the vocabulary, or class, a reference vector has to be determined. Decider has to compare the representation vector of the shape to be classified with the reference vectors and choose the one closer.

Recognition methods are various, so that the kinds of vocabulary studied: That can be static hand postures or dynamic gestures, and in this case, gestures can be isolated, connected or continuous. We have enumerated a lot of studies (around 30), not easy to compare, because of this variety [1]. We indicate here the most common methods, which are template matching, neural networks, dynamic programming matching and hidden Markov models.

3.1 Template matching

The template matching method is the simplest one. This decider is based on a function which compute the similarity between the input and the reference vectors. The input is classified as member of the reference class whose it is the most similar, or closer. Generally, a recognition threshold is defined, below which the input is rejected.

This method is generally used for isolated postures. If some artificial segmentation techniques are added, connected signs can be treated (signs separated by pause or specific configurations). These methods can be used for specific applications with artificial vocabulary [15, 2]. But it not allows us to deal with natural continuous signs, with co-articulation between signs. The use of threshold values provides a higher risk of error, even if these values have been calculated during a learning step, because they are rigid values.

3.2 Neural Networks (NN)

Two kinds of neural networks are generally used in gesture recognition domain. The first one is the multi-layer Perceptron. It is adapted to classify isolated static postures. The second one is called recurrent neural network. Because of its context layer, which is a copy of the hidden layer at the time $t-1$, it can deal with continuous dynamic gestures [9].

Because of a learning process, neural networks are able to recognise a noisy or incomplete template, and they are able to generalise. But this learning process can be very expensive in time, especially with recurrent neural networks. In some studies, this time cost is decreased by using several neural networks. In [7], several NN are used in cascade, allowing to decrease at each step the data research space. In [5], several NN are used in parallel, each dedicated to a different kind of data. In this study, continuous gestures are treated (but not sign language gestures).

NN are not easy to design because the number of unit inside the hidden layer is not known a priori and a lot of tests has to be done. Another problem is that if a new class has to be added to the vocabulary, all the learning process has to be start again. This kind of tool, even if the results are often satisfactory, are nor easy to settle.

3.3 Dynamic programming matching (DP matching)

DP matching consists of computing a temporal transformation function, allowing two dynamic signals to be matched. If we consider a table, and two signals to compare, a temporal transformation function can be seen as a path in the table. The path cost

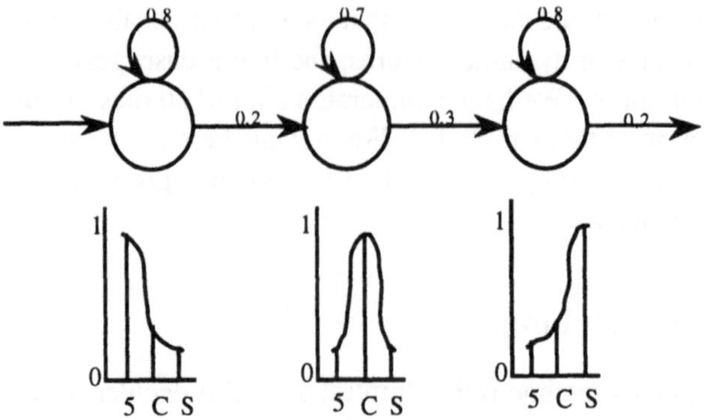

Figure 2: Configurations **5**, **C** et **S**.

represents the dissimilarity note between the two signals. The reference signal with the more little path cost is the closest from the input.

This method allows to classify isolated dynamic gestures [12]. It can be used to classify connected gestures by mean of a recurrent process [3]. In this case, segmentation between gestures is done during the recognition process. It allows to avoid rigid threshold values, and segmentation is more robust.

The problem with this approach is the great amount of time and memory needed (specially for the recurrent version). Some kind of optimisations can be added [3]. But the problem of co-articulation remains, and this technique cannot be used easily for continuous dynamic gesture recognition.

3.4 Hidden Markov models (HMM)

Hidden Markov Models are used with success in speech, writing and vision domains. They allow to deal with time-sequential data. In [14] the transducer used is a camera and the vocabulary is composed of continuous gestures of the two hands. The vocabulary contains gestures for which configuration is not discriminating, because it is difficult with these kind of captor to have precision for fingers. Good results have been obtained when a grammar was used.

Principle of HMM can be explained on the example which follows. In this example, only configurations are described, but the same principle is used for complete gestures, with configuration, location and orientation values.

Let us consider a sequence of three hand configurations: **5**, **C** and **S** (Figure 2). A HMM consists of a given number of states. For example, we can associate a state for each of the three configurations. For each state, a probability of transition to another state is computed, and each state can transit to itself. This allows to represent temporal variability of the data. Moreover, for each state, a probability density function is computed. This allows to represent spatial variability of the data. These probabilities are computed during a learning process. Formula used during the learning and the recognition process can be found in [10] and [13]

For example, for our sequence of three configurations, we can design a HMM like

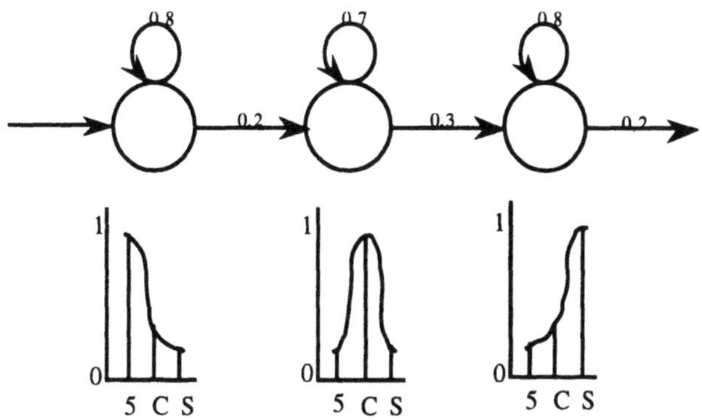

Figure 3: Example of HMM for three configurations.

the one presented in Figure 3. The labelled arrows represent the transition probabilities and the histograms represent the density functions for each state.

The HMMs offer a double approach for recognition, both statistical and structural. The first approach is done by the use of the probability values and density functions. The second approach is done by the mean of the choice of the number of states, which represents the internal structure of the data. Thus for each sign, we can represent a HMM containing the sign itself, but also the transitions before and after the sign.

This method allows us to recognise continuous dynamic gestures. It requires to deal with great learning set of gestures, in order to obtain correct probability density functions. But it is not necessary to start again all the learning step if we want to add a new sign into the vocabulary. And because of the structural capability of this system, it can be easier to settle this kind of tool if the internal structure of the signal is known. Moreover, segmentation between gestures is done during the recognition process, allowing to avoid external segmentation process with rigid threshold values.

HMMs seem to be well-suited for sign sentence recognition, and this is why we have chosen to use them in our recognition system.

4 Our proposal: ARGo

Our recognition system uses for gesture capture a Data Glove from VPL, for the right hand. This glove is composed of two independent measure systems: One is based on optic fibres and can measure hand shape, and the other is based on magnetic fields and can track location and orientation. The first one provides ten angles values (a1 ... a10) and the second provides three coordinates and three Euler angles (x, y, z, and a, b, g).

Our recognition system architecture takes into account the functioning of sign languages and measurement limitations due to the glove used. It is composed of two complementary modules: The first (named Classifier) is used for recognition and the second (named Interpreter), for interpretation (Figure 4).

First, we will describe the recognition module and the experimentation performed with it. Then, the interpretation module will be described.

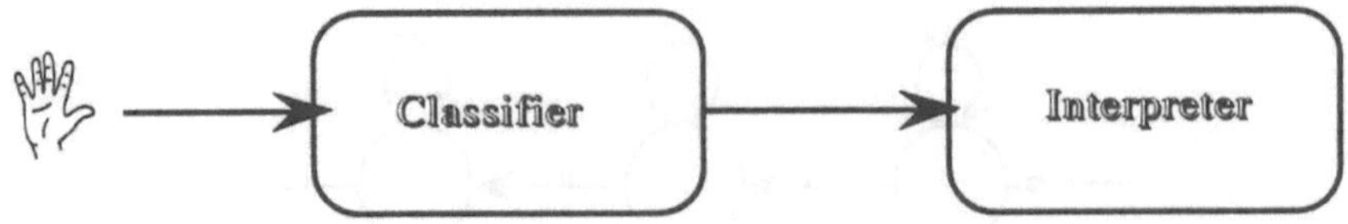

Figure 4: The two modules of ARGo

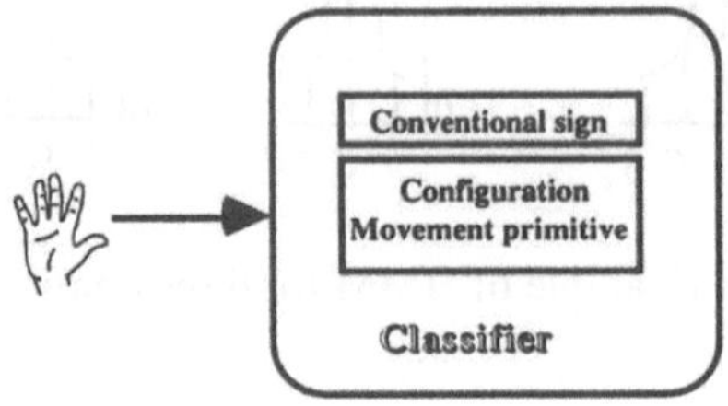

Figure 5: Final recognition module

4.1 ARGo's recognition module

The method chosen for our recognition module is based on HMMs, supported by an initial tool developed in the LIMSI laboratory [6].

4.1.1 Classifier architecture

The recognition module, called **Classifier**, is composed of two sub-modules (Figure 5).

- The first one is dedicated to **Conventional** signs. As we have explained before, only the conventional signs have invariable parameters (independent of context) that can be learned as a whole by a recognition system. This sub-module deals with configuration, location, orientation and movement (location derivative) parameters. It cannot be used to recognise signs with at least one variable parameter (depending on context), as the classificators or the directional verbs.

- The second one is dedicated to non conventional and variable signs. For the classificators, the only invariable parameter, for any context, is the configuration. For the directional verbs, only the movement trajectory primitive is invariable for any context. Thus, the second sub-module deals with **Configuration** and **Movement Primitive** parameters. This second module will be named **Variable** module in the following.

Because all conventional signs have a configuration and a movement primitive, the Variable sub-module is always able to classify data, even for conventional signs. However, the first sub-module dedicated to conventional signs must be able to send a symbol "*Unknown sign*", in case of non conventional or variable sign.

Finally, to allow the classification of a whole sign from the results provided by the two sub-modules, these two classification tools must be synchronised.

Name	Type	Config.	Mvt.	Orient.	Loc.
garçon (boy)	conv.	invariable	invariable	invariable	invariable
gâteau (cake)	conv.	invariable	invariable	invariable	invariable
personne (person)	variable	invariable	invar. prim.	variable	variable
taille (height)	non conv.	invariable	invar. prim.	variable	variable
emplac. (location)	non conv.	invariable	invar. prim.	variable	variable
donner (to give)	variable	variable	invar. prim.	variable	variable
aller vers (to go)	variable	invariable	invar. prim.	variable	variable

Table 1: Corpus's description.

4.1.2 First experimentation

The *Conventional* classifier takes as input all the values given by the glove, and their derivatives:

- (a1 ... a10) for the configuration (two flexion values by finger),
- (x, y, z) for the location,
- $(\sin\alpha, \sin\beta, \sin\gamma, \cos\alpha, \cos\beta, \cos\gamma)$ for the orientation (in order to obtain continuous functions of the a, b and g values).

Let us notice that an imbalance appears between the configuration (ten values), the orientation (six values) and the location (three values). Consequently, we will have to test if signs which differ only by the movement parameter can be differentiate.

The *Variable* classifier takes as input the configuration values and the speed norm (and their derivatives) because for our first experimentation, we have chosen as movement primitives two elementary states: static and dynamic.

Like with the conventional sub-module, because there is a imbalance between the number of values dedicated for configuration (ten values) and those for primitive (one value), we will have to test if signs can be differentiate only with primitive.

In this context, we have defined a corpus by choosing a few quantity of signs, but dispatched in all the types of signs (conventional, variable, and non-conventional). The Table 1 indicates for each sign, its type, and, for each parameter, the behaviour (variable, invariable or, for movement, invariable primitive). These seven signs are shown in Figure 6.

We had a special sign to express the "silence", because our HMM tool requires a sentence to begin and finish with a silence. We have chosen as silence-sign the **i** manual letter staying in front of the torso, because it is not a configuration often used in LSF and it is easy to perform (Figure 7).

Our corpus is composed of 44 different sentences of four signs. Because sign order can be different, co-articulation between signs can vary. Each sign is composed of three parts (co-articulation with the previous sign, current sign, co-articulation with the next sign) and is represented by a HMM with three states. The silence is represented by a one state HMM.

Figure 6: Signs “boy”, “cake”, “person”, “height”, “location.”, “to give” and “to go”

Figure 7: Configuration **i**

The corpus is composed of two sets of 44 different sign sentences, one set for the training process and one set for the recognition process. We have obtain good results, specially for the *Conventional* module. The recognition rates are detailed in the following tables (Tables 2 and 3).

The different kinds of possible errors are substitution, suppression or insertion. With our corpus, no substitution error has been observed. The signs composing this corpus are certainly distinct enough. Suppression errors are not numerous (only one for each module). Insertion errors are more numerous, specially for the *Variable* module. Suppression and insertion errors are due to signs for which only location and movement values differ. A possible reason is the imbalance between the number of values dedicated to the different parameters. It can explain that results are worth for the *Variable* module than for the *Conventional* one.

The recognition rate will certainly decrease as the vocabulary size will increase. But at this moment, we have enough results to try to tackle the interpretation process.

Module	Correct	Errors
Conventional	96	4
Variable	92	8

Table 2: Recognition rates.

Module	Substitution	Suppression	Insertion
Conventional	0	0,5	3,5
Variable	0	0,5	7,5

Table 3: Error rates.

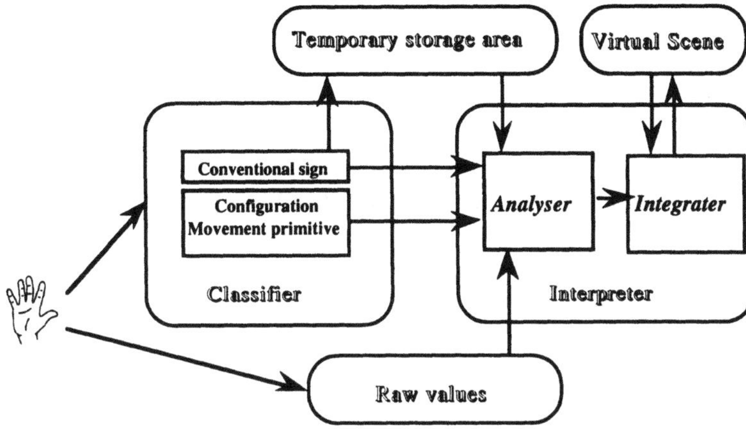

Figure 8: ARGo's architecture.

4.2 Sign Language Interpretation

Because of the constant use of spatial localisation of person or object, to interpret the signer's discourse, we need to reconstruct the scene he has created in order to express a message. Thus, we have to design a computational representation of this scene, called a **virtual scene**, which is used during the interpretation process to complete the interpretation. The complete ARGo's architecture is illustrated in Figure 8.

4.2.1 ARGo's interpretation module

The interpretation module is called **Interpreter**. Gesture interpretation is accomplished in two steps.

In a first step, a tool, called **Analyser**, analyses the kind of classified gesture (directional verb, classificators, conventional sign and so on). Depending on that kind of gesture, the tool retrieves values of orientation and location (x, y, z and α, β, γ) if needed. To deduce the kind of sign, a set of rules is used. Some of them are described later.

In a second step, a tool, called **Integrator**, realises the integration of all the information to produce a final interpretation. These information can be spatial information, like location, direction, or spatial relations.

At Classifier level, when a conventional sign has been recognised, it is added in a **Temporary Storage Area**.

At Analyser level, objects present in the Temporary Storage Area are scanned, in order to disambiguate non-conventional signs, if needed. In case of non-conventional signs, location and orientation values measured by the glove for that sign, are recovered.

At Integrator level, all values needed to located objects in the **Virtual Scene** are computed (location and orientation with respect to the signer's coordinate system, direction in case of directional verbs, spatial relations and so on).

4.2.2 A basis for rules

In order to complete the interpretation of non-conventional and variable signs, we are investigating the definition of a set of rules to solve the possible ambiguities, such as the four described in that follows:

- Localisation classificator.

  It corresponds to a sign with no movement and a configuration corresponding to a classificator. If an object is present in the Temporary Storage Area, the classificator must be one of those dedicated to this kind of object. Location and orientation mean values must be computed.

- Directional verb.

  Configuration and movement primitive must correspond to an existing directional verb (stored in a directional verb database). Movement direction must be computed (with initial and final location values).

- Verb including a classificator.

  Configuration must correspond to a classificator. If an object is present in the Temporary Storage Area, the classificator must be one of those dedicated to this kind of object. Movement primitive must correspond to an existing movement verb (expressing an object moving). No value is needed.

- Directional verb including a classificator.

  Configuration must correspond to a classificator. If an object is present in the Temporary Storage Area, the classificator must be one of those dedicated to this kind of object. Movement primitive must correspond to the one of an existing directional verb. Movement direction must be computed (with initial and final location values).

4.3 Conclusion

Our aim is to deal with sign sentences, composed of conventional, variable and non conventional signs. Because classical recognition system only are able to treat conventional signs, we have proposed a specific system composed of two modules: a recognition module and an interpretation module.

The recognition module is based on HMMs, which are well suited for continuous data recognition. This module is composed of into two sub-modules. The first one is dedicated to conventional signs. The second one allows us to classify the configuration and movement primitive parameters of all kind of signs, including non-conventional and variable ones. We have obtained good recognition rate for these two sub-modules (respectively 96% and 92%) on a corpus of 44 different sign sentences.

The interpretation module's role is to integrate all the recognition results, the raw values, and the context information stored in a virtual scene, in order to complete the interpretation of a sign sentence. A prototype of the interpretation module is under development, which will allow us to interpret signs such as directional verbs or localisation classificators.

References

[1] A. Braffort. *Reconnaissance et compréhension de gestes, application à la langue des signes.* PhD thesis, L'université d'Orsay, 1996.

[2] A. Braffort, T. Baudel, and D. Teil. Utilisation des gestes de la main pour l'interaction homme-machine. In *GDR-PRC-CHM (Ed.), IHM'92*, pages 193–196, Paris, 1992.

[3] J. Cagin. Une étude sur la reconnaissance de formes dynamiques - application à la langue des signes. Projet de fin d'études de l'ENSTA, Paris, 1993.

[4] C. Cuxac. Autour de la langue des signes. Journée d'études n°10, Université Paris V, Paris, 1983. (In French).

[5] S. S. Fels. *Glove-TalkII: Mapping Hand Gestures to Speech Using Neural Networks-An Approach to Building Adaptive Interfaces.* PhD thesis, Department of Computer Science, University of Toronto, Canada, 1994.

[6] J. Gauvain, L. Lamel, and M. Adda-Decker. Developments in large vocabulary dictation: The LIMSI Nov94 NAB system. In *ARPA SLT'95*, Austin (Texas), 1995.

[7] L. Messing, R. Erenshteyn, R. Foulds, S. Galuska, and G. Stern. American Sign Language computer recognition: Its present and its promise. In *ISAAC'94*, pages 289–291, Maastricht, NL, 1994.

[8] B. Moody. *La langue des signes. Histoire et grammaire.* Ellipses, Paris, 1983. (In French).

[9] K. Murakami and H. Taguchi. Gesture recognition using recurrent neural networks. In *CHI '91 Proceedings*, pages 237–242, New Orleans (Louisiana), 1991.

[10] L. R. Rabiner. A tutorial on Hidden Markov Models and selected applications in speech recognition. *IEEE ASSP Magazine*, 77(2):257–285, 1989.

[11] D. Rubine. *The automatic recognition of gestures.* PhD thesis, Carnegie Mellon University, 1991.

[12] H. Sagawa, H. Sakou, and M. Abe. Sign Language translation using continuous DP matching. In *MVA'92-IAPR Workshop on Machine Vision Applications*, Tokyo, 1992.

[13] T. Starner. Visual recognition of American Sign Language using Hidden Markov Models. Master's thesis, Media Arts and Sciences, MIT, 1995.

[14] T. Starner and A. Pentland. Visual recognition of American Sign Language using Hidden Markov Models. In M. Bichsel, editor, *Proceedings of the International Workshop on Automatic Face- and Gesture-Recognition*, pages 189–194, 26-28 June 1995.

[15] D. Sturman. *Whole-hand Input*. PhD thesis, MIT, 1992.

Real-time Video-based Recognition of Sign Language Gestures using Guided Template Matching

A. Sutherland

Hitachi Dublin Laboratory, O'Reilly Institute, Trinity College, Dublin 2, Ireland

E-mail: alistair@hdl.ie
Telephone: +353 1 6798911 Fax: +353 1 6798926

Abstract

We present a system for recognising hand-gestures in Sign language. The system works in real-time and uses input from a colour video camera. The user wears different coloured gloves on either hand and colour matching is used to distinguish the hands from each other and from the background. So far the system has been tested in fixed lighting conditions, with the camera a fixed distance from the user. The system is user-dependent.

The system is implemented on a Datacube platform, which contains specialised image processing hardware and allows real-time operation. Hand-shapes are recognised using template-matching implemented using the Datacube's NMAC module. Different sets of templates can be matched at each frame depending on the absolute positions of the hands within the frame and their relative positions with respect to each other.

Results are presented for a set of 25 gestures from Irish Sign Language. 22 of the gestures involve motion and we show how the structure of the gestures may be used to guide the template-matching algorithm. Dynamic gestures are recognised by identifying sequences of distinct hand-shapes/positions. Recognition rates will be presented for a set of 500 example video sequences.

1 Introduction

We describe a hand-gesture recognition system which is currently under development. The system can recognise 25 gestures from Irish Sign Language (ISL) from real-time video sequences acquired in controlled conditions. Our long-term aim is to build a system which can translate a sign language like ISL into a spoken language like English. Such a system would need to recognise not only hand-gestures but also facial expressions. Work on facial expression recognition is being carried out within Hitachi [3]. It would need a vocabulary of 5000 gestures to cope with everyday conversation. Such a system will probably take many years to develop but we have a short-term aim which is a system with a vocabulary of around 300 gestures which would suffice for certain stock situations such as a visit to a shop or a bank or to the doctor. This system would need to operate in a number of lighting conditions, be physically lightweight and be robust to the user's distance from the camera. The system described in this paper is still not near achieving these objectives but is a first step along the road.

Previous systems which attempt to solve the same problem include T. Starner and A. Pentland's [4] which uses coloured gloves to segment the hands from the rest of the image. Two parameters are used to describe the shape of the hand: the eccentricity and angle of the major axis of the bounding ellipse. These parameters together with the *xy*position of the hand are fed into a Hidden Markov Model (HMM) classifier to carry out the recognition. The system can recognise 40 gestures in American Sign Language.

The system of T. Darrel and A. Pentland [1] uses Dynamic Time Warping (which is similar to HMMs.) The input is the correlation scores of the hand-image with a set of view models. The system is tested on two gestures.

The system of Brigitte Dorner [2] uses coloured markers placed on the finger joints of each hand. A deformable 3D model of a hand is fitted to the observed positions of the coloured markers at each frame.

The system described in this report uses coloured gloves to segment the hands as does Starner and Pentland's system. The system compares the segmented image with a set of templates. A different set of templates is used depending on the positions of the two hands. The best match template plus the *xy*positions of the hands are fed into a simple classifier which recognises the gesture. We present the results of current system on a set of 25 ISL gestures.

The system is implemented on Datacube hardware.[1] The Datacube is a real-time image processing system which contains specialised hardware such as look-up tables, adders, Hough transform units etc. For this particular algorithm we use a device called an NMAC (Neighbourhood Multiplier and Accumulator) which carries out convolutions. We also use an additional board called a MaxBolt which contains four parallel CPUs. Current serial workstations and PCs are unable to give the necessary power to carry out sufficient template matching in real-time. In future, however, relatively cheap specialised template matching boards should become available which can be inserted into a PC providing adequate power.

This system is based on the following view of sign language gestures. We view gestures as consisting of a series of easily identifiable and momentarily static hand configurations - where the hands assume a particular pair of shapes in a particular pair of positions. For example the ISL sign "evening" is as shown in Figure 1 below.

It consists of two configurations: in the first the hands are spread wide and held upwards, in the second they are still spread wide but are pointing horizontally. Our system identifies the two configurations independently and if it perceives the first followed by the second within some predetermined period of time it decides that the gesture "evening" has occurred.

This view of sign language may seem too primitive. It could be criticised on the

[1]"Datacube" is a trademark of Datacube Inc., Danvers, MA, USA.

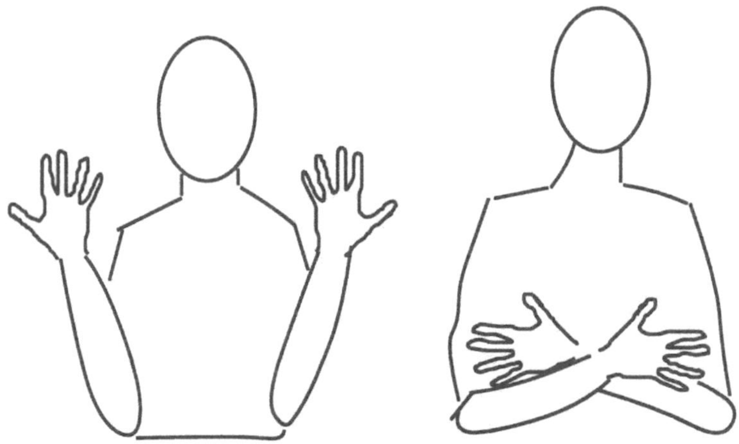

Figure 1: The gesture "evening".

grounds that sign language is not a series of static configurations but a continuous flow. This may well turn out to be the case when we start to look at sign language performed at normal speed by a native signer. However, for the gestures so far considered our assumptions have proved adequate. We feel that if in future these assumptions prove too restrictive it will be easy to modify them by producing some continuous output (along the lines of Starner or Darrel and Pentland) rather than a series of discrete symbols. Or alternatively by increasing the frame rate of the camera.

2 Colour segmentation

The video sequences used are acquired under the following conditions. They are all taken in the same room with the signer sitting in a fixed position with respect to the camera. The background contains many different objects but remains constant throughout the procedure. The signer always wears the same clothes. Lighting is provided by overhead fluorescent strip lights. There is no natural lighting.

The colour segmentation is based on the hue spectrum of each of the two gloves. Hue is used rather than red, green and blue values because it is less invariant to changes in lighting intensity or distance from the camera. Gloves with hue spectra which do not overlap with each other or with the hue spectra of the background or the signer's clothes or skin are used.

A look-up table is used to select those pixels which have hue values within the spectrum of each of the gloves. The 8-bit brightness values of each of these pixels is recorded and the local region of the image around each hand is extracted and loaded onto the NMAC in preparation for template matching.

3 Template Matching

The original video image is 512x576 pixels in size. However, at this resolution the hand occupies too large an area of the image to allow template matching in real-time. Therefore the image is subsampled by 5 in the horizontal and vertical directions. Each hand now occupies at most 16x16 pixel region of the image. The signer is seated sufficiently far away from the camera that the image of the hand does not vary greatly in size as the hand moves along the line of sight.

The template matching process is carried out as follows. Each template is 16x16 pixels in size and each pixel has an 8-bit brightness value. We utilise the pipeline architecture of the Datacube to speed up the process. The templates for one of the hands are laid out in an array within one of the Datacube's special dedicated image memories. Such an array can hold up to 1000 templates. The local region of the image around the hand is loaded onto the NMAC. The array of templates is then passed through the NMAC which, together with the MaxBolt, calculates the Euclidean distance of each of the templates from the image. We can then find the template with the minimum Euclidean distance. We can choose to match a subset of the set of all templates by choosing a rectangular sub-array of the array of all templates. The Datacube allows this to be done with no computational overhead. We do not need to read new templates off the disk. We use two NMACs - one for each hand - each with its own array of templates. Our current implementation allows one subset of 16 templates to be matched per hand per frame at 25 frames per second.

4 Selecting templates on the basis of the positions of the two hands

Figures 2–4 show some of the hand configurations which arise in ISL. As stated in the introduction we view signs as consisting of a series of these configurations. In order to reduce the number of templates which must be matched at a given frame we use the positions of the two hands to determine which subset of templates to be used. Because the signer always sits in the same position within the frame we use the positions of the hands with respect to the frame to select the subset. In a future system we may have to use the positions of the hands with respect to the signer's body in order to give the signer more freedom of movement.

In Figure 2 (left) the hands are held close together at stomach level. This is the beginning of the gesture "book". Figure 2 (right) shows another gesture "break" in which the hands are held in the same region but with a different shape. The templates for these two configurations would therefore be placed in the same subset. However, Figure 1 shows the final configuration of the gesture "evening" (see above) where the hands have crossed over, so the right hand is to the left of the left hand. This configuration is easily distinguishable from the previous two, so the templates would be placed in a different subset. Other easily distinguishable configurations are shown in Figure 3. In the first the hands are held at the sides but at different heights. In the second they are held at the same height. In the third they are held at face height.

Gestures which involve only one hand (usually the right hand) are identified when

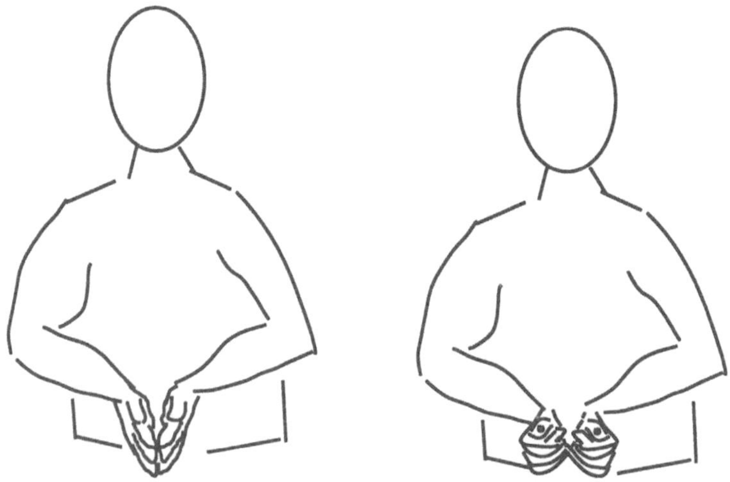

Figure 2: Hand configurations from the gestures "book" (left) and "break".

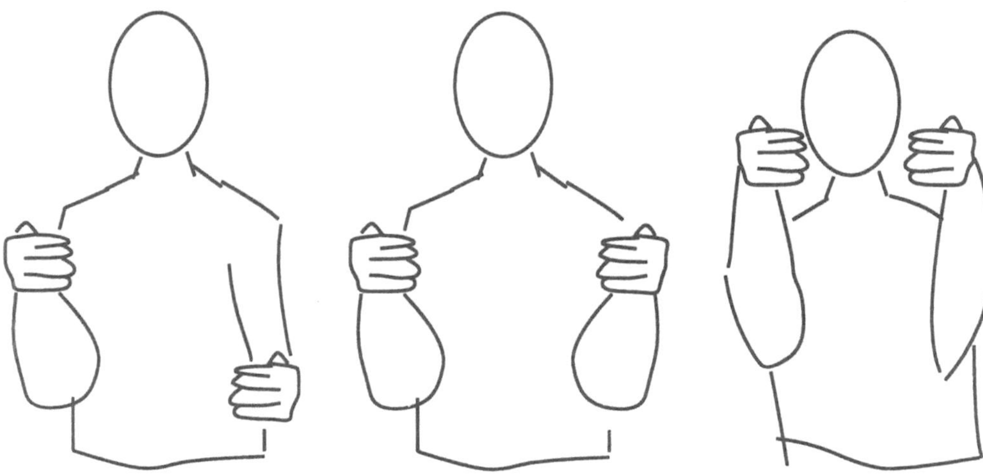

Figure 3: Configurations from the gestures "car" (left), "agree" (middle) and "be-cause'.

Figure 4: The gesture "me".

the redundant hand drops below a certain level in the image. See Figure 4 the gesture "me".

5 Results

A set of 25 gestures from ISL was collected. The user sat at a fixed distance from the camera of about 10 m. All gestures were performed by the same person. The user always positioned himself within the image in the same position. The user was able to see himself on a monitor.

Twenty examples of each gesture were recorded. Each example was performed separately and recorded in a 4 second (100 frame) video sequence. The sequences were digitised in real time and stored on disk. Ten examples of each gesture were selected as a training set from which templates were computed and region boundaries for each subset of templates were determined. The remaining ten examples of each gesture were used as a test set.

The templates were computed by manually stepping through each of the test sequences frame by frame and selecting those frames which corresponded to the appropriate configurations mentioned above. At those frames the local region around each hand was extracted and the hand positions recorded. For each configuration the centroids of the hand images were matched and the mean hand image calculated. This mean hand image was used as the template for that configuration. In future we intend to use multiple templates for each configuration which should be chosen after some clustering procedure has been applied to the data. A total of 54 templates were used for the left hand and 60 templates for the right hand. There are more templates for the right hand because it is used in one-handed gestures whereas the left is not.

The recognition rate obtained was 91%. One should bear in mind that this was obtained in very controlled rather artificial conditions. Much work remains to be done before this result can be replicated in a more realistic situation. There were two main sources of error. The first occurred when the correct subset of templates was selected but the wrong template within that subset was matched. This suggests that either the training set was not typical of the whole population or that a greater number of different templates are required. The solution to this is to acquire a much larger training set and do some clustering before selecting the templates. The second type of error occurred when the wrong subset of templates was selected. This suggests that the spatial boundaries for the different subsets determined from the training data are incorrect. Again the solution is to acquire a much larger training set which is more likely to be typical of the whole population.

6 Future Work

With a capacity of more than 1000 templates for each hand we can clearly build up a larger vocabulary of gestures in the present set of conditions. However, we have to confront issues such as multiple users and changes in lighting conditions. For these even a large body of templates may not be sufficient. To achieve this we intend to experiment with a principal components analysis rather than straight template matching. We would gather a large set of examples of different hand-shapes in each region of the image in different lighting conditions and possibly from different users. The principal components are found by finding the eigenvectors of the covariance matrix of the data. Since principal components are the most efficient way of representing multivariate data they should allow the recognition of a much larger variety of shapes than normal template matching.

A further possibility is to model the spatial distribution of each hand-configuration. At the moment the categorisation into different spatial regions imposes abrupt boundaries on the spatial distribution, which is hardly realistic. A better technique would be to use a Bayesian approach where the spatial distribution of template T is modelled by a smooth probability distribution $P(T|x,y)$. The match score of a given template would then be given by combining $P(T|x,y)$ with $P(T|Z)$ where Z is the image data. It would also be possible to include the probability of T given the data in the previous frame thus spreading the recognition over two frames and reducing the possibility of errors.

Thirdly, we could use HMMs to model the time variation of the gestures. The input to the HMM could be the best matching templates plus their match scores at each frame plus the*xy*co-ordinates of each hand. Velocity and acceleration could also be included. Acceleration could be used as a cue for the beginning and end of each gesture since the hand tends to slow down or speed up at these points.

7 Conclusions

A video-based hand-gesture recognition system has been described. It is based on template matching and can select different sets of templates depending on the positions of the two hands within the video frame. It works in real-time and has been tested on a set of 500 video sequences of 25 ISL gestures. The next objective is to increase the vocabulary of the system and broaden the conditions in which it can be used.

References

[1] T. Darrel and A. Pentland. Space-Time Gestures. In A. Pentland, editor, *Looking at People Workshop, IJCAI 93*, 1993.

[2] B. Dorner. Hand shape identification and tracking for Sign Language interpretation. In A. Pentland, editor, *Looking at People Workshop, IJCAI 93*, 1993.

[3] H. Sako, M. P. Whitehouse, A. V. W. Smith, and A. I. Sutherland. Real-time facial feature tracking based on matching techniques and its applications. In *Proceedings of the International Conference on Pattern Recognition*, pages B320–4, 1994.

[4] T. Starner and A. Pentland. Visual recognition of American Sign Language using Hidden Markov Models. In M. Bichsel, editor, *Proceedings of the International Workshop on Automatic Face- and Gesture-Recognition*, pages 189–194, 26-28 June 1995.

Analyzing Human Gestural Motions using Acceleration Sensors

F. G. Hofmann and G. Hommel
Department of Computer Science, Technical University of Berlin, Real-Time Systems and Robotics Research Group, FR2-2, Franklinstr. 28/29, D-10587 Berlin, Germany

E-mail: {fgh, hommel}@cs.tu-berlin.de
Telephone: +49 30 314-25403 Fax: +49 30 314-21116

Abstract

A novel approach to human gestural motion analysis and recognition on the basis of acceleration sensors is proposed. Using accelerometers for motion analysis has the advantage of very high temporal resolution (measurement rates $\geq$ 1 kHz are easily possible) and low instrumentation overhead. In this paper, a theoretical model for the description of gestural motion trajectories and the derivation of expected accelerations as well as the estimation of trajectories from measured acceleration data is presented. The theory is applied to measurements performed with a system of two combined triaxial accelerometers. Applying results from the theory of curves and differential geometry, features for pattern classification are extracted from the data. As an example, the nearest-neighbour classificator is used to match the features of gestural trajectories against stored templates. Preliminary trials indicate good recognition rates for a set of 9 different elementary gesture motions of varying size and speed. Also, a short overview of the interdisciplinary research project "Gesture Recognition with SensorGloves" at the Technical University of Berlin is given.

1 Introduction

There are many possible solutions to the problem of capturing human gestural motions. At the input level, the tracking problem can be divided into two main parts:

- The tracking of the fingers, for which various types of datagloves [19, 12, 6, 8] and other methods like computer vision exist (a selection of which can be found in [2]), and
- the tracking of hand-, arm- and body movements, for which such different devices as magnetic trackers [9], ultrasonics [7], infrared diodes and cameras [17], computer vision methods [2], bodysuits [18] and accelerometers [11], [1] are available.

Here we focus on the second problem, particularly on the tracking of the human hand. Each applicable input method possesses various advantages and disadvantages:

Magnetic trackers (being rather expensive) give a reasonably high data rate (about 100–200 frames / second) and good spatial resolution (about ± 1 mm) — as long as interfering electrical fields and metal objects are kept away from the experimental setup and as long as certain distance constraints concerning the ranges between magnetic emitter and receiver are observed. Using *ultrasound* is an easily implementable low-cost method but is limited by the speed of sound (10–50 measurements / second) and its accuracy is impeded by temperature shifts and air turbulence (± 1 cm resolution). *Infrared trackers* achieve moderate data rates (100 samples / second) and good accuracy (± 1 mm), but suffer the occlusion problem common to all vision-based methods. *Computer vision*-based motion tracking gives a wealth of information, its spatial resolution depending on camera resolution and the number of cameras used, but is computationally expensive, suffers from lighting problems and currently results in low data rates (25–50 samples / second). All above-mentioned methods are only workable in a stationary environment.

In this paper, we take a different approach, namely using *acceleration sensors* for motion analysis. Using accelerometers has the advantage of very high temporal resolution (1000 samples per second and more are easily possible) and low instrumentation overhead. No external reference systems or stationary cameras are needed — in fact, the measurement system is small enough to fit onto a glove. When an infrared or radio link to the host computer is used, a test person can move freely. The disadvantages of an accelerometer-based system are the accumulation of measurement errors over time, as only relative measurements are possible, and the need for an additional system for frequent recalibration if absolute position tracking is required. Also, accelerometers are rather shock-sensitive.

It seems that as yet accelerometers have been rarely used by the HCI community for gesture input, even though they have a long tradition in biomechanics [13], navigation and space applications [3]. Recently, they have been used as input sources for computer music applications [16, 10]. Commercially, they seem to have been included in a VR headset as position trackers for head movements.

The objective of our work is to show that the analysis and recognition of gestural motions using accelerometers as input devices is feasible and good recognition rates are possible. In Section 2, we present a formal framework for the description of gestural motion trajectories based upon a kinematic formulation of a subset of HamNoSys, the Hamburg Notation System for Sign Languages [14]. Section 3 contains a description of the conducted experiments. In Section 4, methods for feature extraction from acceleration data and its subsequent classification are derived; Section 5 discusses preliminary results. In Section 6, we give a survey of ongoing work in our interdisciplinary research project at the Technical University of Berlin; Section 7 suggests directions for further investigations.

2 KINOTE — A Kinematic Notation for Gestural Motion Trajectories

The first question one has to answer when analyzing human gestural movements is which types of movement are to be investigated. Using a system currently consisting only of acceleration sensors implies that only relative movements can be distinguished. Searching for meaningful movements, we came across Chapter 4 of the HamNoSys manual, in which basic hand movement types are listed. In order to simulate data from accelerometers for later comparison with real data, it was necessary to transform the HamNoSys symbols into trajectory information. For this, KINOTE — a kinematic transcription of a subset of HamNoSys — was developed, which will be described after a brief discussion of the sign notation system.

2.1 HamNoSys

HamNoSys [Prillwitz et al 1989] is a general iconic notation system for sign languages, developed at the Hamburg Centre for German Sign Language and the Communication of the Deaf. It combines icons for body parts, hand shapes, -position and -orientation with icons for trajectory-, movement type- and manner-of-movement information. In principle, it can be used to denote any sign language, not only German Sign Language (GSL), though this is its prime application.

Just to give a general idea, eg. "HamNoSys" itself is written as , meaning "sign writing" in GSL.

We only use a subset of the system, which is described in chapter 4 of the manual. There are symbols for straight linear movements (→↘↓↙←↖↑↗, movements with different spatial orientations (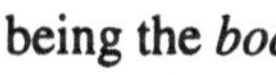, the straight line next to the arrow being the *body referent*), curved (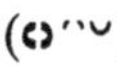) and circular movements (). Wavy, zigzag and cross-shaped movements are written , and  or , respectively. It is also possible to combine symbols, eg. resulting in a *widening clockwise horizontal spiral movement upwards* 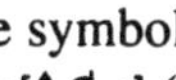 ( widening spiral,  narrowing).

To use these symbols for gesture trajectory description, they have to be mapped onto precise kinematic meanings, which is the topic of the next section.

2.2 A Kinematically Inspired Parametric Description of Trajectories

In this section, a parametric description of simple trajectories for the use with HamNoSys is proposed. In the following discussion, homogeneous coordinates and matrices (so-called *frames*) for the description of three-dimensional positions and orientations are always used [5]. Parameters and variables are printed in *italics*, functions in plain type, vectors and matrices in **bold** type.

Trajectories are ordered sequences of dimensionless, orientation-free points. The order is determined by a trajectory parameter u [15], which in turn may be a function of time: $u = \mathrm{u}(t) \cdot \mathrm{u}(t)$ is assumed to be a monotonic nondecreasing function.

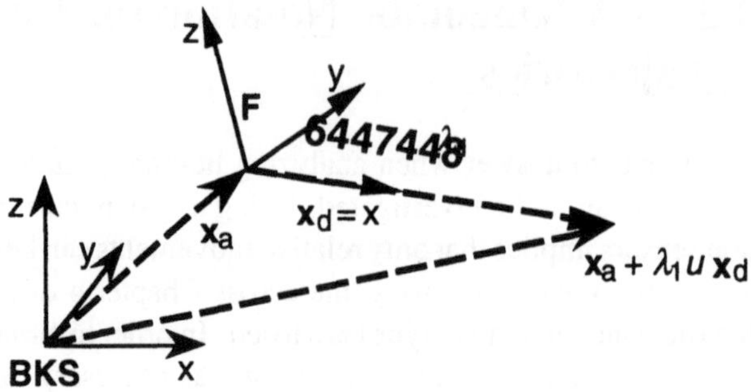

Figure 1: The straight line $G_{\lambda_1}(u, \mathbf{F}, \lambda_1)$.

A trajectory function **b** may be denoted as a homogeneous vector function $\mathbf{b}(u) = (b_x(u), b_y(u), b_z(u), 1)^{\mathsf{T}}$ (with the exception of the neutral trajectory $\mathbf{b}_\nu = (0,0,0,1)^{\mathsf{T}}$, being a point).

Each trajectory has a starting or base point $\mathbf{x}_a = (x_{a_x}, x_{a_y}, x_{a_z}, 1)^{\mathsf{T}}$ and an initial orientation **R**. Both parameters can be combined to form an initial frame **F** by multiplying a translational frame **T** (for $\mathbf{x}_a$) with the rotational frame **R** ($\mathbf{R}_{3\times3}$ being the rotational component of **F**):

$$\mathbf{F} = \mathbf{TR} = \begin{bmatrix} 1 & 0 & 0 & x_{a_x} \\ 0 & 1 & 0 & x_{a_y} \\ 0 & 0 & 1 & x_{a_z} \\ 0 & 0 & 0 & 1 \end{bmatrix} \begin{bmatrix} r_{11} & r_{12} & r_{13} & 0 \\ r_{21} & r_{22} & r_{23} & 0 \\ r_{21} & r_{32} & r_{33} & 0 \\ 0 & 0 & 0 & 1 \end{bmatrix} = \begin{bmatrix} & \mathbf{R}_{3\times3} & & \vdots \\ & & & \mathbf{x}_a \\ & & & \vdots \\ 0 & 0 & 0 & \vdots \end{bmatrix} \tag{1}$$

Each trajectory is described by at least u and **F**. Depending on the trajectory type, additional parameters may be necessary, as the trajectory length λ for a straight line $G_\lambda(u, \mathbf{F}, \lambda)$ or the principal axes radius r_a, r_b for an ellipse $E(u, \mathbf{F}, r_a, r_b)$. Trajectory parameters may also be functions of u, for example $r_a(u)$ and $r_b(u)$. In the case of **F** being parameterized with u, only $\mathbf{R}_{3\times3}$ should depend on u, as otherwise $\mathbf{x}_a(u)$ would form a trajectory of its own, contradicting the meaning of $\mathbf{x}_a$ as the trajectory's starting point (in the same sense, one should not parameterize ψ in $G_{\sin}(u, \mathbf{F}, a, \omega, \psi)$).

For each trajectory B, there is a trajectory function **b**. The term *trajectory* (or *trajectory description*) is used if trajectories or combinations thereof are spoken about generally; the term *trajectory function* is used when the specific vector function is meant.

There are three different types of trajectories: *Basic*, *combined* and *assembled* trajectories. Assembled trajectories are constructed piecewise from other trajectories (all three types possible); combined trajectories may contain other combined as well as basic trajectories; basic trajectories are indivisible (*with reference to a joining operator* J).

2.2.1 *Basic Trajectories*

Basic trajectories are the building blocks of all other trajectories discussed in this paper. They are defined as follows:

DEFINITION 1
A trajectory B *is* basic *(*with reference to a joining operator J*), if its vector function* **b** *can neither be broken up into simpler trajectories by eliminating vector components, nor by decomposing it into a combination of simpler trajectories (by applying* J^{-1}*, nor by decomposing it into intervals consisting of simpler trajectories.*

For example, $G_{\lambda 3}$ (3) is elementary with reference to $\mathsf{J} \equiv \oplus$ (definition see below), but not elementary with reference to $\mathsf{J} \equiv \otimes$ ($\otimes$ is the elementwise multiplication of vectors and/or matrices and is also known as the Hadamard product). For the rest of the paper, "basic" always means "basic with reference to $\mathsf{J} \equiv \oplus$".

The definition implies that only such trajectory functions are basic which use only one vector component as a function of u.

There are many mathematical functions f depending on the parameter u which can be used to describe the progress of a vector component $x_j = \mathrm{f}(u)$. For our purposes, two suffice:

- $\mathrm{f}(u) = \lambda_i u^i$ with $i \in \mathbb{N}_0^+$ and
- $\mathrm{f}(u) = a \sin(\omega u + \psi)$

Using these, two basic trajectory functions — the straight lines $G_{\lambda_i}(u, \mathbf{F}, \lambda_i)$ and $G_{\sin}(u, \mathbf{F}, a, \omega, \psi)$ — can be defined as follows:

DEFINITION 2 (TRAJECTORY DESCRIPTION)

$$G_{\lambda_i}(u, \mathbf{F}, \lambda_i) \tag{2}$$

DEFINITION 3 (TRAJECTORY FUNCTION)
Figure 1 shows the different parameters in context for i = 1.

$$\mathbf{g}_{\lambda_i}(u, \mathbf{F}, \lambda_i) = \mathbf{F}(\lambda_i u^i, 0, 0, 1)^{\mathsf{T}} = \mathbf{x}_a + \lambda_i u^i \mathbf{x}_d \tag{3}$$

where $\lambda_i \in \mathbb{R}$ *is the trajectory length,* $\mathbf{x}_a = \mathbf{F}(0,0,0,1)^{\mathsf{T}}$ *(See Equation 1) and* $\mathbf{x}_d = \mathbf{F}(1,0,0,0)^{\mathsf{T}}$*; with* $\mathbf{x}_a$ *being the starting point of the line and* $\mathbf{x}_d = (r_{11}, r_{21}, r_{31}, 0)^{\mathsf{T}}$ *(first column of* **F***) the direction vector.*

DEFINITION 4 (TRAJECTORY DESCRIPTION)

$$G_{\sin}(u, \mathbf{F}, a, \omega, \psi) \tag{4}$$

DEFINITION 5 (TRAJECTORY FUNCTION)

$$\mathbf{g}_{\sin}(u,\mathbf{F},a,\omega,\psi) = \mathbf{F}(a\sin(\omega u+\psi),0,0,1)^{\mathsf{T}} = \mathbf{x}_a + a\sin(\omega u+\psi)\mathbf{x}_d \qquad (5)$$

where a is the amplitude, $\omega = 2\pi f$ *(f being the frequency),* ψ *is the phase shift and* $\mathbf{x}_a, \mathbf{x}_d$ *are the same as in Equation 3.*

As a special case of G_{λ_i}, $\mathrm{G}_{\lambda_1}(u,\mathbf{F},\lambda_1)$ *denotes the normal straight line* ($\lambda_1 \geq 0$, *see Figure 1).* $\mathrm{G}_{\cos}(u,\mathbf{F},a,\omega,\psi)$ *is simply* $\mathrm{G}_{\sin}(u,\mathbf{F},a,\omega,\psi+\frac{\pi}{2})$.

2.2.2 Combined Trajectories

One way to join trajectories is to *combine* their vector functions by overlapping them on a uniform parameter interval $[u_{\min}, u_{\max}]$. Their combination can be described on two levels — firstly, the trajectory level and secondly, the vector function level which can be derived from the trajectory description. In a first approximation, the combination of trajectories can be denoted as follows:

$$\mathrm{C} = \mathbf{F}_{\mathrm{C}}[\mathrm{B}_1,[\mathrm{B}_2,[\ldots,[\mathrm{B}_{n-1},\mathrm{B}_n]_{\mathsf{J}}\ldots]_{\mathsf{J}}]_{\mathsf{J}}]_{\mathsf{J}} \qquad (6)$$

$\mathbf{F}_{\mathrm{C}}$ is the initial frame (Equation 1) of the resulting trajectory C, $\mathrm{B}_{1,\ldots,n}(n \geq 2)$are the component trajectories and $[\ldots]_{\mathsf{J}}$denotes the joining of their vector functions. In the case of J being the addition operator ("$[\ldots]_{\oplus}$"), J can be omitted in writing ("$[\ldots]$"). It is assumed that J is an associative and commutative function, so that the combination of trajectories may also be written in a shorter form:

$$\mathrm{C} = \mathbf{F}_{\mathrm{C}}[\mathrm{B}_1,\ldots,\mathrm{B}_n]_{\mathsf{J}} \qquad (7)$$

The combination of the trajectory vector functions is defined analogously:

$$\mathbf{c}(u,\mathbf{F}_{\mathrm{C}},\ldots) = \mathrm{F}_{\mathrm{C}} \cdot \mathsf{J}(\mathbf{b}_1(u,\mathbf{F}_1,\ldots),\mathbf{b}_2(u,\mathbf{F}_2,\ldots),\ldots,\mathbf{b}_n(u,\mathbf{F}_n,\ldots)) \qquad (8)$$

where $\mathbf{c}(\ldots)$ is the vector function of the resulting trajectory C, $\mathbf{b}_{1,\ldots,n}$ are the vector functions of the component trajectories, u is the trajectory parameter, the $\mathbf{F}_i$are the initial frames of the component trajectories and "$\cdot$" stands for the multiplication of the homogeneous matrix $\mathbf{F}_{\mathrm{C}}$ with the homogeneous vector function created by the combination of $\mathbf{b}_1,\ldots,\mathbf{b}_n$. To obtain more complicated trajectories, (Equations 7 and 8) can be used recursively.

The joining operator J must be defined in such a way that the combination of the homogeneous constituent vector functions $\mathbf{b}_{1,\ldots,n}$ results in a homogeneous vector function $\mathbf{c}$. Simply adding up the different $\mathbf{b}_i(1 \leq i \leq n)$ would give $(\mathrm{c_x}(u),\mathrm{c_y}(u),\mathrm{c_z}(u),n)^{\mathsf{T}}$ as a result, which is not correct. Thus $\mathsf{J} \equiv \oplus$ is defined as follows:

$$\mathsf{J}(\mathbf{x},\mathbf{y}) \equiv \oplus(\mathbf{x},\mathbf{y}) := \mathbf{x}+\mathbf{y}-(0,0,0,1)^{\mathsf{T}} \qquad (9)$$

$\mathsf{J}(\mathbf{x})$ can be used as an abbreviation for $\mathsf{J}(\mathbf{x},\mathbf{b}_{\mathrm{v}})$, $\mathbf{b}_{\mathrm{v}}$ being the neutral element for the trajectory combination operator J with $\mathsf{J}(\mathbf{x},\mathbf{b}_{\mathrm{v}}) = \mathbf{x}$. For $\mathsf{J} \equiv \oplus$, $\mathbf{b}_{\mathrm{v}} = (0,0,0,1)^{\mathsf{T}}$.

The previously defined notation only allows for the combination of trajectories for the same trajectory interval, that is for $u_{c[a_c,b_c]} = u_{1[a_1,b_1]} = \ldots = u_{n[a_n,b_n]}$, with $u_{c[a_c,b_c]}$

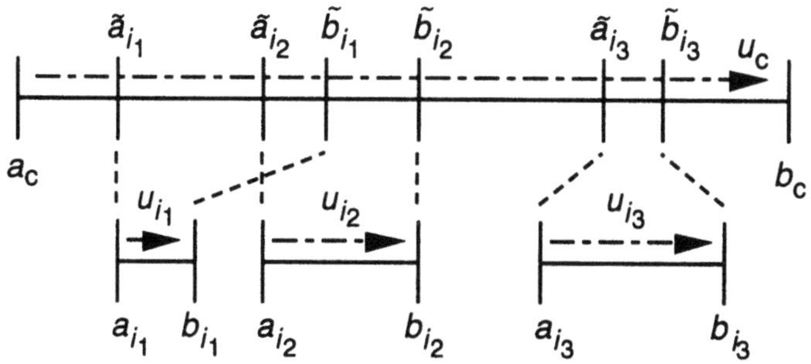

Figure 2: Context of the meanings of the different parameter interval limits for assembled trajectories ($1 \leq i_{1,2,3} \leq n$ and $i_1 \neq i_2 \neq i_3 \neq i_1$).

being the interval $[a_c, b_c]$ of the resulting trajectory C, on which the vector function $\mathbf{c}$ is defined for u_c, and $[a_i, b_i]$ being the intervals of the local parameters u_i for the respective vector functions $\mathbf{b}_i$.

For a more general notation, scaling functions $\sigma_i : [a_c, b_c] \rightarrow [a_i, b_i]$ can be introduced to scale the resulting trajectory's parameter interval $[a_c, b_c]$ onto the different intervals $[a_i, b_i]$ of the component trajectories' parameters u_i. Formally, this can be denoted on the trajectory level as

$$\mathrm{C}(u_{[a_c,b_c]}, \mathbf{F}_\mathrm{C}, \ldots) = \mathbf{F}_\mathrm{C}[\mathrm{B}_1(u_{[a_1,b_1]}, \mathbf{F}_1, \ldots), \ldots, \mathrm{B}_n(u_{[a_n,b_n]}, \mathbf{F}_n, \ldots)]_\mathrm{J} \tag{10}$$

and on the trajectory function level as

$$\mathbf{c}(u, \mathbf{F}_\mathrm{C}, \ldots) = \mathbf{F}_\mathrm{C} \cdot \mathrm{J}(\mathbf{b}_1(\sigma_1(u), \mathbf{F}_1, \ldots), \mathbf{b}_2(\sigma_2(u), \mathbf{F}_2, \ldots), \ldots, \mathbf{b}_n(\sigma_n(u), \mathbf{F}_n, \ldots)) \tag{11}$$

In the simplest case, σ_i is a linear function:

$$\sigma_i : [a_c, b_c] \rightarrow [a_i, b_i] \quad \text{with} \quad \sigma_i(u_c) = a_i + \frac{(b_i - a_i)(u_c - a_c)}{(b_c - a_c)} \tag{12}$$

To simplify matters, from now on the following convention for combined trajectories is obeyed: All trajectory parameter intervals are restricted to the interval $[0, 1]$, thus all σ_i represent the identity function ($\sigma_i \equiv \mathrm{id}$). If scaling is needed, it is provided through such trajectory parameters as trajectory length λ_i, amplitude a, or circular frequency ω.

If parameters of combined trajectories remain unused (through neutral instantiation, for example as with the ellipse by setting one principal axis radius to 0), the resulting trajectory may correspond to a simpler or even to a basic trajectory. In such a case, the combined trajectory is called *degenerate*.

DEFINITION 6 (DEGENERATE)

- A degenerate *trajectory* $\mathrm{C}(p_{11}, \ldots, p_{nm_n}) = \mathbf{F}[\mathrm{B}_1(p_{11}, \ldots, p_{nm_n})]_\mathrm{J}$ *is a non-elementary trajectory with at least one of its parameters p_{ij} instantiated neutrally in such a way that at least one of its constituent trajectories* B_i *ceases to contribute* *to the overall shape of* C*, thus being removable from the combination without affecting the shape of* C*. Formally,* C *is degenerate iff (with* $\mathbf{F}_\mathrm{C} = \mathbf{F}_\mathrm{D}$*)*

$$\begin{aligned}\mathrm{C}(p_{11},\dots,p_{nm_n}) &= \mathbf{F}_\mathrm{C}[\mathrm{B}_1,\dots,\mathrm{B}_{i-1},\mathrm{B}_i,\mathrm{B}_{i+1},\dots,\mathrm{B}_n]_\mathrm{J}\\ &= \mathbf{F}_\mathrm{D}[\mathrm{B}_1,\dots,\mathrm{B}_{i-1},\mathrm{B}_{i+1},\dots,\mathrm{B}_n]_\mathrm{J}\end{aligned}$$

- C *is degenerate except for* **F** *iff* $\mathbf{F}_\mathrm{C} \neq \mathbf{F}_\mathrm{D}$
- *The number m of neutralized* B_i *determines the order m of trajectory degeneration, for example* $m = 2$ *means* C *is* twofold *degenerate.*

Examples for combined trajectories can be found in Table 2.

2.2.3 Assembled Trajectories

Another way to join trajectories is to *assemble* their vector functions by adding one piece after another. In contrast to combined trajectories, where all component trajectories affect the shape of the resulting trajectory over its whole length (giving a uniform *trajectory segment*), in each segment of an assembled trajectory, its shape is normally dominated by only one or a few trajectory functions (all other functions are "dormant" with respect to this segment).

On the trajectory description level, an assembled trajectory is denoted as follows:

$$\mathrm{C} = \mathbf{F}_\mathrm{C}\{\mathrm{B}_1,\dots,\mathrm{B}_n\}_\mathrm{J} \tag{13}$$

The corresponding vector function is

$$\mathbf{c}(u_c,\mathbf{F}_\mathrm{C},\dots) = \begin{cases}\mathbf{b}_1(\sigma_1(u_c),\mathbf{F}_1,\dots) & ; \quad \tilde{a}_1 \le u_c \le \tilde{b}_1\\ \vdots & \\ \mathbf{b}_n(\sigma_n(u_c),\mathbf{F}_n,\dots) & ; \quad \tilde{a}_n \le u_c \le \tilde{b}_n\end{cases} \tag{14}$$

where C, $\mathbf{F}_\mathrm{C}$, B_i, J, **c**, u_c, $\mathbf{b}_i$, $\mathbf{F}_i$, a_i, b_i, a_c, b_c are as above (see combined trajectories) and where different possibilities for the ordering of the $\tilde{a}_i$, $\tilde{b}_i$ with respect to the resulting interval $[a_c,b_c]$ are possible:

1. $a_c = \tilde{a}_1 < \tilde{b}_1 = \tilde{a}_2 < \dots < \tilde{b}_{n-1} = \tilde{a}_n < \tilde{b}_n = b_c$ where $\tilde{b}_{i-1} = \tilde{a}_i$ for $i = 2,\dots,n$

2. $a_c = \tilde{a}_1 < \tilde{a}_2 < \dots < \tilde{a}_n < b_c \quad ; \quad a_c < \tilde{b}_1 \le \tilde{b}_2 \le \dots \le \tilde{b}_n = b_c \quad ; \quad \tilde{a}_i < \tilde{b}_i$ for $i = 1,\dots,n$
   (For $\sigma_i = \mathrm{id}$ and $\mathrm{J} = \oplus$ this also covers the interval definitions of natural spline functions — if different G_{λ_i} are used in combination with this, it is straightforward to formulate the spline functions.)

3. $a_c = \tilde{a}_1 < \tilde{b}_1 = b_c \quad ; \quad \tilde{a}_1 \le \tilde{a}_2 < \tilde{b}_2 \le \tilde{b}_1 \quad ; \quad \dots \quad ; \quad \tilde{a}_{n-1} \le \tilde{a}_n < \tilde{b}_n \le \tilde{b}_{n-1}$
   (Each interval $[\tilde{a}_i,\tilde{b}_i]$ contains the next smaller interval $[\tilde{a}_{i+1},\tilde{b}_{i+1}]$; setting $a_c = \tilde{a}_1 = \tilde{a}_2 = \dots = \tilde{a}_n$ and $\tilde{b}_1 = \tilde{b}_2 = \dots = \tilde{b}_n = b_c$ results in the special case of a *combined trajectory*.)

Synopsis	Trajectory Description	HamNoSys (with $\mathbf{F} = \mathbf{I}_4$)
Cross $C_{rs}(u,\mathbf{F},\lambda_{a1},\lambda_{a2},\lambda_{b1},\lambda_{b2}) =$ $\mathbf{F}\{G_{\lambda 1},E,G_{\lambda 1})\}$	$C_{rs}(u,\mathbf{F},\lambda_{a1},\lambda_{a2},\lambda_{b1},\lambda_{b2}) =$ $\mathbf{F}\{G_{\lambda 1}(u,\mathbf{F}_{\lambda a},\lambda_{a1}+\lambda_{a2}),$ $E(u,\mathbf{F}_E,\lambda_{b1},\lambda_{a2},\frac{\pi}{2},0),$ * $G_{\lambda 1}(u,\mathbf{F}_{\lambda b},\lambda_{b1}+\lambda_{b2}\}$	
Curves $C_{vs}(u,\mathbf{F},\lambda_1,a,n) =$ $\mathbf{F}\{C_{v_1},\dots,C_{v_n}\} =$ $\mathbf{F}\overset{n}{\underset{i=1}{\{}}\, C_{v_i}\}$	$C_{vs}(u,\mathbf{F},\lambda_1,a,n) =$ $\mathbf{F}\overset{n}{\underset{i=1}{\{}}\, C_v(u,\mathbf{T}(((i-1)\lambda_1,0,0,1)^{\mathsf{T}}),\lambda_1,a)\}$	
Triangle (Sawtooth) $T_r(u,\mathbf{F},\lambda_1,a) =$ $\mathbf{F}[G_{\lambda 1},G_{\lambda 1},G_{\lambda 1}]$	$T_r(u,\mathbf{F},\lambda_1,a) =$ $\mathbf{F}[G_{\lambda 1}(u,\mathbf{F}_{T_{r1}},l_a),G_{\lambda 1}(u,\mathbf{F}_{T_{r2}},l_b),$ † $G_{\lambda 1}(u,\mathbf{F}_{T_{r3}},l_a)]$	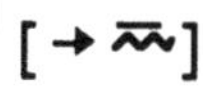
Triangles (Sawteeth) $T_{rs}(u,\mathbf{F},\lambda_1,a,n) =$ $\mathbf{F}\{T_{r_1},\dots,T_{r_n}\} =$ $\mathbf{F}\overset{n}{\underset{i=1}{\{}}\, T_{r_i}\}$	$T_{rs}(u,\mathbf{F},\lambda_1,a,n) =$ $\mathbf{F}\overset{n}{\underset{i=1}{\{}}\, T_r(u,\mathbf{T}(((i-1)\lambda_1,0,0,1)^{\mathsf{T}}),\lambda_1,a)\}$	

*$\mathbf{F}_{\lambda a} = \mathbf{T}((0,0,\lambda_{a1},1)^{\mathsf{T}})\mathbf{R}_y(\frac{\pi}{2})$, $\mathbf{F}_{\lambda b} = \mathbf{T}((-\lambda_{b1},0,0,1)^{\mathsf{T}})$, $\mathbf{F}_E = \mathbf{T}((-\lambda_{b1},0,-\lambda_{a2},1)^{\mathsf{T}})\mathbf{R}_x(\frac{\pi}{2})$ and $\lambda_{a1,2}$, $\lambda_{b1,2}$ as shown in Figure 3a.

†$l_a = \sqrt{\left(\frac{\lambda_1}{4}\right)^2 + a^2}$, $l_b = \sqrt{\left(\frac{\lambda_1}{2}\right)^2 + 4a^2}$, $\mathbf{F}_{T_{r1}} = \mathbf{R}_z(\alpha_{T_r})$, $\alpha_{T_r} = \arctan(\frac{4a}{\lambda_1})$, $\mathbf{F}_{T_{r2}} = \mathbf{T}((\frac{\lambda_1}{4},a,0,1)^{\mathsf{T}})\mathbf{R}_z(-\alpha_{T_r})$, $\mathbf{F}_{T_{r3}} = \mathbf{T}((\frac{3\lambda_1}{4},-a,0,1)^{\mathsf{T}})\mathbf{R}_z(\alpha_{T_r})$ (for l_a, l_b, a and λ_1 see Figure 3b .)

Table 1: Some assembled trajectories.

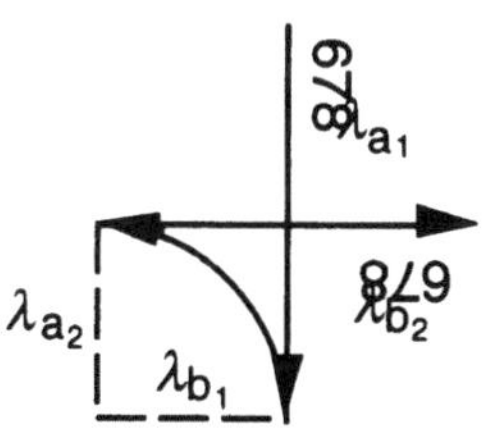

(a) $\lambda_{a_{1,2}}$ and $\lambda_{b_{1,2}}$

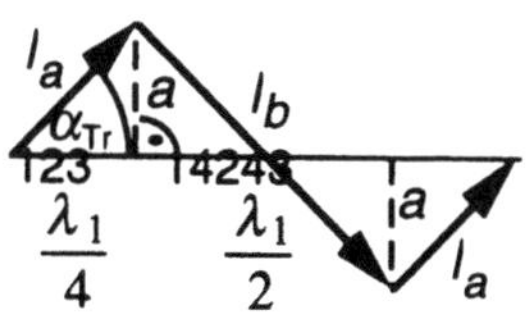

(b) $\lambda_{a,b}$ and λ_1

Figure 3: Lengths for assembled trajectories

Of course, Equations 13 and 14 can be applied recursively to create more complicated trajectories. Compared to Equation 12, the scaling functions σ_i now scale the values of u_c from a different range onto the component parameter intervals $[\tilde{a}_i, \tilde{b}_i]$ — in the simplest case, the σ_i are linear functions again:

$$\sigma_i : [\tilde{a}_i, \tilde{b}_i] \rightarrow [a_i, b_i] \quad \text{with} \quad \sigma_i(u_c) = a_i + \frac{(b_i - a_i)(u_c - \tilde{a}_i)}{(\tilde{b}_i, \tilde{a}_i)} \tag{15}$$

The connection between the interval limits a_i, b_i of the component trajectory parameters u_i and the $\tilde{a}_i$, $\tilde{b}_i$ of Equation 14 is illustrated in Figure 2.

The joining operator J is used to combine component trajectories in the case of two or more of them overlapping partly or completely.

Equation 14 is the most general formulation for assembling trajectory functions. At the moment, we only make use of it in a simplified form, using similar conventions to those of combined trajectories: Per default, we set $\mathrm{J} \equiv \oplus$ and use the interval ordering of case a) (see above), with each interval $[a_i, b_i] = [0, 1]$ and with $[a_c, b_c] = [0, 1]$ too. Thus σ_i becomes

$$\sigma_i : [\tilde{a}_i, \tilde{b}_i] \rightarrow [0, 1] \quad \text{with} \quad \sigma_i(u_c) = n(u_c - \tilde{a}_i) \quad \text{and} \quad [\tilde{a}_i, \tilde{b}_i] = \left[\frac{i-1}{n}, \frac{i}{n}\right] \tag{16}$$

Examples for assembled trajectories can be found in Table 1.

2.3 Describing a Subset of HamNoSys by Parametric Trajectories

In this section, examples for the mapping of symbols and simple expressions from HamNoSys to their parametric trajectory equivalents are given. Each movement symbol implies a three-dimensional direction which can be expressed by an appropriate initial frame **F**. With reference to the human body, the axes of the frame of reference — the Basic Coordinate System (**BCS**) — are defined as follows (with $\mathbf{BCS} = \mathbf{I}_4$ and $\mathbf{I}_4$ being the 4×4 identity matrix). The z-axis runs the length of the body, pointing upwards; the x-axis follows the outstretched right arm and the y-axis points along the horizontally extended (left or right) arm pointing to the front. The following matrices are used: $\mathbf{F}_x = \mathbf{I}_4, \mathbf{F}_y = \mathbf{R}_z(\frac{\pi}{2})$ and $\mathbf{F}_z = \mathbf{R}_y(-\frac{\pi}{2})$ where

$$\mathbf{R}_x(\alpha) = \begin{bmatrix} 1 & 0 & 0 & 0 \\ 0 & \cos\alpha & -\sin\alpha & 0 \\ 0 & \sin\alpha & \cos\alpha & 0 \\ 0 & 0 & 0 & 1 \end{bmatrix} \tag{17}$$

$$\mathbf{R}_y(\alpha) = \begin{bmatrix} \cos\alpha & 0 & \sin\alpha & 0 \\ 0 & 1 & 0 & 0 \\ -\sin\alpha & 0 & \cos\alpha & 0 \\ 0 & 0 & 0 & 1 \end{bmatrix} \tag{18}$$

Synopsis	Trajectory Description	HamNoSys ($\mathbf{F} = \mathbf{I}_4$)
Wave $\mathrm{W}(u, \mathbf{F}, \lambda_1, a, \omega, \psi) =$ $\mathbf{F}[\mathrm{G}_{\lambda_1}, \mathrm{G}_{\sin}]$	$\mathrm{W}(u, \mathbf{F}, \lambda_1, a, \omega, \psi) =$ $\mathbf{F}[\mathrm{G}_{\lambda_1}(u, \mathbf{F}_x, \lambda_1),$ $\mathrm{G}_{\sin}(u, \mathbf{F}_y, a, \omega, \psi)]$	
Curve $\mathrm{C}_v(u, \mathbf{F}, \lambda_1, a) =$ $\mathbf{F}[\mathrm{G}_{\lambda_1}, \mathrm{G}_{\sin}]$	$\mathrm{C}_v(u, \mathbf{F}, \lambda_1, a) =$ $\mathbf{F}[\mathrm{G}_{\lambda_1}(u, \mathbf{F}_x, \lambda_1),$ $\mathrm{G}_{\sin}(u, \mathbf{F}_z, a, \pi, 0)]$	
Ellipse $\mathrm{E}(u, \mathbf{F}, r_a, r_b, \omega, \psi) =$ $\mathbf{F}[\mathrm{G}_{\sin}, \mathrm{G}_{\sin}]$	$\mathrm{E}(u, \mathbf{F}, r_a, r_b, \omega, \psi) =$ $\mathbf{F}[\mathrm{G}_{\sin}(u, \mathbf{F}_y, r_a, \omega, \psi + \frac{\pi}{2}),$ $\mathrm{G}_{\sin}(u, \mathbf{F}_z, r_b, \omega, \psi)]$	 ($\omega > 0$ or $\omega < 0$)
Cylindrical Spiral $\mathrm{E_Z}(u, \mathbf{F}, \lambda_1, r_a, r_b, \omega, \psi) =$ $\mathrm{F}[\mathrm{G}_{\lambda_1}, \mathrm{G}_{\sin}, \mathrm{G}_{\sin}]$	$\mathrm{E_Z}(u, \mathbf{F}, \lambda_1, r_a, r_b, \omega, \psi) =$ $\mathrm{F}[\mathrm{G}_{\lambda_1}(u, \mathbf{F}_x, \lambda_1),$ $\mathrm{G}_{\sin}(u, \mathbf{F}_y, r_a, \omega, \psi + \frac{\pi}{2}),$ $\mathrm{G}_{\sin}(u, \mathbf{F}_z, r_b, \omega, \psi)]$	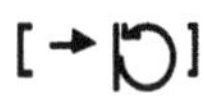 ($\omega > 0$) or 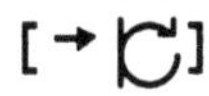 ($\omega < 0$)
Opening / Closing Spiral $\mathrm{S}(u, \mathbf{F}, \lambda_1, \mathbf{r}_a, \mathbf{r}_b, \omega, \psi) =$ $\mathbf{F}[\mathrm{G}_{\lambda_1}, \mathrm{G}_{\sin}, \mathrm{G}_{\sin}]$ with $\mathbf{r}_a = (r_{a_1}, r_{a_2})^\mathsf{T}$ $\mathbf{r}_b = (r_{b_1}, r_{b_2})^\mathsf{T}$	$\mathrm{S}(u, \mathbf{F}, \lambda_1, \mathbf{r}_a, \mathbf{r}_b, \omega, \psi) =$ $\mathbf{F}[\mathrm{G}_{\lambda_1}(u, \mathbf{F}_x, \lambda_1),$ $\mathrm{G}_{\sin}(u, \mathbf{F}_y, r_{a_1} + u(r_{a_2} - r_{a_1}),$ $\omega, \psi + \frac{\pi}{2}),$ $\mathrm{G}_{\sin}(u, \mathbf{F}_z, r_{b_1} + u(r_{b_2} - r_{b_1}),$ $\omega, \psi)]$	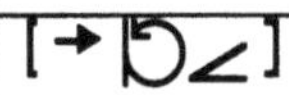 ($\omega > 0, r_{a_1} < r_{a_2}, r_{b_1} < r_{b_2}$) 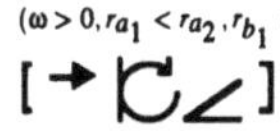 ($\omega < 0, r_{a_1} < r_{a_2}, r_{b_1} < r_{b_2}$) 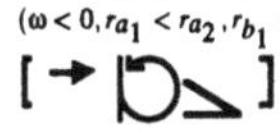 ($\omega > 0, r_{a_1} > r_{a_2}, r_{b_1} > r_{b_2}$) 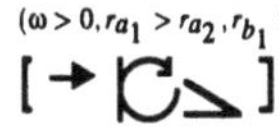 ($\omega < 0, r_{a_1} > r_{a_2}, r_{b_1} > r_{b_2}$)

Table 2: Some combined trajectories.

$$\mathbf{R}_z(\alpha) = \begin{bmatrix} \cos\alpha & -\sin\alpha & 0 & 0 \\ \sin\alpha & \cos\alpha & 0 & 0 \\ 0 & 0 & 1 & 0 \\ 0 & 0 & 0 & 1 \end{bmatrix} \tag{19}$$

$$\mathbf{T}(\alpha) = \mathbf{T}\left(\begin{bmatrix} v_x \\ v_y \\ v_z \\ 1 \end{bmatrix}\right) = \begin{bmatrix} 1 & 0 & 0 & v_x \\ 0 & 1 & 0 & v_y \\ 0 & 0 & 1 & v_z \\ 0 & 0 & 0 & 1 \end{bmatrix} \tag{20}$$

2.4 Deriving Acceleration Data From Parametric Trajectories

Deriving acceleration data from KINOTE is straightforward: As the trajectory function $\mathbf{s}(t) = \mathbf{b}(\mathrm{u}(t))$ gives the actual position of a trajectory point in time, its first derivative $\mathbf{v}(t) = d\mathbf{s}(t)/dt$ provides the velocity and the second derivative $\mathbf{a}(t) = d\mathbf{v}(t)/dt$ the acceleration.

Space is lacking in this paper to go into the details of how whole configurations of acceleration sensors can be formally described to fit in with KINOTE, so that the acceleration function for each sensor can be derived directly from the trajectory description B and the configuration description C. This can be used to build a theoretical model of the sensor configuration and compare its data predictions with real measurements. Details of this will be published elsewhere.

3 Experiment

In this section, the experiments we conducted to measure gestural hand movements with accelerometers are described. The purpose of the experiments was to obtain trajectory data for analysis and classification in the framework of KINOTE.

Different kinds of motion were recorded using a combination of two triaxial accelerometers (three monoaxial accelerometers ADXL50 [Analog Devices, 1994] and one triaxial accelerometer 8692B5 [Kistler, 1994]). The two types of accelerometers differ in accuracy and measurement ranges. Whereas the micromachined silicon ADXL50 has a range of ±50 g (threshold at 0.1 g) and is capable of measuring "static" accelerations (eg. earth's gravity) as well as "dynamic" accelerations (vibrations), the piezoelectric 8692B5 has a measurement range of ±5 g (threshold 120 μg) and measures vibrations from 0.5 Hz onwards. It was hoped that by combining the measurements of the two sensor pairs, the quality of the resulting data could be improved (high dynamic accuracy and greater g-bandwidth). Through a defect in the x-axis of the 8692B5 (to some extent in the y- and z-axis as well), this was only marginally possible and for current motion classification purposes, only data from the three ADXL50 sensors was used.

The sensors were fastened to a small platform and aligned in such a way that their x-, y- and z-axes pointed into the same direction, respectively. The platform was attached to a glove which was worn on the experimenter's right hand. All motions were digitized at 500 samples/second with a 12 bit-resolution and had an overall duration of 5–10 s (depending on the size and speed of the motion). For the ADXL50, noise levels were so high that a simple 8 bit analog-to-digital converter (ADC) would have easily been enough.

The motions matched a selection of basic HamNoSys motion symbols for which the kinematic transcription was given in Section 2. They consisted of a straight line (↗), a circular movement (C), sine (∿) and sawtooth (⩘) movements, a cross (✢), one curved arc ([→⌒]), multiple curved arcs ([→⌒⌒]), a cylindrical spiral (→C) and a closing cylindrical spiral (CƆCƆCƆ). Even though the selected movements may seem somewhat artificial when compared to "real" sign language gestures, they contain similar elementary movement patterns, so that the same analysis techniques used with them should also be applicable to more realistic gestures.

Each movement was executed in a variety of different ways, including small, medium sized and large expansive movements at three different speeds (slow, medium speed, fast). All motions were made using a fixed hand orientation with reference to a stationary basic coordinate system, some motions (line, sine, cross, single curved arc) were also made with a varying (free) orientation. Each motion was repeated 10 times in front of a video camera and a paper screen marked with horizontal and vertical lines (equally spaced at 1 cm) for later reference.

For a total of almost 1200 recorded movements, about 20MB of raw data were obtained. At present, only a small portion has been evaluated as indicated in the next section and much work must still be done. Even so, the preliminary results are encouraging.

4 Using Acceleration Data for Trajectory Classification

In this section, the processing techniques and analysis methods are described which were used on the data obtained from the experiments.

4.1 Preprocessing of Accelerometer Data

For gesture template acquisition the continuous data stream of the accelerometers is sampled in windows of width W. Each gesture begins some time after the start of a new window and ends before the time index t reaches W. Typical values for W are $W = 2500$ and $W = 5000$.

For further processing the raw data must be filtered. A sample mean filter is used with a filter width of $N = 100$ sample points corresponding to a time interval of 0.2 s (different filter widths were experimented with), where the data points are denoted as $a_{x,y,z}(t)$ and the filtered data points as $\hat{a}_{x,y,z}$(t), with time index $t = 1,2,\ldots,W$:

$$\hat{a}_{x,y,z}(t) = \frac{1}{N}\sum_{i=0}^{N-1} a_{x,y,z}(t+i) \tag{21}$$

Filter (Equation 21) is used on each of the 6 input channels of acceleration data: Channels 1–3 correspond to the x-, y- and z-axis of the ADXL50 sensor configuration; channels 4–6 to the three axes of the 8692B5. As mentioned above, only the first three channels were fully operational and are subsequently referred to as $a_{x,y,z}$.

The sensors were calibrated against earth gravity to give off a voltage swing corresponding to about ±5 g for the 0–5 V input of the ADC. No exact calibration is needed as the main interest lies in the classification of *relative* trajectory shapes and sizes, not their precise three-dimensional position and shape (the effect of gravity on the ADXL50 is neglected in this paper, but will be considered in further investigations). Thus in addition to the g range calibration only a simple "online"-calibration for the zero offset is needed (See Equation 22): $\hat{\mathbf{a}}_m$.

For feature extraction, three different profiles are calculated from the filtered data: a velocity profile $\mathrm{v}_{\mathrm{abs}}(t)$, a curvature profile $\kappa^2(t)$, and a winding profile $\mathrm{w}(t)$ (Section

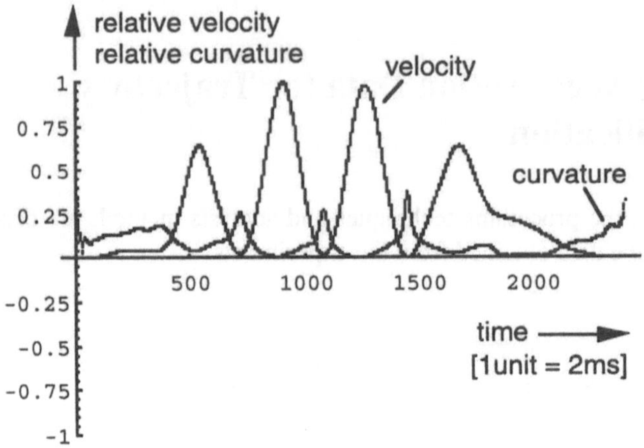

(a) Velocity and curvature profile

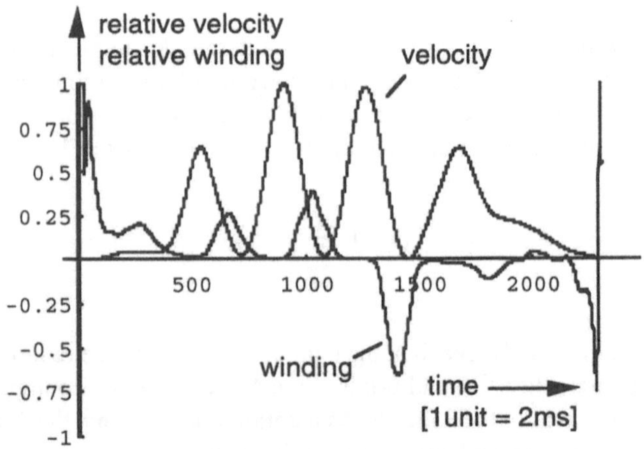

(b) Velocity and winding profile

Figure 4: Profiles for a medium size and speed cylindrical spiral.

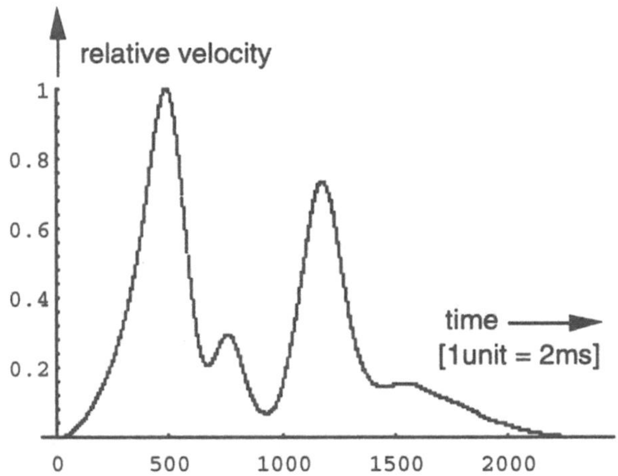

Figure 5: Velocity profile for a medium size and speed cross

4.3.2.2 of [4]). They are obtained as follows:

$$\mathrm{v}_{\mathrm{abs}}(t) = |\mathbf{v}(t)|, \quad \text{where} \quad \mathbf{v}(t) = \sum_{\tau=1}^{t} (\hat{\mathbf{a}}(\tau) - \hat{\mathbf{a}}_m) \tag{22}$$

$$\kappa^2(t) = \frac{(\mathbf{v}(t)\cdot\mathbf{v}(t))\,(\hat{\mathbf{a}}(t)\cdot\hat{\mathbf{a}}(t)) - (\mathbf{v}(t)\cdot\hat{\mathbf{a}}(t))^2}{(\mathbf{v}(t)\cdot\mathbf{v}(t))^3} \tag{23}$$

$$\mathrm{w}(t) = \frac{1}{\kappa^2(t)} \frac{\left|(\mathbf{v}(t),\hat{\mathbf{a}}(t),\hat{\mathbf{r}}(t))^{\mathsf{T}}\right|}{(\mathbf{v}(t)\cdot\mathbf{v}(t))^3} \tag{24}$$

where $\hat{\mathbf{a}}(t) = (\hat{a}_x(t), \hat{a}_y(t), \hat{a}_z(t))^{\mathsf{T}}$, $1 \leq t \leq W - N + 1$, $\hat{\mathbf{a}}_m$ is the vector of the overall mean of the acceleration values in the current data window (with $N = W$ and $\hat{\mathbf{a}}_m = (\hat{a}_x(1), \hat{a}_y(1), \hat{a}_z(1))^{\mathsf{T}}$ in Equation 21), $\mathbf{r}(t) = d\hat{\mathbf{a}}(t)/dt$ and $\hat{\mathbf{r}}(t)$ is obtained by applying filter (Equation 21) with $N = 100$ to $\mathbf{r}(t)$.

This form of representation of a gestural motion trajectory has the advantage of an inherent translational and rotational invariance, as compared to the normal cartesian x(t), y(t), z(t) representation. A typical example of a velocity-, curvature- and winding profile is shown in Figures 4a and 4b.

Whereas the *amplitude* of the velocity profile depends on gesture speed, its *shape* generally remains the same for the three gesture speeds used in the experiment. The other two profiles, curvature and winding, ideally only depend on the size and shape of the accelerometers' motion path, but not on gesture speed. Taken in combination, the three profiles provide a good basis for the extraction of sample points to form feature vectors for curve classification.

4.2 Feature Extraction for Pattern Classification

As was observed in the experiments, the shape of the velocity profile of the gestural movements remains quite constant for similar gestures, but differs from gesture type to gesture type (See Figure 4 vs. Figure 5). For classification, typical aspects of the curve must be extracted from it and converted to a form suitable for pattern recognition methods such as the nearest neighbour classificator.

Here, the relative position rx_j and height ry_j of the curve of the extrema $\mathbf{e}_j = (x_j, y_j)^\mathsf{T}$, $(j = 1, \ldots, m)$ are extracted as typical features (assuming that for classification purposes, the curve is described by its extrema in sufficient detail). The curve extrema in each data window (or *time series* $Z = (d_1, \ldots, d_n)$ with $n = W$) are extracted from the data, resulting in a list $E = (\mathbf{e}_1, \ldots, \mathbf{e}_m)$ of extrema. Each y_j corresponds to a d_i of Z with $x_j = i$. In order to compensate for differences in time scale and amplitude when comparing two time series $Z_{1,2}$, both coordinate components of the $\mathbf{e}_j$ are rescaled to the interval $[0,1]$, giving $\mathbf{re}_j = (rx_j, ry_j)^\mathsf{T} = z_j$:

$$
\begin{aligned}
ry_j &= (y_j - y_{\min})/y_{\text{pp}} && (25)\\
rx_j &= (x_j - x_{j-1})/x_{\text{pp}} \quad (\text{with} \quad x_0 = x_{\min}) && (26)\\
y_{\text{pp}} &= y_{\max} - y_{\min} && (27)\\
x_{\text{pp}} &= x_{\max} - y_{\min} && (28)\\
x_{\max} &= \max(x_j) && (29)\\
x_{\min} &= \min(x_j) && (30)\\
y_{\max} &= \max(y_j) && (31)\\
y_{\min} &= \min(y_j) && (32)
\end{aligned}
$$

Rescaling the complete list of extrema of the time series Z gives its *vector representation* $\mathbf{z} = (z_1, \ldots, z_m)^\mathsf{T} = \left((rx_1, ry_1)^\mathsf{T}, \ldots, (rx_m, ry_m)^\mathsf{T}\right)^\mathsf{T}$. In this way, a vector representation $\mathbf{z}_v$ of the velocity profile $\mathrm{v}_{\text{abs}}(t)$ (or rather, of $Z_{\mathrm{v}_{\text{abs}}} = (\mathrm{v}_{\text{abs}}(1), \ldots, \mathrm{v}_{\text{abs}}(W))$) is obtained. It is important to note that the vector representation may vary in length, as in some gesture data sets certain features may be missing. This has to be compensated for in the matching procedure (Section 4.3).

Including the curvature and winding profiles into this representation for classification is straightforward: After going through a similar scaling process[1] for $\kappa^2(t)$ and $w(t)$ (this time not only the extrema, but *all* data points are scaled), the vector representation $\mathbf{z}_v$ is extended as follows and used for pattern matching in the next section:

$$
\begin{aligned}
\mathbf{z}_{v\kappa w1} &= (z_{v\kappa w1}, \ldots, z_{v\kappa w1})^\mathsf{T}\\
&= \left(\left(rx_1, ry_1, r\kappa^2(x_1), rw(x_1)\right)^\mathsf{T}, \ldots, \left(rx_m, ry_m, r\kappa^2(x_m), rw(x_m)\right)^\mathsf{T}\right)^\mathsf{T}
\end{aligned} \tag{33}
$$

[1] The scaling process for the curvature and winding profiles includes the application of the logarithm function to $\kappa^2(t)$ and $w(t)$.

4.3 Pattern Classification

For the recognition or *classification* of gesture movements, the vector representation $\mathbf{z}$ of the last section is used in conjunction with the nearest neighbour classificator and a special matching algorithm.

The nearest neighbour classificator is a simple but effective pattern classification method: Each new unknown vector $\mathbf{x}$ which is to be classified (that is have a class name or index assigned to it) is compared with prototype vectors $\mathbf{p}_{kl}$ of $k = 1, \ldots, K$ classes and $l = 1, \ldots, \mathrm{P}_k$ prototypes per class. The comparison of $\mathbf{x}$ and $\mathbf{p}_{kl}$ involves the calculation of some type of distance measure d; often the euclidean distance $||\mathbf{x} - \mathbf{p}_{kl}||$ is taken for simplicity. $\mathbf{x}$ is assigned to the class k for which $\mathrm{d}(\mathbf{x}, \mathbf{p}_{kl})$ is smallest.

In principle, the matching of two vector representations $\mathbf{z}_1, \mathbf{z}_2$ (one being the newly input gesture, the other a stored prototype) simply consists of "flattening" the vector representations to one-dimensional lists — Equation 33 becomes

$$\left(rx_1, ry_1, r\kappa^2(x_1), rw(x_1), \ldots, rx_m, ry_m, r\kappa^2(x_m), rw(x_m)\right)^{\mathsf{T}}$$

— then of applying the nearest neighbour classificator.

A special matching algorithm is necessary because the nearest neighbour classificator can only match vectors of the same length, which is not always the case for $\mathbf{z}_{1,2}$. So before $\mathbf{z}_{1,2}$ are "flattened" for direct comparison, the longer vector must be reduced to the same size as the shorter one. It is assumed that $\mathbf{z}_1$ always represents the longer vector. The process of shortening is described first, after which the matching is explained.

There are many ways to shorten $\mathbf{z}_1$ to give $\mathbf{z}_1'$ — here, a very simple approach is taken. Shortening $\mathbf{z}_1$ of previous length l_p to a final length l_f simply consists of dropping $l_p - l_f$ elements and reprocessing the remaining elements as follows: for each dropped element $\mathbf{z}_i$, the value of rx_i is retained and added to the value of rx_{i+1} (if consecutive elements of the vector are dropped, this results in an accumulation of the rx_i in the next rx_j which is not dropped). If z_{l_p} is dropped, the value of rx_{l_p} simply "vanishes". When enough elements have been dropped, the value of the new rx_1 is set to 0. The remaining rx_i are normalized such that $\sum rx_i = 1$ and represent — as before — the mutual relative distances of the remaining curve extrema.

As for the dropping itself, in principle there are $l_p!/\left(l_f!(l_p - l_f)!\right)$ possibilities of dropping $l_p - l_f$ elements from $\mathbf{z}_1$. The simplest way is to try out all combinations and match each resulting $\mathbf{z}_1'$ with $\mathbf{z}_2$ (in practice, one will adopt certain heuristics to reduce the computational cost). The smallest distance found in this way is taken to be the (unnormalized) distance $\mathrm{d}(\mathbf{z}_1, \mathbf{z}_2)$. Normalizing d simply consists of division by l_f. (Another, perhaps better way to normalize the distance measure would be to scale $\mathbf{z}_1'$ and $\mathbf{z}_2$ both to length 1, then take the dot product $\mathbf{z}_1' \cdot \mathbf{z}_2$ as a distance measure instead. With $||\mathbf{z}_1'|| = ||\mathbf{z}_2|| = 1$, $\mathbf{z}_1' \cdot \mathbf{z}_2$ represents the cosine of the angle between $\mathbf{z}_1'$ and $\mathbf{z}_2$, 1 being the smallest and 0 the largest possible distance. This distance measure was not yet implemented and remains to be evaluated at some future time.)

Using this method for pattern classification, it is now possible to look for sections in the continuous acceleration data stream which match stored templates or even only parts of templates with a given minimum length (vector representation shortening need not be restricted to $\mathbf{z}_1$ — for example for the evaluation of our experimental data, a minimum match length of 90% for $\mathbf{z}_2$ was required).

5 Preliminary Results

As mentioned above, a defect in one of the sensors hampered the combination of measurements, so that for the current analysis only the ADXL50 data was used. The noise levels were high as compared to the y- and z-axis of the 8692B5, but even so, good recognition rates could be achieved.

As already early surveys of the collected data have shown, the velocity profile serves as a good gesture segmentation cue. Its curve extrema taken as sampling points for curvature and winding profiles provide good feature vectors for classification.

For the estimation of recognition rates, two main tests were conducted:

1. *Intraclass* classification of equal gesture movement types but of different size and speed and

2. *interclass* classification of different gesture movement types of approximately equal size and speed.

For the second test, good recognition rates (94%) could be achieved simply by using the velocity profile of the gesture movements; using the same method for the first test, recognition rates were about 80%. Adding the curvature and winding profiles to the feature vectors increased recognition rates in the second case to nearly 100%, in the first case to about 93%.

These preliminary results suggest a good performance of the measurement system and the implemented classification algorithm, even though the tests were conducted on only about 20% of the data set. Until the complete set has been covered, no final statements are possible on the overall performance of the system. Nevertheless, a short survey of the remaining data seems to imply at least equally good performance.

6 The Interdisciplinary Research Project "Gesture Recognition with SensorGloves"

The presented work originates in the context of the interdisciplinary research project "Gesture Recognition with SensorGloves" sponsored by the Technical University of Berlin. At current, the project approaches the end of its first of two two-year phases. Three project partners (the university departments of computer science, electrical engineering and a semiotics research group) work together on the problem of automatic recognition of human gestures with the aid of a glove and various attached sensors.

The computer science research group is concerned with the actual acquisition of gesture data using the TUB-SensorGlove, its analysis and recognition as well as the compilation of the three project partners' results into a prototypical gesture recognition system. The electrical engineers (a microsensors research group) simulate, develop and test new sensors for the TUB-SensorGlove (at current, silicon chip based 3D-accelerometers). The semiotics research group formalizes and categorizes gestures for a dictionary of local Berlin emblems and occupation-related specific gestures, such as gestures used by the police, firemen, divers etc. The dictionary is electronic and contains HamNoSys-transcriptions, verbal descriptions and digitized examples of the collected emblems. It also serves as a basis for the computer science research group's collection of gesture data.

7 Future Work

Much work must still be done. First of all, the analysis of the collected data must be completed, then the data set will have to be expanded. More examples of similar gestures as well as different, more "natural" gesture movements must be collected. The recognition algorithm can still be improved and preprocessing must be expanded to deal with more data from different sensor sources. Certain aspects of the special matching algorithm of Section 4.3 remind of dynamical programming; further investigations are needed to explore the interrelationship of both techniques.

The use of the kinematic notation system proposed in Section 2 for parametric trajectory matching and methods for the transcription of raw gesture data into (sub-) HamNoSys symbols must be investigated with a view to automatically generating recognition algorithms (or data templates) for new gestures simply by giving the recognition system a gesture's description in HamNoSys. For this, the description of finger movements has to be integrated into KINOTE.

Finally, an appropriate test application (for example robot control by gestures) for the developed gesture recognition system must be implemented.

8 Conclusion

In this paper, we propose a new approach to human gestural motion analysis and recognition on the basis of acceleration sensors. A formal method for the mapping of HamNoSys symbols to analytical gesture trajectories is presented, which will serve as a basis for future gesture analysis in our project. We discuss some first ideas and results of ongoing research. Details of this will be the subject of future presentations.

9 Acknowledgements

This work was supported by an internal funding grant of the Technical University of Berlin for the interdisciplinary research project IFP N13/22.

References

[1] Analog Devices. ADXL50 Accelerometer Data Sheet, 1994.

[2] M. Bichsel, editor. *Proceedings of the International Workshop on Automatic Face- and Gesture-Recognition*. Zürich, Switzerland, June 26–28 1995.

[3] K. R. Britting. *Inertial Navigation Systems Analysis*. Wiley-Interscience, 1971.

[4] I. N. Bronstein and K. A. Semendjajew. *Taschenbuch der Mathematik.* B.G. Teubner Verlagsgesellschaft, Stuttgart Leipzig und Verlag Nauka, Moskau, 25th edition, 1991.

[5] J. J. Craig. *Introduction to Robotics: Mechanics & Control.* Addison-Wesley, Reading, Massachusetts, 1986.

[6] F. G. Hofmann. Entwurf und implementierung eines sensorhandschuhs zur steuerung der USC/Belgrad hand. Studienarbeit am institut, Technische Informatik der TU Berlin, November 1991.

[7] F. G. Hofmann. Entwurf und implementierung einer ultraschallbasierten stellungserkennung für den TUB-Sensorhandschuh. Diplomarbeit am institut, Technische Informatik der TU Berlin, June 1993.

[8] G. Hommel, F. G. Hofmann, and J. Henz. The TU Berlin high-precision sensor glove. In *Proceedings of the WWDU'94, Fourth International Scientific Conference*, volume 2, pages F47–F49, University of Milan, Italy, 1994.

[9] Kaiser. *Polhemus, 3 Space user's manual.* A Kaiser Aerospace & Electronics Company, 1987.

[10] T. Kanamori, H. Katayose, Y. Aono, S. Inokuchi, and T. Sakaguchi. Sensor integration for interactive digital art. In *Proceedings of the International Computer Music Conference ICMC '95*, pages 265–268, Banff, Canada, September 3–7 1995. International Computer Music Association.

[11] Kistler. 8692b5 Accelerometer data sheet, 1994.

[12] B. Marcus, T. Lawrence, and P. Churchill. Hand position/measurement control system, US Patent No. 4 986 280, January 1991.

[13] J. R. W. Morris. Accelerometry — A technique for the measurement of human body movements. *Journal of Biomechanics*, 6:729–736, 1973.

[14] S. Prillwitz, R. Leven, H. Zienert, T. Hanke, J. Henning, et al. HamNoSys (version 2.0) — Hamburg Notation System for Sign Languages / An introductory guide. In *International Studies on Sign Language and the Communication of the Deaf*, volume 5, Hamburg, Germany, 1989. Signum Press.

[15] M. Rusch. *Beitrag zur Führungsgrößenerzeugung für freie und kraftschlüssige Bewegungen von Industrierobotern.* Carl Hanser Verlag, Munich, Vienna, 1993. Also: Dissertation at the Technical University of Berlin, 1992.

[16] H. Sawada, S. Ohkura, and S. Hashimoto. Gesture analysis using 3D acceleration sensors for music control. In *Proceedings of the International Computer Music Conference ICMC '95*, pages 256–260, Banff, Canada, September 3–7 1995. International Computer Music Association.

[17] V. Tartter and K. Knowlton. Perception of sign language from an array of 27 moving spots. *Nature*, 289, 1981.

[18] TCAS Datawear. Bodysuit manufactured by Twenty-First Century Actuators and Sensors Ltd., Cardiff, Wales, UK.

[19] T. Zimmermann, J. Lanier, C. Blanchard, S. Bryson, and Y. Harvill. A hand gesture interface device. In *Proceedings of CHI + GI '87 Human Factors in Computing Systems*, pages 189–192, Toronto, Canada, 5–9 April 1987. ACM Press.

Architectural Models of Gesture Systems

M. Bordegoni† and G. P. Faconti‡

†P.F.R. c/o ITIA-CNR, Viale Lombardia, 20/a - 20131 Milano - Italy.
E-mail: mb@itia.mi.cnr.it
Telephone: +39 2 7064 3953 Fax: +39 2 7063 8035

‡CNUCE-CNR, Via S. Maria, 36 - 56126 Pisa - Italy.
E-mail: g.faconti@cnuce.cnr.it
Telephone: +39 50 593 241 Fax: +39 50 904 052

E-mail: {fgh, hommel}@cs.tu-berlin.de
Telephone: +49 30 314-25403 Fax: +49 30 314-21116

Abstract

Gesture systems have been developed following different strategies and approaches. This applies to the technology, the gesture recognition engine, and the application areas. From the technological point of view, we distinguish the gesture devices in two broad classes, depending on the type of data they send to the gesture recognition engine: graphical devices and pictorial devices. Gesture recognition engines have been built based mainly on pattern recognition, neural networks, and statistical classification. Similarly, the potential applications range from signs, system commands, text editing, gesticulation, robot control, etc. This paper tries to compare different architectures of gesture systems, highlighting their strength and weakness.

1 Introduction

In literature, several research works can be found dealing with systems for gesture recognition, used in specific application domains. The application domains can be classified, according to the level of awareness the user has of interacting with a machine. These broaden from applications dealing with gesticulations and virtual reality, to those supporting sign languages and direct manipulation. Each of these applications is characterized by an architecture and an engine used for recognizing gestures. Typically, a recognition system works sequentially, receiving data sampled from a device, analyzing these data, and sending them to an interpreter, that gives to user's gestures some meaning within an application context.

A variety of technologies have been used to capture mechanical and gestural information from the hand [17]. Basically, technology provides position tracking devices using optical, magnetic or acoustic sensing to determine the position of the hand in space, and glove-like devices, which use an electro-mechanical device fitted over the hand and fingers to determine hand shape. An alternative approach, less intrusive than those mentioned, uses a video camera to track the human's hand movement and shape.

Gesture recognition engines are characterized by the algorithm used for gesture recognition, and by the type of gestures they are able to recognize. Generally, the algorithm used is one between pattern recognition, neural networks and statistical classification. They basically differ on the type of training required, and on the accuracy of recognition. From the literature, it seems that no system is capable of accurately recognizing full, dynamic hand gestures. Some recognition engines deal with postures, simply recognizing hand shape. Others deal with gestures, dealing with sequences of postures. Finally, some others deal with dynamic gestures, also taking into account hand shape evolution in space over time. The problem is related to gesture temporal scaling, not easy to compute, and spatial scaling, nearly impossible to compute given the difficulty in modeling the trajectory. Thus, the problem is that algorithms necessary for matching time-space curves are computationally too much expensive.

The location of the interpreter and the feedback module within the system architecture is often constrained by the application domain the recognition system is used for. In systems supporting gesticulation and virtual reality, the interpretation is left to the application, that associates an application semantic with the performed gesture. In systems recognizing sign languages, the interpretation is done within the recognition system, since a meaning is previously associated with the gesture. Finally, in systems dealing with direct manipulation, the interpretation is done in parallel with the recognition, supporting continuos feedback.

This paper discusses different aspects of gesture systems and proposes a taxonomy for their categorization that is driven by the needs of the application domains.

2 Recognition Engines

In existing systems, three algorithms are basically used for gesture recognition: pattern recognition [3, 15], neural networks [10, 14, 18] and statistical classification [16].

In systems based on pattern recognition, the problem of gesture recognition is seen as a problem of pattern matching. Raw data from the device (an image, a record of sensor data, etc.) are elaborated for providing a representation of the pattern, which consists of a set of features extracted from the raw data. The pattern is then classified and compared with the set of known patterns, looking for a matching one. Recognition engines based on pattern recognition are more suited to detect static postures and poses.

In systems using neural networks, the network is configured on the base of training examples. The advantage of these systems is that gestures are recognized also in the presence of noise or incompleteness. One of the drawbacks of these recognition engines is that thousands of examples are required to train the network for having an accurate recognition.

Statistical gesture recognition works by representing a gesture by means of a vector of features, extracted from a set of training gestures, that are subsequently used to derive a set of gesture classes. The gesture recognition problem is consequently stated as

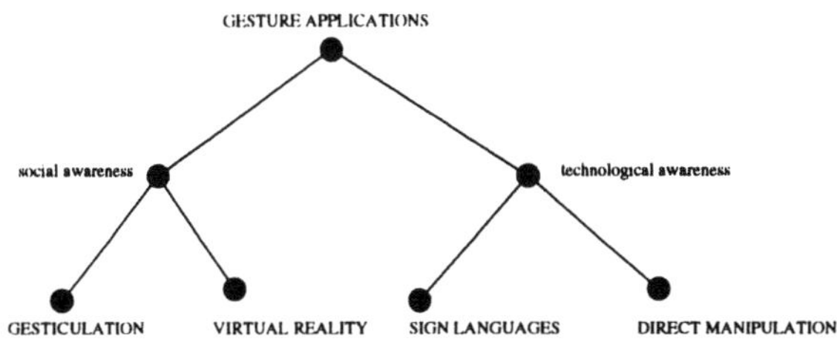

Figure 1: Gesture systems application distinguished on the level of user awareness regarding the technology mediating the communication.

to determine the class to which an input gesture belongs (i.e. the class whose training examples are most like the input gesture). This is done by assuming that each class has a certain probability distribution over the space of gestures, that the training examples of each class were drawn according to this class's distribution, and that the recognition problem is to choose the class whose distribution is the most likely to have produced the input gesture. This methodology allows to realize *eager* recognizers particularly suited for direct manipulation. Such recognizers try to recognize an input gesture as soon as enough postures have been seen in order for the gesture to be unambiguously classified from its feature vector.

3 Applications

The application domains where recognition and/or interpretation of gestures can be useful to augment the knowledge about input data streams can be distinguished in two broad classes, depending on the level of awareness of the user in providing this input to the system (Figure 1). In one case, a human behaves naturally following the social convention shared within specific constituencies and we call it *social awareness*. A second case refers to a user that is aware of interacting with a machinery and adapting his behaviour to its capabilities, and we call it *technological awareness*. In the following, these two classes are detailed, referring to examples of existing applications.

3.1 Social Awareness

In the state of social awareness, the user doesn't take care or even perceive that her behaviour is captured by a computing system that mediates interactions with other humans (i.e. as in the case of cooperative working) or with virtual environments. On the contrary, she fills and, consequently, behaves naturally as in everyday life either making fluent multimodal presentations or using effectively virtual tools as they where real ones. Two application areas can be envisaged at this purpose, namely *gesticulation* and *full immersion* systems.

3.1.1 Gesticulation

Humans interact among themselves by exploiting the potential of their effectors in enriching the semantic content of information to be communicated. Here, humans are fluent in presenting information for communication by blending modalities such as speech, gestures and gazes. In general, none of the modalities is intended to convey a completely refined information although one of them will play a predominant role; rather, each of the modalities can be differently perceived and interpreted in distinguished social contexts for the purpose of adding further details to the communicated information.

Within this framework, true empty-hand gestures are of interest that do not have a unique predefined meaning so that they are not used, in general, to formulate a concept in isolation. On the contrary, they can be interpreted only when performed in a specific context. Changing the context may lead to a changing interpretation of the same gesture. In this sense, gesticulation departs from more traditional approaches since gestures are meaningful only when they hold a proper spatio-temporal relationship with other modalities in the same context.

This form of communication is native to humans: children communicates by means gesticulation before they are able to speak, many people always perform gestures while speaking, and people speaking different languages are often able to communicate simple concepts via gestures. Unfortunately, there has been not much research on the field until recently and the known works are addressing the problem from the very bottom [19]. In fact, all the responsibility of interpreting the gesture is left to the application that potentially requires the availability of a non trivial body of knowledge. In fact, one of the more interesting areas of investigation would be the relationship between multimedia presentation, multimodal interaction and knowledge engineering.

3.1.2 Full-Immersion Systems

The virtual reality [13] technology has made possible to develop systems where the user is able to interact with objects in a simulated world. Currently, such systems are built around the direct manipulation paradigm and use an enhanced technology to *cheat* the human sensors.

In most of the system currently available, users are not allowed to perform natural gestures; rather, in order to interact with objects in a simulated worlds, only a number of predefined gestural commands can be made. Each gesture is defined over a specific hand configuration/motion and is mapped into a defined command [12, 4]. From this point of view, the expressive power of such interfaces is not higher than a typical drawing application. The use of gestures in this context adds very little to the functionality of the system that doesn't justify the requirements for extra cognitive load. In particular, the technology doesn't provide the user with proprioceptive feedback making the interaction almost painful for any non high-skilled and well-trained user.

Hopefully, new technological advances [2] will provide new possibilities for the kind of applications in a very similar way as gesticulation. Here, interaction with virtual objects will be mainly driven by collision detection algorithms with the user being visually and tactually aware of the collision. Examples can be found in the field of robotics and telepresence.

3.2 Technological Awareness

Within technological awareness the user perceives the machine as his primary interacting partner, independently from the fact that it acts as an agent mediating the communication with other humans, or as the final destination of the communication. With this view, the user tends to perceive the modalities potentially available to interact with the system as separate entities and to stress this distinction by reinforcing and highlighting those acts that imply a conjoint participation of different modalities. In this way each act is performed to communicate the intended information with great details. In general, this behaviour suggests that a single modality is used at a time to communicate a complete information. Although the available technology and software development techniques would allow the use of different modalities in a synergistic way, the analysis of the user behaviour with this awareness state demonstrates that such a system would be used in the more simplistic way. For example, [6] gives a formal proof that a user may not be able to carry out the context switching required to locate a value for deictic reference (i.e. saying "find all flights to *this* city" while pointing to a city name referring to the *this* utterance). In this case, she would prefer to formulate the query by using a single modality instead of the *more natural* combination of speech and gestures. Examples of existing applications are direct manipulation interfaces and sign languages where postures and motion are recognized and used as a direct command input. Consequently, gestures form a command language used to give directions to applications.

3.2.1 Direct Manipulation Interfaces

Direct manipulation interface systems are found addressing both 2D and 3D spaces, using traditional devices such as mice/notepads, and more sophisticated technologies such as different kinds of hand-input devices (gloves), and video-camera systems. The goal is to combine gesturing and direct manipulation with the intent of retaining the intuitiveness of both interaction styles while combining their power. Examples of such applications deal with pointing, grabbing and manipulating objects in 2D or 3D scenes [3, 16, 18]. As an example, an object can be created following the recognition of a specific gesture and subsequently be dragged or resized depending on the continuation of the gesture. In this way, the gestures can be interpreted by the system both as commands, or as attributes of a command already input. In this last case, the information carried by the gesture and embedded within the attribute is quantitative, referring to precise locations in space.

One main characteristic of gesture driven direct manipulation interfaces is that only manipulation commands are pre-defined for a given application in terms of the tasks a user is permitted to perform. In general, gestures are dynamically bound to commands so that each user can define her own set of gestures and to train the system to explicitly recognize only gestures from this set. Moreover, gestures can be reproduced by a simulation function. This approach has a number of advantages:

- the gestures do not need to be physically performed for the teaching procedure,
- the human effort is considerably reduced, and

- gestures can be defined by a single user and used by any number of people.

In [7] and [8] some of the problems arising with gesturing and direct manipulation are highlighted. In particular, it is shown how the system might misinterpret a gesture possibly breaking safety properties of the system or causing confusion to the user up to a level in which she is unable to complete her task.

3.2.2 Sign Languages

Sign languages have been developed to define conventions in the communication amongst humans in presence of disable persons; the American, British and Japanese Sign Languages are just a few of many possible examples.

Sign languages are languages per se: they are precisely described by a grammar. In general, they are generative in the sense that new signs can be created, used and adopted into the standard vocabulary. They are also combinatorial so that existing signs can be merged to form a new sign. Contrary to the other mentioned applications, gestures underlying signs must be taught to users that are assumed always to use a common set. With respect to this, sign languages demand for robust recognizers [10, 14] that are able to interpret correctly gestures also in presence of noise and of poor user's performance.

4 System architecture and Recognition Engines

Each type of application seen in the previous section is characterized by a particular architecture, where the discerning element is the location of the interpreter and therefore of the feedback module within the system.

4.1 External Interpretation

In applications recognizing gesticulation, the information carried by the gesture is simply qualitative, providing parameters and attributes of a command given through another modality. This implies that no meaning can be associated with the gesture while it is performed, until it is considered in a broader and more general context. This certainly influences the system architecture, consisting of a module for gesture segmentation analysis, providing input data to an external interpreter (Figure 2).

Given this type of architecture, feedback can be provided only when a gesture is blended with a contextualizing command. Really, these kinds of application do not need specific feedback, as the gesture is often non determinant in the conversation, but it just enriches it. An example of such a system is described by [19]. It is a continuous-gesture recognizer, where no trigger mechanism is used to indicate the start and stop of a gesture. The gesture analyser produces in output symbolic and numeric information, from which the interpreter extracts only the information of interest and meaningful within a context. The symbolic and numeric information represents a high level of gesture description, that has no meaning yet associated with. Their interpretation is done within the interpreter, that is application-context dependent.

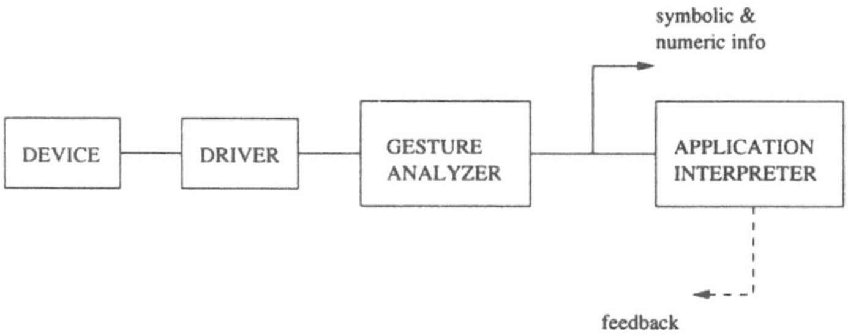

Figure 2: Gesture systems architecture, with the interpreter located outside the system.

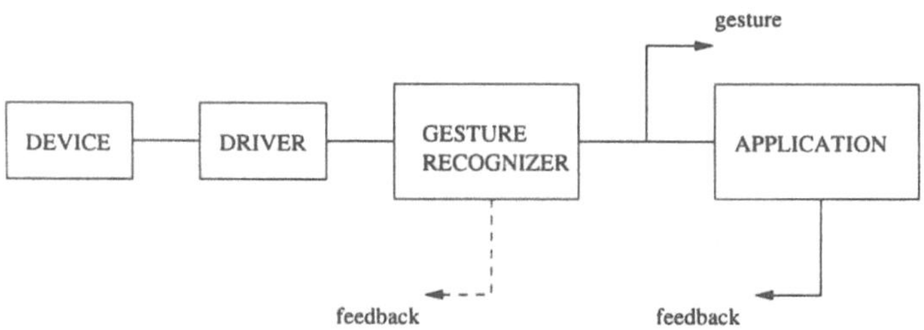

Figure 3: Gesture system architecture, with the interpreter located inside the system.

4.2 Internal Interpretation

In applications supporting the recognition of sign languages, the system behaves as a mediator between two entities, that are in general two humans. In this case, the system is required to interpret the gesture when the "speaker" has finished performing it. The meaning of the sign is embedded into the system, and therefore the interpreter is part of the system architecture. Thus, in these types of systems, the gesture interpretation sequentially follows its segmentation. Feedback is provided when the sign has been completely performed, and intermediate feedback is useless in this kind of application.

This system architecture is adopted in [10] where the gesture recognizer is fed with raw data, it works on them, and when a gesture is recognised, the corresponding word, rate and stress are sent to a speech synthesizer that speaks out the word. In [14], a sign is produced when the gesture has been recognised. Raw data are not sent to the application, and everything coming from the device is computed by the recognition engine.

4.3 Parallel Interpretation

In the last type of applications considered, dealing with direct manipulation interfaces, the gestures performed can be both commands and attributes/parameters of a command. Consequently, the interpretation of gestures is twofold:

- a hand configuration or specific motion is recognized and used as a direct command input or to enter a specific environment, or

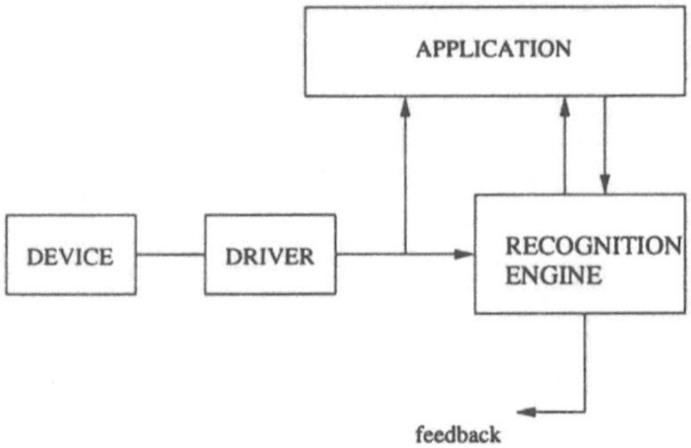

Figure 4: Gesture system architecture, with the interpreter working in parallel with the segmentation analyser.

- the user's hand is used as a (3D) mouse to move a *virtual* hand that may intersect objects invoking the execution of manipulation commands.

In this sense, gestures are used for having a control on the system, and for carrying quantitative information. In this case, the interpretation of the performed gesture is done in parallel with its segmentation (Figure 4).

Depending on the type of recognition algorithm used, feedback on the state of the recognition process can be continuously updated or not. In fact, using for example neural networks, feedback on intermediate steps of the recognition process cannot be provided, whereas it can be using pattern recognition or statistical classification algorithms. As used for interacting with direct manipulation interfaces, it is important that the user is continuously updated on the system status. In [3], the system is notified continuously about the gesture recognition. This is possible thanks to the recognition algorithm that is based on pattern matching. In [18], the system, based on neural networks, is notified about the gesture recognition status only at the end of the process. In the first case, the system might provide gesture feedback when the recognition is still in progress.

Studies in the field of cognitive psychology as applied to human-computer interaction [1], and a number of research works [5, 7, 6, 8, 9] aiming at formally capturing the underlying cognitive theory, have shown the importance of providing real-time feedback when gestures are combined with direct manipulation.

This is even more true, in virtual environments when using new devices such as the one described in [2]. In this case, the tactile perception of the collision with the objects in the environment will cause enormous problems (in the sense of cognition) if this perception is not properly supported by a coherent visual perception matching the tactile one.

5 A Categorization of Gesture Systems

Following the above made considerations, an initial taxonomy can be developed in order to characterize gesture systems. The resulting 3-dimensional space includes as co-

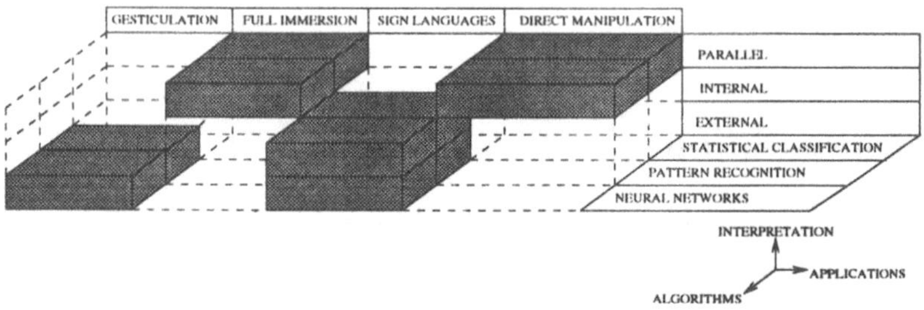

Figure 5: An initial taxonomy to characterize gesture systems.

ordinate axes the type of application, the location of gesture interpretation, and the algorithm used by the gesture recognizer (Figure 5). Further axes could be eventually added to take into consideration for example the type of input data stream, the kind of devices and the requirement for gesture segmentation.

As is appears from the figure, gesticulation and sign languages applications can both use pattern recognition and neural networks algorithms, but statistical classification is not suggested. Clearly, these applications require that the end of gesture is noticed explicitly for the gesture to be successfully recognized. Although in principle the detection of a gesture up to its end can also apply to statistical classification, the underlying recognition algorithm looses much of its interest since its most distinguished feature, namely *eager* recognition, is not addressed at all.

Within gesticulation only external interpretation is possible. In fact, the context in which gestures are interpreted is known only to the application that needs to access sources of knowledge about other modalities, the user's behaviour and the environment. This knowledge varies across applications and is located in different places, external to the gesture system. On the contrary, sign languages applications can use indifferently internal or external interpretation as all the knowledge necessary to interpret a gesture can be centralized in a unique self-consistent source, namely the grammar describing the language.

Parallel interpretation is not a requirement at all. The architectural complexity of parallel interpretation, where the logical components act as a set of processes running in parallel with communication constraints, is not justified in both cases and even not possible within gesticulation.

Similarly, full immersion and direct manipulation systems address parallel interpretation through the use of statistcal classification and pattern matching algorithms.

The parallel interpretation architecture finds its justification in that a continuous near real-time feedback is required conveying both application semantics and gesture perception. Apart from this general requirement, there is a major difference in the two cases. In direct manipulation the semantic of the gesture is explicitly defined and the recognition directs the subsequent execution of a manipulation command on an (possibly not yet) identified object. In full immersion systems the semantic of the gesture is given implicitly and the manipulation is contextually dependent from some characteristics (i.e. physical properties) of an already identified object.

In both cases, the feedback requirements justify also the suitability of eager recognition methods for gestures.

6 Segmentation

Segmentation refers to the capability of determining when a gesture ends and a new one begins. It is one of the major issues currently on the table in gesture recognition. Different solutions have been proposed and adopted at this purpose, most of which are noy satisfactory.

For example, in [16], dealing with 2D gestures made with a mouse or a pen, the solution is rather obvious. One of the mouse buttons is used to trigger the starting of a new gesture which may be recognized before the button is released due to the peculiarities of the recognizer. A similar solution could be applied also to 3D hand gestures by using a further device as the trigger. However, this will mostly inhibit the natural performance of dynamic gestures. Other approaches [3, 14] use gestures all starting with a different posture leading to the problems highlighted in [7]. The use of hand velocity and trajectory solves these problems [19] but it can lead to false segmentation when the user is not making intentional gestures. In [11] a hand tension model is proposed to discriminate between gestures in sign languages applications.

Obviously, a unique solution cannot be adopted at the current state of the art. We prefer to explore the requirement for segmentation depending from the kind of application in which gestures are recognized. This requirement is indeed quite different so that we add a further axis to our taxonomy in order to characterize gesture systems (Figure 6).

We start by distinguishing the requirement of social and of technological awareness. In the first case, segmentation of gestures is not crucial. In fact, a gesture is not recognized per se but within a much broader context.

In gesticulation, a gesture can have different meanings and one is not forced to enter a recognition process. The goal is to extract some features from (part of) the hand posture, velocity and trajectory at different levels of granularity, at specific instants in time, synchronized with other interaction modes. For example, a user may repetitively say *faster* while performing a fast hand rotation that can span a period of time longer than the speech. If this is the case, there is a *semantic transfer* from speech to gesture mode that associates the meaning of the *faster* word with the rotating hand. The semantic association holds up to when the hand keeps rotating. There is no need to completely recognize the gesture, but only to extract from it the trajectory and velocity information as values that are kept (almost) constant for a period of time beginning in synchrony with the spoken word. In this case, the solution proposed in [19] might be the appropriate one.

Similarly, in full immersion systems gestures might not be recognized. The user moves her hands in the environment colliding with objects. On collision detection, a force feedback is given to the user so that she perceives a number of properties of the collided object. Conversely, the object is manipulated by the system that infers the semantic of the gesture from the same object properties. In robot control, the different phases of a complex gesture address different features that are of interest. For example, teaching to a robot to grasp an object implies the robot to be trained to recognize ob-

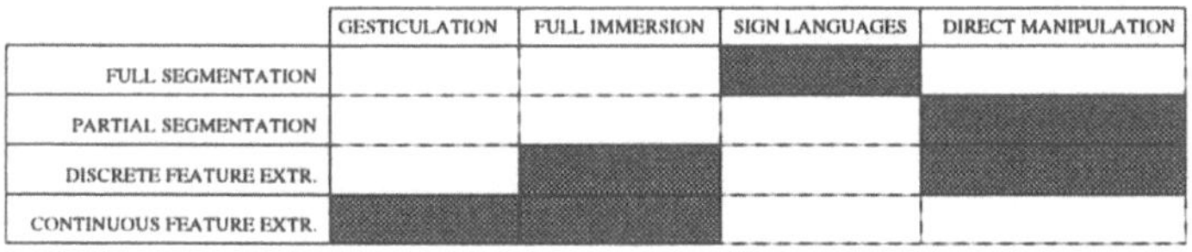

Figure 6: Segmentation requirements.

ject shapes and orientations, to follow a trajectory for approaching the object from a limited number of direction, and to perform the *grasp* gesture. Although, this may be a very complex task in general terms, the beginning of a full gesture recognition can be constrained to specific time intervals whose starting point is derived from alternative information acquired from the environment.

Technological awareness is much more demanding with respect to segmentation. In both sign languages and direct manipulation gestures are recognized as having an associated semantics. Consequently, there is a need to unambiguously distinguish and to make a clear separation between them.

The solution adopted in 2D direct manipulation are not readily transferable to the 3D case. On the other end, the approach taken by [3] is justified taking into account that the number of gestures needed in such an application is small. A relatively small number of postures can accordingly be defined to disambiguate between gestures both by defining unique initial postures and diverging sequences of postures. In this view, the problem can be stated as to find the set of gestures that minimizes the intersection of all the subsequences of postures of a given length that are possible.

[11] takes a more comprehensive approach to gestures in the context of sign languages. The work suggests that gesture recognition and segmentation take into account the overall scope of an interaction. In this way, the gesture recognizer has some knowledge about what to expect, for example, by inferring it from task analysis. This certainly applies to sign languages, and it might apply also to direct manipulation, where the grammar of the interaction is well established so that the relations between raw data of hand motion and high level features of gesture segmentation can be anticipated.

7 Conclusions

Gestures play an important role in person-to-person communication since they are a natural mean of expression of humans supplementing the spoken language. Gestures are commonly used also to describe the shape and size of objects, and how to manipulate them once a context is known in which these objects may exist. Despite the natural capability of communicating through gestures, gestural interfaces in human-computer interaction has started only very recently as a stimulating new area of research. Consequently, no general models and theories exist than can be effectively applied.

In this paper we have argued that, like in person-to-person communication, gestures play different roles depending on the application in which they are used. This difference results in different computational requirements that can be used to characterize gesture systems. At this purpose, we have started developing an initial taxonomy that helps in reasoning about the relationship between technologies and application contexts.

References

[1] P. J. Barnard and J. May. Interactions with advanced graphical interfaces and the deployment of latent human knowledge. In *Design, Specification and Verification of Interactive Systems*, pages 15–49. Springer-Verlag, Berlin, 1995.

[2] M. Bergamasco. Haptic interfaces: a new way for improving realistic interaction with virtual environments. In *Human Comfort and Security*. Springer Verlag, Berlin, Germany, 1995.

[3] M. Bordegoni and M. Hemmje. A dynamic gesture language and graphical feedback for interaction in a 3d user interface. In *Proceedings of Eurographics'93*, pages 1–9. NCC Blackwell, Cambridge, UK, 1993.

[4] C. Codella. Interactive simulation in a multi-person virtual world. In *Proceedings of CHI'92*, pages 329–334. ACM Press, New York, New York, 1992.

[5] D. A. Duce and D. J. Duke. Syndetic modelling: A new opportunity for formal methods. Amodeus Project Document: ID/WP_57 (submitted for publication), 1996.

[6] D. Duke, P. Barnard, D. Duce, and J. May. Systematic development of the human interface. In *APSEC'95: Second Asia-Pacific Software Engineering Conference*, pages 313–321. IEEE Computer Society Press, 1995.

[7] D. J. Duke. Reasoning about gestural interaction. In *Proceedings of Eurographics '95*, pages 55–66. NCC Blackwell, Cambridge, UK, 1995.

[8] G. Faconti and A. Fornari. Syndetic modelling and gestural interaction. In *User Interfaces for All*. European Consortium for Informatics and Mathematics - ERCIM, Paris, 1995.

[9] G. P. Faconti and D. J. Duke. Device models. Amodeus Project Document: ID/WP_56 (submitted for publication in Proceedings of Design, Specification and Verification of Interactive Systems., 1996.

[10] S. Fels. Building adaptive interfaces with neural networks: The glove-talk pilot study. In *Human-Computer Interaction - INTERACT'90*, pages 683–688. Elsevier Science Publishers B.V., Amsterdam, The Netherlands, 1990.

[11] P. A. Harling and A. Edwards. Hand tension as a gesture segmentation cue. In *this book*. 1996.

[12] M. Hemmje. Lyberworld - a 3d based user interface for computer-supported information retrieval in document sets a 3d user interface. In *Journal of the German Research Center for Computer Science*, pages 56–63. GMD Spiegel, Sankt Augustin, Germany, 1993.

[13] M. W. Krueger. *Artificial Reality II*. Addison-Wesley Publishing Company, 1991.

[14] K. Murakami. Gesture recognition using recurrent neural networks. In *Proceedings of CHI'91*. ACM Press, New York, New York, 1991.

[15] F. Quek. Toward a vision based hand gesture interface. In *Virtual Reality Systems and Technology*. ACM Press, New York, 1994.

[16] D. Rubine. Specifying gestures by example. In *Computer Graphics 25, 4*, pages 329–337. ACM Press, New York, New York, 1991.

[17] D. J. Sturman. A survey of glove-based input. In *Computer Graphics & Applications*. IEEE, New York, New York, 1994.

[18] K. Vaananen. Gesture driven interaction as a human factor in virtual reality environments - an approach with neural networks. In *Virtual Reality Systems*, pages 94–106. Academic Press Ltd, New York, New York, 1993.

[19] A. Wexelblat. An approach to natural gesture in virtual environments. In *ACM ToCHI*, pages 179–200. ACM Press, New York, 1995.

Hand Tension as a Gesture Segmentation Cue

P. A. Harling and A. D. N. Edwards
Department of Computer Science, University of York, YORK, YO1 5DD, UK.

E-mail: philiph@cs.york.ac.uk
Telephone: +44 1904 432765 Fax: +44 1904 432767

Abstract

Hand gesture segmentation is a difficult problem that must be overcome if gestural interfaces are to be practical. This paper sets out a recognition-led approach that focuses on the actual recognition techniques required for gestural interaction. Within this approach, a holistic view of the gesture input data stream is taken that considers what links the low-level and high-level features of gestural communication. Using this view, a theory is proposed that a state of high hand tension can be used as a gesture segmentation cue for certain classes of gestures. A model of hand tension is developed and then applied successfully to segment two British Sign Language sentence fragments.

1 Definitions

Posture. A *posture* in this paper is considered to be a static hand shape where only the positions of the fingers are important. Hand orientation, location in space and any movement are not included.
Gesture. A *gesture* is a series of *postures* over time that also include information about hand orientation and location in space.

2 Introduction

Hand gestures are used as an important part of everyday communication that can enhance and clarify what is spoken. The urge to use gestures to communicate is present with us from birth; indeed, it has been noted [12] that long before an infant is able to use adult language (spoken or signed), she is able to manipulate objects and gesticulate to her parents to communicate her wants and needs. Clearly, gestural communication forms an integral and important part of everyday human communication, but the use of manual gestures in the human-computer interface is non-existent. The gestures we make are able to both clarify what is spoken, and also able to describe objects (their size, location in space, relative motion, etc.) more intuitively and with less effort than spoken language. This suggests that we should consider our innate capability for gestural communication and study how gestures are used in human communication, and then apply what we have learnt to the human-computer interface. If gestural communication is indeed as important as it seems, then this should then allow us to develop and implement an interface with a style of interaction that is natural, intuitive and powerful.

The first major problem to overcome before we can implement a gestural interface is the recognition of gestures. Gesture recognition involves many different tasks and problems of its own and in this paper we are primarily concerned with a solution to the problem of discriminating two or more fluidly connected gestures (the *segmentation problem.*) Because this problem is complex and does not offer itself to a trivial solution, we present an approach that further work can be framed in. Further in this paper we then use this framework to develop a hand tension model to aid with segmentation.

3 Recognition-led Approach

The hand tension model that is presented in this paper has been developed within the context of a recognition-led approach to gestural interfaces. This approach concentrates on the development of gesture recognition algorithms, their accurate and reliable implementations, and then finally considers how these gesture recognisers may be used in a gestural interface. The alternative interface-led approach is to consider what gestures would be appropriate for a given interface and then attempting to construct a gesture recogniser to recognise those gestures.

The recognition-led approach is important because it focuses on the development on the recognition process. This attention is required because of the infancy of gesture recognition as a field and the relative slow progression of gesture recognition systems. There comes a point when it is fruitless to proceed with a gestural interface that is unreliable and inaccurate because not enough attention has been paid to the actual recognition.

However, the recognition-led approach has a possible disadvantage in that it may lead to the development of a gesture recogniser that is not adequate for the implementation of a usable gestural interface, as it is not able to recognise appropriate gestures. Yet, the process of developing an accurate and reliable recogniser that is able to recognise certain *subclasses* of all possible gestures is useful. This process may reveal techniques, problems (their possible solutions), and further avenues of research which will enable us to pursue a recogniser that can recognise more complex classes of gestures. In effect, we forget what gestures are demanded by the interaction and simply attempt to recognise any possible gestures and then apply what has been learnt to the recognition of more complex and useful gestures.

Therefore, rather than designing a gestural interface and then forcing the requirements of its interaction to direct and push the development of a gesture recogniser that may not meet the demands placed upon it, the emphasis here is to design a gesture recogniser which is able to recognise a useful class of gestures (see later) and then to see what usable gesture interface could be constructed with that recogniser. This way, any gestural interface created should allow productive work to be done without hindering the user with recognition problems of accuracy and reliability. An interface that re-

Class	Description
SPSL	static hand posture, static hand location
DPSL	dynamic hand posture, static hand location
SPDL	static hand posture, dynamic hand location
DPDL	dynamic hand posture, dynamic hand location

Table 1: Classification of gestures

peatedly requests that you remake a gesture that it could not correctly recognise first time will be tiresome to use, and the user will cease to use it. The emphasis of this research is to eventually produce a working prototype gesture interface that will not unduly hinder the user with recognition errors. The next problem to address is how gestures may be generally classified.

4 Gesture Classes

The first step in designing a gesture recogniser is to consider exactly what gestures are. If we proceed with this study it may be possible to group certain gestures together that have similar characteristics, in the hope of constructing different classes of gesture. Then we might be able to order the classes depending upon how complex the gestures in each class are, and then construct a gesture recogniser for the least complex gesture class on the assumption that it is easier to build a recogniser for a less complex class of gesture than a more complex one. If we order and construct the classes in such a way that a higher order class is more complex and inherits characteristics of the previous class, we can then use our knowledge about (and techniques for) the less complex recogniser to help build a recogniser for the more complex class.

For the purposes of classification, gestures here are considered simply to be any possible movement that the human hand can make, including both movement of the fingers and of the hand in space. Any meaning which may be attached to any gesture is ignored. From this point of view, it is possible to build up two general groups of gestures. The first group consists of static hand shapes where only the positions of the fingers at one particular time are important; the second group consists of dynamic hand shapes, where the gesture is considered to be solely finger motion over some time period. If hand motion and hand orientation are considered, these two groups can be further subdivided to give four general classes of gesture, listed in Table 1.

The least complex class of gesture is SPSL (because only hand posture is important) with class DPDL being the most complex because both changing hand posture and hand location need to be considered. Class SPDL is considered to be more complex than class DPSL because no additional algorithm has to be used to take account of hand location; the already existing technique for recognising static postures can be adapted to work with dynamic postures. Thus the classes are ordered as they appear in Table 1 (from least to most complex): SPSL, DPSL, SPDL, DPDL.

5 Gesture Segmentation

One of the fundamental building blocks of a gesture recogniser is the ability to distinguish and recognise static hand shapes, i.e. gestures that belong to class SPSL. Static hand shapes can be recognised adequately using methods such as neural networks with an accuracy of about 96%-98% [2, 5, 6, 9]. These postures can be recognised successfully when they occur singly. However, when postures occur one after another, posture recognition is more difficult because the recogniser also needs to determine the point where one posture begins and another ends in order to output a single symbolic token. It is easy to see that a naïve recogniser could generate many tokens during the change between one posture and the next, as the user's fingers go from one position to another. Determining where one gesture begins and the next ends is termed the *segmentation problem.*

5.1 What is really meant by "segmentation"?

Before examining previous attempts at gesture segmentation, it is important to be clear about what segmentation really means. This standard view of gesture 'segmentation' might indeed be a misleading one, hindering the aim of recognising fluidly connected gestures. Gestures made by people are not naturally segmented. That is we do not make distinct gestures one after another, but rather the gestures flow together. This is analogous to how speech is produced in that we say continuous streams of words rather than saying each word individually with a pause between the words. In effect, people do not simply make a stream of distinct gestures, each individually made from their "gesture lexicon." Instead they make a stream of gestures that when made in a particular order, are made in a particular way; if they were to use the same gestures but order them differently, we would end up with each gesture being made in a different way to accommodate the overall flow of the gesture stream.

What we eventually want as the output of our gesture recogniser is a stream of *distinct* symbolic tokens for the *fluidly connected* gestures that appear at the input. This is what should be meant by the usual notion of segmentation—not the false idea that it is the input that is clearly segmented, but instead it is the output that is segmented. Instead of concentrating on this notion that gestures are clearly segmented and potentially being misled, an approach suggested here is to work with a wider view of the input stream by considering how individual gestures are physically affected when they appear as part of a string of gestures. Perhaps certain types of gestures (e.g. different gesture classes, gestures that are made across large distances, repeated gestures, etc.) have particular effects on the way that the entire string of gestures is constructed. This holistic view of the gesture input stream and how it is related to output tokens is discussed further when we propose our approach to segmentation.

5.2 Segmentation Difficulties

The recognition of the more complex class of gestures that include dynamic hand motion is complicated by the uncertainty in being able to clearly define when one gesture involving two distinct hand motions is indeed one *atomic* gesture, and not actually two separate sequential gestures. If we consider a dynamic gesture to be simply a sequence of static hand postures that we sample at discrete points in time, we could imagine a recogniser that would recognise each of these separate hand postures as components of the dynamic gesture. However, we must also remember the physical limitations and practicalities constraining the human making gestures. Each time the gestures will be slightly different; perhaps the gesture will be made larger, will take a longer time to perform, or different parts of the same gesture will not repeatedly be made with the same speed or emphasis. So the simple notion of recognising a gesture by recognising its component hand postures is not as appropriate as it first seemed. We need to consider in more depth how static hand postures connect together to make a gesture, and how gestures are connected together to make a dialogue.

5.3 Existing Segmentation Problem Solutions

Segmentation problem solutions have been suggested for both 2D and 3D input. With 2D input the choice of input device can effectively eliminate the problem, by causing the user to explicitly indicate with the press of a mouse button [10] the beginning and end of a gesture. Using a pen-based tablet [8] can make explicit delimitation involve less effort on the user's part, as pressing a pen onto a tablet is the natural way to make a gesture with a tablet. However, user explicit segmentation means that the gestures used must be simple ones as they cannot consist of two connected gestures, else the user will have to either pick up the pen and press it down again or click the mouse. This technique is not readily transferable to hand gesture input as instrumented gloves do not have any natural delimitation due to their construction.

Several different approaches have been taken for 3D input. Mostly these methods [1, 3, 9] involve the recogniser initially looking for the starting posture of a gesture before attempting to recognise a gesture. The problem with this approach is that each gesture that is to be recognised must have a different starting posture. Other works have used low-level features of the gesture data, such as hand velocity [7] and hand trajectory [5] to indicate when the start of a gesture was about to begin. This approach solves the problem that each gesture must have a different starting posture, but it can be prone to false triggering when the user is not making an intentional gesture and is simply moving his or her arm. One final solution [11] that has been suggested is that the user is forced to maintain a posture for the duration of one minute before it is recognised. However, this is not a practical solution as it will cause problems with fatigue and interfere with the natural flow of interaction.

6 An Approach to Segmentation

A gesture recogniser must be able to recognise isolated gestures; it must also be able to recognise gestures when they follow on from each other, one after another. Therefore it is important that the gesture recogniser be able to segment gestures from the stream of raw input data. This segmentation task will be more difficult for a string of gestures from a more complex class than a string of gestures from a less complex class. For example, segmenting gestures from class DPDL which involve both dynamic finger movements and dynamic hand gestures is difficult. With this class, it is possible that one atomic gesture may include two distinct hand motions that *could* be considered to be two separate gestures. The issues in gesture segmentation are complex and require a more in-depth discussion, and the mostly naïve approaches that have been taken before are inadequate to even become a basis for a segmentation rationale.

Much of the previous work on the topic of gesture recognition and segmentation has relied upon statistical methods of pattern recognition, or artificial neural networks. These methods take no account of any meaningful information that could be supplied about the gesture communication—they simply look at the data and attempt to classify gestures based solely upon an analysis of the numerical data. However, if we consider what knowledge we have available when we attempt to recognise a gesture we see it is much more than just the raw measurements we received from the input device. The interaction that takes place is within a context; the user is attempting to achieve some task and will go about it in a meaningful way, starting and ending at some logical point. This knowledge allows us to constrain the size of the dictionary that the current gestures needs to be recognised from, but more importantly, allows the gesture recogniser some knowledge about *what to expect.*

6.1 Higher-level Data Features

The gesture recognition and segmentation algorithm design approach suggested here is that we should not just look at the low level raw data, but also take into account the higher level features of gestural interaction. In effect we need to consider the grammar of the interaction as well as the gestures that we wish to use. It is important to realise that there is a large gulf of understanding between the raw data and the grammar. How is one connected to the other? By attempting to answer this question we will acquire an understanding of just what the important features of gestural interaction are. What we must do in effect, is to look at the higher level information and also at the lower level information and construct a theory about how the two join together.

At the lowest level, we can look at what is physically happening with the user's hand and construct a model of where the user's fingers are and how they are interconnected [4]. There are positions that the human hand is unable to reach, for example the little finger and thumb will not cross over the back of the hand. A model which allows us to constrain where digits may be placed will be useful for cleaning up the raw input data, which will contain noise due to the imperfections of the input device. However useful this basic model may be to stabilise the input data, it still does not help us close the gap between the higher and lower features of gesture interaction. The path of the research proposed here is to take the notion of a hand model and expand upon it to produce a theory linking the physical motion of the hand (or fingers) and the higher level feature of gesture segmentation.

7 Hand Tension as a Segmentation Cue

One level up from modelling the physical motion of the hand is to consider what is happening to the muscles in the fingers. As the hand is moved from one posture to another the amount of tension in the fingers will change and some postures will be more tense that others. More energy will have to be expended for some positions than others, and hence the person will have to exert more effort to keep the hand in that posture. A good practical demonstration of this is to place your elbow on a desk, with your arm in a vertical position. Allow your hand to go limp at the wrist and you will notice that your fingers will fall into a naturally relaxed position and you will not have to make much effort to keep your hand in this position. As a contrast, keep your wrist relaxed, now stretch your fingers outwards and upwards and try and hold your fingers in this position for, say, a minute. You should notice that this position is more difficult to maintain than the first, as it is more tense and you are required to exert more energy and effort.

The theory proposed here is that intentional gestures will be made with a tense hand position rather than a relaxed one. This is based upon the idea that if a person is trying to convey some meaning using gestures, she or he will have to actively exert effort to do this and so consciously move her or his hand into a position that has a generally understood meaning. These positions are more likely to be tense ones (such as index finger pointing, a shaking fist or a 'V' victory sign) than relaxed, as relaxed hand positions would generally happen when the gesturer was not paying conscious attention to what her or his hands were doing (consider how people's hands hang by their sides when they walk.) So, there is a natural relaxed state for the hand and when it is being used to convey meaning it moves into a tense state.

Now let us consider what happens when two gestures are made sequentially (for the moment we shall only consider gestures that are of class SPSL, i.e. static finger position, hand location in space ignored.) The hand will be in one tense hand posture and then it will move to another. During the period that the hand changes shape, the tension in each finger will change and so the tension in the hand overall will change. Brief analysis of a few signs of British Sign Language (BSL) suggests that during this transition from one intentional tense hand position to another, the hand goes through a relaxed hand state. If we were to consider a graph of hand tension over time during this transition, we would expect that initially the hand tension would be high, the tension would fall as the hand went into a more relaxed state as the hand shape change, and then the tension would start to rise again. This graph would have at some point a minimum of hand tension, where the shape of the hand would be some mix of the start and end hand position.

Immediately this minimum of hand tension between the two postures gives us a point at which we are able to segment the two postures. We can now delimit the continuous input data and say that chunks of data between the two marks represent a definite atomic posture that we can then pass onto a recogniser. However, the data in this segment also contains information about the change from the preceding posture to the posture of interest, to the next posture. So somewhere in between the start and end of the segment there will be some data that represents the hand shape we are interested in, and will probably be at the point of maximum hand tension. Effectively, we need an algorithm that will take hand tension over time, locate a minimum (relaxed hand), locate the next maximum and then attempt to recognise the hand posture at that point in time. No attempt to recognise a posture should occur until we find the next minimum. Some preliminary research has be done on using hand tension and relaxation as a segmentation cue and is reported later in this paper.

This type of segmentation should work well for gestures of class SPSL as long as there is there is a significant difference between the hand tension of the current gesture and the next gesture that is to be made. This can be investigated by using the finger-spelling signs of American Sign Language (which are mostly gestures of class SPSL) and if this works it will be possible to say that this type of segmentation is adequate for this class of gesture. This method of segmentation will fail if two gestures which are identical follow each other, i.e. there is no significant difference between the two gestures. However, with gestures of class SPSL there would be no way of indicating that two identical gestures were made sequentially, so this is not such a severe limitation of this segmentation method as it first appears.

This segmentation method works best on gestures that do not involve dynamic finger motions (classes DPSL and DPDL) as hand tension is constantly changing during the course of one gesture, so a different approach will have to be taken with these classes. It is not clear how segmentation on these classes of gestures could yet be done although one approach would be to look at higher order features of gestural communication, perhaps building upon hand tension as a segmentation cue along with other physical hand properties.

7.1 Fingertip acceleration

One such additional physical hand property that would be worth investigating is the acceleration of the hand in space. By examining the acceleration of the hand over time, it could be possible to recognise identical sequential gestures that belong to class SPDL. In BSL the number '888' is signed by holding the hand in the posture for '8' (the fingers are static) and then making three rapid movements of the whole hand away from the body while the hand moves horizontally across the body. A proposed line of research would be to consider the components of hand acceleration in the x, y and z directions relative to the body. In this case, we would expect maxima of acceleration to occur on each rapid movement away from the body, which we would be able to interpret as the intention of the user to produce another gesture. This method could also be used in conjunction with the hand tension model to give a more coherent model of segmentation in gestures of class SPDL.

7.2 Tension Graph Shape

In addition to aiding gesture segmentation, the study of the physical characteristics of hand tension and acceleration could also be applied to gesture recognition, especially of gestures with dynamic finger movements. Considering the graph of hand tension over time, as well as using the appearance of minima of hand tension to help segmentation, we could also use the shape of the graph to help classify gestures. It is worth investigating whether the change of hand tension during an atomic dynamic hand gesture would have a tension curve that could be used as a defining characteristic of that particular gesture, and so be used to aid classification. Furthermore, the way in which these particular tension curves change, as they appear within a sequence of gesture, may also aid segmentation and overall recognition of a sequence of gestures. This same approach may likewise be used with graphs of hand acceleration over time.

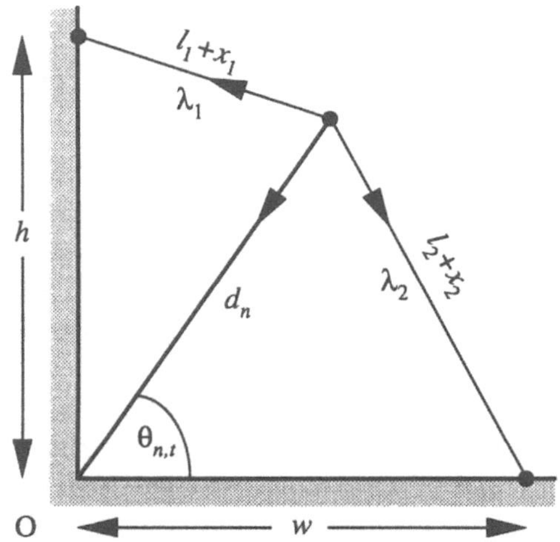

Figure 1: Diagram of finger tension model

8 Hand Tension Model

Physical finger tension is not readily measured directly using current input technology, so a model of the finger tension is needed that will represent the amount of tension in a finger depending upon parameters that can be measured, i.e. finger-joint angles. As gestures often do not take long to make, the measurements taken over a short time interval will be pertinent and contain important information, so the model is required to be simple enough to compute many times a second. For this reason, a simple model was initially constructed to confirm that it was adequate; if not a more complex model would be considered. Therefore, in the model, a finger is considered to be a light rigid rod of a fixed length, with two light elastic strings attached to the end of the rod (Figure 1). The elastic strings are used to measure the amount of force required to place the rod in a desired location; this is analogous to attaching two rubber bands to a finger, fixing the rubber bands to two points and then trying to move the finger—the amount of tension required to stretch a rubber band will be the amount of tension exerted by the finger. The first elastic string is attached to some point vertical above the pivot of the finger, and the second to some point horizontally from the pivot.

Using Hooke's law and resolving the forces along the finger, gives the amount of tension in finger number n at time t as:

$$T_{n,t} = \frac{\lambda_1 x_1}{l_1}\sqrt{1 - \frac{h^2\cos^2\theta_{n,t}}{(l_1+x_1)^2}} + \frac{\lambda_2 x_2}{l_2}\,\frac{(d_n - w\cos\theta_{n,t})}{l_2+x_2} \qquad (1)$$

where the extensions of the two elastic strings, x_1 and x_2, are given by

$$x_1 = \sqrt{h^2 \cos^2 \theta_{n,t} + (d_n - h \sin \theta_{n,t})^2} - l_1 \tag{2}$$

$$x_2 = \sqrt{w^2 \sin^2 \theta_{n,t} + (d_n - w \cos \theta_{n,t})^2} - l_2 \tag{3}$$

where d_n is the length of finger n, $\theta_{n,t}$ is the angle of elevation of finger n at time t, h is the height of the first elastic string about the finger pivot, w is the horizontal distance of the second elastic string from the pivot, l_1 and l_2 are the natural lengths of the respective elastic strings, and λ_1 and λ_2 are the respective moduli of rigidity of the elastic strings.

While these equations give the tension exerted by finger n at time t, what is required by the hypothesis is the total amount of tension in the hand at time t. Now, $T_{n,t}$ represents the amount of tension required to move one finger from its relaxed position. The proposed method to compute the total hand tension is to simply sum the tension for each finger, giving total hand tension at time t as:

$$T_{H,t} = \sum_{n=1}^{5} T_{n,t} \tag{4}$$

This is considered to be appropriate because as the tension in one finger increases, the total hand tension will increase. Conversely, a decrease in finger tension in another finger will also produce a decrease in total hand tension. Therefore the total amount of hand tension will be representative of the total amount of tension in each finger.

9 Model Tests

During development of this model, a spreadsheet was used to construct the model to allow easy alteration. A real-time version is currently being developed using integer calculations and trigonometric function look-up tables to increase computation speed.

For all of the tests done, d_n, w, l_1, l_2, λ_1 and λ_2 were all defined to be 1.

9.1 Finger Tension Model Test

The finger tension model was initially tested with simulated finger angle data to confirm that it produced high finger tension when the finger was either fully stretched, or fully clenched. The finger angle, $\theta_{n,t}$, was allowed to range from 0 to $\frac{\pi}{2}$ and a graph of finger tension, $T_{n,t}$ (Expression 1) was plotted. As expected, the graph produced (Figure 2) had a minimum of hand tension when the angle of the finger was at the expected relaxed position, halfway between being fully stretched and fully clenched, and maxima of hand tension when at both extremes.

9.2 Hand Tension Model Tests

The hand tension model was tested with a set of data collected from four test subjects (one deaf, the other three having at least 3 years' experience in sign language). The

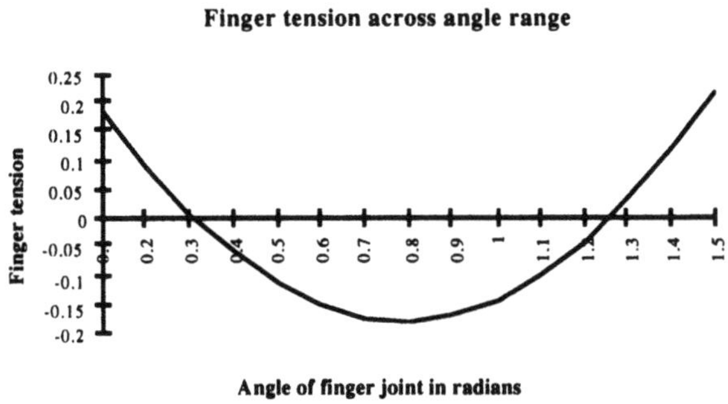

Figure 2: Graph of finger tension model over angle range

subjects were asked to sit in front of the computer wearing the data suit pictured in Figure 3. The suit has 32 sensors split equally on the left and right sides. There are 6 sensors in each arm: horizontal and vertical arm movement (2), elbow movement (1), forearm rotation (1) and wrist bend and yaw (2). Each hand has ten sensors: thumb (4), index finger (3) and one sensor at the base of each of the middle, ring and little fingers (3).

9.2.1 Experiment

The subjects were asked to place their hands on the desk in front of them and watch the computer screen. The computer would then instruct them to make the fingerspelling sign of British Sign Language that corresponded to the letter shown on screen. The computer would then pause and ask the user to make a second sign. After the second sign had been made the computer asked the user to place their hands back on the desk. A typical sequence from the experiment would be: "relax ... make the sign for 'A' ... make the sign for 'B' ... relax" where ' ... ' indicates a pause and "relax" is when the user has his hands on the desk.

Each user was asked to make 676 transitions from 'AA' to 'ZZ'. Each set of transitions included 26 transitions that were identical ('AA', 'BB', 'CC' and so on), 56 transitions of near-identical signs ('A', 'E', 'I', 'O', 'U', 'J', 'L', 'T'), one sign including motion ('J') and 593 other transitions. In total 2704 transitions were collected from all 4 subjects.

9.2.2 Results

The data from the experiments were post processed to remove noise and to automatically detect segments (the process is not described here for reasons of space). The results are given in Table 2.

The results for the identical and near-identical postures are as expected – the hand tension model of segmentation works by determining when a change in hand tension occurs, and as this only occurs when there is a change in hand shape then we should expect low recognition when contiguous hand shapes are identical or near-identical as there is little or no hand shape change to produce a change in hand tension. We really

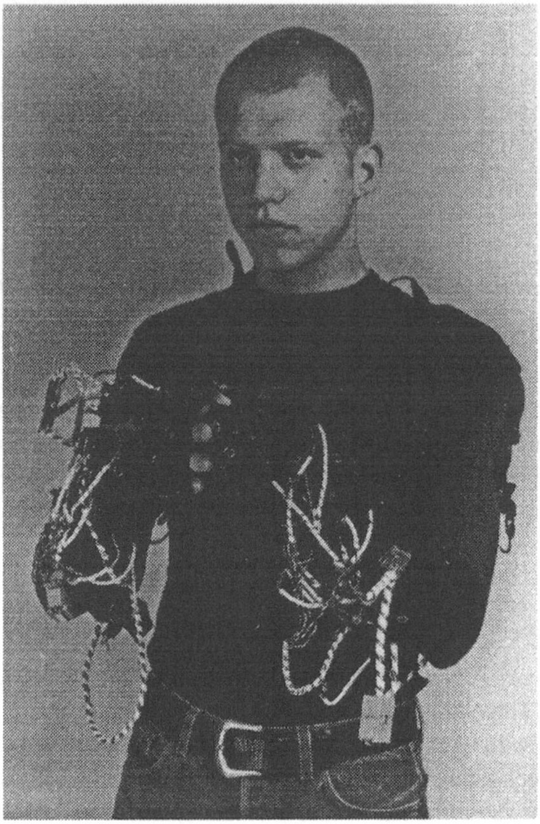

Figure 3: TCAS Data wear, 32 sensor suit

Type of transition	Successful detections
Identical postures	38.5%
Near-identical postures	64.9%
Others	90.4%
Just middle segment	92.0%

Table 2: Results from Hand Tension Model Tests

should expect no recognition of these transitions at all if the user kept their hands completely still, but in BSL it is usual to remake a sign when duplications occur by 'squeezing' the current hand shape. Although this change is small, it is still being picked up by the segmentation algorithm.

The results for all other transitions are very promising at 90.4% for *all* transitions including the ones between when the first and last relaxations. A lot of noise was discovered upon inspection of the raw data for these transitions which upon examination of the suit was attributed to lose connections between the sensors and the connection leads. It seems that when the subject put his hands on the desk, he crushed the leads in the process which caused the noise. In order to determine how well the segmentation algorithm worked without this noise, the middle transition between signs was inspected. It generally was less noisy and provided a better recognition rate of 92%.

10 Conclusions

The results from the experiments are extremely promising. The hand tension model was successfully used to determine 92% of 2704 transitions of the fingerspelling signs of BSL. In doing so, no actual knowledge of the signs of BSL were used so the method should work for other sign languages (such as American or Irish Sign Language).

There are some obvious cases when this method does not work well, for example when two contiguous signs are identical or near-identical which was not unexpected. The hand tension model is not expected or intended to be able to successfully segment all possible transitions, but instead it is intended to be used as a *cue* along with other methods to determine segments. These other segmentation cues are the subject of current further work (such as acceleration, arm tension, finger-tip proximity).

11 Acknowledgements

We would like to thank both David Adger and John Local of the Language and Linguistic Science Department of the University of York for providing thoughtful discussion on many of the ideas in this paper.

This research was funded by the UK Engineering and Physical Sciences Research Council (EPSRC) studentship grant 93313798.

References

[1] T. Baudel and M. Beaudouin-Lafon. CHARADE: Remote control of objects using free-hand gestures. *Communications of the ACM*, 36(7):28–35, 1993.

[2] R. Beale and A. D. N. Edwards. Recognising postures and gestures using neural networks. In R. Beale and J. Finlay, editors, *Neural Networks and Pattern Recognition in Human-Computer Interaction*, pages 163–169. Ellis Horwood, New York, 1992.

[3] M. Bordegoni and M. Hemmje. A dynamic gesture language and graphical feedback for interaction in a 3D user interface. *EUROGRAPHICS '93*, 12(3):C1–C11, 1993.

[4] A. Braffort, C. Collet, and D. Teil. Anthropomorphic model for hand gesture interface. In *CHI '94 Conference Companion*, pages 259–260, Boston, MA, 1994. ACM Press, New York, NY.

[5] S. S. Fels and G. E. Hinton. Glove-Talk: A neural network interface between a data-glove and a speech synthesizer. *IEEE Transactions on Neural Networks*, 4(1):2–8, 1993.

[6] P. A. Harling. Gesture input using neural networks. BEng project report, Department of Computer Science, University of York, Heslington, York, YO1 5DD, UK, Mar. 1993.

[7] J. Kramer. The Talking Glove in action. *Communications of the ACM*, 32(4):515, 1989.

[8] J. S. Lipscomb. A trainable gesture recognizer. *Pattern Recognition*, 24(9):895–907, 1991.

[9] K. Murakami and H. Taguchi. Gesture recognition using recurrent neural networks. In *CHI '91 Proceedings*, pages 237–242, 1991.

[10] D. Rubine. Specifying gestures by example. *Computer Graphics*, 25(4):329–337, 1991.

[11] T. Takahashi and F. Kishino. A hand gesture recognition method and its application. *Systems and Computers in Japan*, 23(3):38–48, 1992.

[12] C. Trevarthen. Form, significance and psychological potential of hand gestures of infants. In J.-L. Nespoulous, P. Perron, and A. R. Lecours, editors, *The Biological Foundations of Gestures: Motor and Semiotic Aspects*, pages 149–202. Lawrence Erlbaum Associates, Hillsdale, New Jersey, 1986.

Gesture in Human-Machine Communication: capture, analysis-synthesis, recognition, semantics

S. Gibet, A. Braffort, C. Collet, F. Forest, R. Gherbi and T. Lebourque
Department of Human Machine Communication, LIMSI-CNRS, B.P. 133, 91403 ORSAY, France

E-mail: {gibet, braffort, collet, ff, gherbi, lebourqu}@limsi.fr
Telephone: +33 69858104 Fax: +33 69858088

Abstract

This paper presents an overview of the different works around gesture conducted at LIMSI Laboratory. Different kinds of capture devices are available, which allow us to deal with 2D or 3D gestures. Depending on projects, gestures are studied alone (monomodality), or combined with other modalities (speech). Different approaches are used, from analysis and synthesis to recognition and interpretation, along with knowledge representation.

1 Introduction

Gesture is studied within Human-Machine Communication purpose. We both consider here gesture as a single modality, and gesture combined with other modalities.

Considering the gesture modality alone, we are interested in two main objectives: *the recognition of gestures* and the *synthesis of gestures*, both of these approaches involving preliminary *analysis* of gesture. Multimodality projects use also gesture, but involve other modalities such as speech, sound and vision. The recognition of gestures is studied for 3D human hand-movements, from signals captured with a VPL Data-Glove.

The synthesis of gestures integrates psycho-motor principles into a control movement model, and is applied to the animation of a simulated hand-arm system and more generally to the animation of poly-articulated systems. In the latter case, synchronization and coordination of movements are derived from motor program concepts.

An application to Sign Language gestures is developed, for hand gesture recognition as well as for hand-arm gesture generation. These researches necessitate the definition of different levels of abstraction. Recognition is then used in a more global hybrid learning system in which gesture is a mean for building semantic representation of knowledge.

Finally, the capacity of other devices such as cameras to capture gesture is explored. This kind of devices provides an interesting alternative to other devices, appropriate for some movement capture, such as the capture of head or eye movements, when a good accuracy is not required.

Some research areas such as analysis, recognition, synthesis of gestures and knowledge representation have already led to partially implemented systems. Other areas of interest present some preliminary ideas (capture of gestures by cameras).

2 Gesture Analysis

The analysis of gesture has three main objectives : the first one consists in acquiring some signal expertise for recognition purpose.

The second one is synthesis. An analysis by synthesis approach is studied which extracts from recorded signals significant features and uses these features to re-synthesize the gestures.

Finally, the analysis can be used to validate the generated gestures, by comparing real signals and synthesized gestures and showing that both signals verify invariant rules of movement.

The analysis of gestures depends on the kind of information captured from physical devices. We study 3D hand gestures from a VPL DataGlove, and 3D body gestures from the SELSPOT device.

2.1 Analysis of hand gestures

Hand gestures are captured by means of a DataGlove and are stored into files. These files can be used to analyse some parts of the signal in order to get some expertise on it, or they can be used as learning or test corpus by the recognition tools.

Within these aims, a software named VAG2 have been developed [4]. This software is composed of two parts :

The first part is a visualization tool which gives visual information on gesture files: gesture is filtered, and visualized by means of a wired hand. It is also possible to visualize the signals and their corresponding derivatives, both on finger flexions, and hand location and orientation.

The second part allows us to segment the learning files, which leads to a learning gesture corpus for recognition. This segmentation is done manually, by means of a "visual expertise" of the signal.

2.2 Analysis of human body gestures

A project has been defined, which is conducted simultaneously by the Laboratory of Movement Physiology and the LIMSI laboratory. This project consists into the conception and the realisation of a gesture corpus and an automatic gestural analysis system from 3D corporal gestures. This system will be a basis tool for recognition, synthesis and validation purposes.

We use the SELSPOT system, which is an optoelectronic system with two infra-red cameras and 24 active diodes, to capture the following of moving corporal points.

We dispose of N gestural 3D signals, each signal being defined by the cartesian point $P(t) = (x(t), y(t), z(t))$ evolving with time. The analysis operates on kinematic data extracted from these 3D signals. We calculate the successive derivative of signals, the tangential velocity and the radius of curvature. Results highlighted by psychomotrician are tested on the synthesized signals at the output of the model.

3 Recognition of gestures

At this moment, we are dealing with right hand gestures, captured through a VPL DataGlove, with the aim of treating sign sentences for the French Sign Language (LSF).

In a first step, the analysis of a corpus based on a LSF dictionary [9] and composed of 1359 signs has been performed. We have designed a data base allowing us to get some statistical informations on gesture parameters.

Based on this study and with the help of VAG2 (previously described), a recognition system has been developed and is currently under evaluation. It is composed of two main modules:

- a classification module which architecture takes into account the characteristics of gestural signals. The algorithms used are based on Hidden Markov Models.
- an interpretation module, that takes into account the context, necessary for the global understanding of Sign Language sentences; this module is based on the conception of a virtual scene.

More details can be found in these proceedings [3].

4 SAGA: Synthesis and Analysis of Gesture for Animation

Principles of sensori-motor control are integrated into a control movement model. We adopt a synergetic view in which we assume that the movement patterns are not explicitly programmed but rather are emergent properties of a dynamic system constrained by physical laws in space and time [7, 6]. We solve an inverse problem of finding the appropriate control parameters of a non-linear multi-dimensional system to achieve a desired end-point position. The model is composed of a servo-motor loop dedicated to the command of a multi-joint articulated system. The method is based on a gradient descent minimization of the error between a desired "target" position and the current arm location. The introduction into the feedback loop of a non-linear function (sigmoïd function) and a second order filter gives rise to natural behaviours. Using psychomotor results, we show indeed that such a model generates gestures which keep some features of human gestures.

An application to the *control and the animation of a hand-arm system* is presented in these proceedings [8].

A more generic application, dedicated to the animation of articulated figures is developed through the **SAGA** project (Synthesis and Analysis of Gestures for Animation). The aim of this project is to control and animate geometrical poly-articulated systems with different levels of control corresponding to human motor control levels. This approach is based on evidence for *generalized motor programs*, that is to say we suppose that movements have a common set of movement pattern characteristics (such as relative timing or relative force) but slightly different specific characteristics (such as overall time). One of the main assumption of the generalized motor control is that the global temporal structure is invariant across certain phases in the behaviour.

The motion generation system is composed of several sensori-motor loops, each loop controlling a multi-articulated system.

Above this system, motor programs of higher level coordinate and synchronize the articulated chains. These motor programs are based on temporal features for some classes of gestures (upper-limb movements, locomotion, posture) and can be represented by means of temporal chronograms.

The motor programs are translated into parallel sequences of elementary tasks, each task being associated to a particular articulated chain. The elementary tasks are composed of sequences of spatio-temporal targets (goals to reach for a specific articulated chain). An editor enables to build these elementary tasks in an interactive way (graphical edition of targets). Events, such as timing events or asynchronous events generated by external tasks, can synchronize the different tasks. The running of the set of tasks is therefore dependent on the evolution of the different sensori-motor systems associated to each articulated chain.

A compartmental and reactive language (ELECTRE) is used to describe the set of tasks. The motor programs written with this language are compiled and produce finite-state automata, which will drive the multi-articulated system.

5 Semantics of gestures

Our interest for the semantic of gesture covers several aspects. First, we assume that gesture is part of human communication. Thus, information from the speaker's body is of great importance to understand the verbal message and we are interested by the possible meaningful typologies of communicative gesture. Second, we assume that gestural language may be a shorter way to semantics than vocal languages are. That is to say that gesture gives information about the way the speaker imagines the situation being described. It is true for coverbal gesture, and even more for sign language gesture. We use these characteristics to build semantic representations of such situations. Thirdly, from the automatic understanding point of view, we state that the experience accumulated by an individual plays a central part in the process of building the meaning of an utterance, in a situation of communication. The meaning of a message is built using information from that previous experience as much as from information extracted from the message itself. We state that the use of a good knowledge base may help for the message to be understood. In that way, semantics are useful even in the process of analysis and recognition of gestures in CHM.

The work presented in this workshop addresses the problem of the original contribution of gesture in the building of semantic knowledge. Sign Language gesture is used to express simple concrete situations in which few entities are involved through an interaction process. The gesture "draws" in the space, in front of the speaker, the situation being described. This spatial expression suggests a spatio-temporal format for representing the situations which have been memorized during the stage of language learning [5].

6 Movement passive capture system

Vision is studied as a communication modality allowing the user to visually interact with the machine. In particular, we aim to detect head, gaze, posture or hand movements of the user. However, it is necessary to develop systems to capture such movements (positions, movements, directions, etc.). It is obvious that we do not try to compete with, in terms of localization precision, systems based on active captors like DataGlove, Elite, Selspot or EyeTracker. Indeed, these systems give reliable localization and movement data. Unfortunately, such systems present two major drawbacks. First, they are restricted to a particular application and they capture data from either hand, eyes or posture. Second, the user may be disturbed by the device he has to put on in order to communicate with the machine. Thus, he can not perform natural gestures.

We hope that systems based on passive captors (cameras) can replace, or at least add additional information to those based on active captors. The passive systems do not bother the user and do not make him feel uncomfortable . Besides, the same system can be used to detect both head and gaze movements. We describe below our the architecture of our future system called CADRE to capture continuous coarse positions and orientations of both head and eyes.

The CADRE project consists in developing an experimental plate-form to capture the head and eyes movements of a user in front of a machine so that he can interact with an interactive application. For this purpose, we have a video capture system on a Silicon Graphics workstation. We use two cameras, one (main) is placed in front of the user's face and the other (secondary) on the side of the user. Our system will use the main camera to detect the presence/absence of the user, then to localize the head and to determine if the user's face is in front the screen (with several orientation degrees). The system then localizes the image area of the eyes. From this area, the system interprets the significant iris movements in order to get a continuous trace of the user gaze. The role of the secondary camera is to evaluate the distance between the screen and the user in order to help the main one. For our application, we trace 9 possible directions in the screen (top, bottom, right, left, 4 corners and center). The system's architecture is based on a multi-layer specialised modules. Each parent module communicates it's results to it's child. Each child module, when it can not deliver reliable data, invokes it's parent in order to re-compute the necessary data. This architecture guarantees us two properties. First, the system operates in quasi real time because each module is dedicated either to a specific processing or to a small image area. This property is important for interactive applications. Second, the backtracking allows the system modules to be helped by their parents. This assures the reliability of the trace data.

7 Conclusion

The study of gesture depends strongly on the kind of information captured from physical sensors, and to the aimed task. We essentially work on 3D gestures, captured from a DataGlove device and from the Selspot system. We also study head and eyes movements from two cameras in front of a computer.

A recognition system (ARGo) for isolated gestures is currently implemented for one hand movements; this system is based on Hidden Markov Models and applied to Sign Language gestures. We plan to extend this system by adding a second hand and some head and eye movements (CADRE).

The recognition system will integrate in the near future an interpretation module, which takes into account the context, necessary for the global understanding of Sign Language sentences.

Generation of movements gives rise to two kinds of applications : the first one concerns the generation of sign language gestures, which can help deaf people to communicate with other people via a computer. The second one concerns the animation of realistic movements, improved by the introduction of motor patterns concepts (SAGA).

Multimodal applications which have been developed at LIMSI - MIX3D [2] and Meditor [1] will integrate the visual trace of the eyes movements to detect the attention of the user and to detect the impact of the user's gaze on the screen. This integration is a way to make the interface adaptive to the user behaviour.

References

[1] Y. Bellik and D. Buger. The potential of multimodal interfaces for the blind: an exploratory study. In *RESNA'95*, Vancouver, Canada, 1995.

[2] P. Bourdot, M. Krus, and R. Gherbi. Mix3d: une palte-forme expérimentale pour des interfaces multimodales dédiées à la cao. In *IHM 6th conference*, Toulouse, France, 1995.

[3] A. Braffort. ARGo: An architecture for sign language recognition and interpretation. In *Gesture Workshop '96*, York, 1996.

[4] A. Braffort, C. Collet, and D. Teil. Anthopomorphic model for hand gesture interface. In *CHI '94*, pages 259–260, Boston, MA., 1994.

[5] F. Forest. Semantic representaion of situations which fit their description in a sign language. In *Gesture Workshop '96*, York, 1996.

[6] S. Gibet. Modèle sensori-moteur pour la génération de mouvements. Notes et Documents 95-09, LIMSI, 1995.

[7] S. Gibet and P. Marteau. A self-organized model for the control, planning and learning of nonlinear multi-dimensional systems using a sensory feedback. *The International Journal of Artificial Intelligence*, 4:337–349, 1994.

[8] T. Lebourque and S. Gibet. Synthesis of hand-arm gestures. In *Gesture Workshop '96*, York, 1996.

[9] B. Moody. *La langue des signes – Tome 2: Dictionnaire bilingue élémentaire.* Ellipses, Paris, 1986.

Navigating in 3D using the "Flying Fish"

D. Allport
Hewlett Packard Research Laboratories, Filton Road, Bristol BS12 6QZ, UK.

E-mail: dea@hplb.hpl.hp.com
Telephone: +44 117 922 8391 Fax: +44 117 922 8925

Abstract

We have developed a novel input device called the "Flying Fish" [2], which uses Electric Field (EF) sensing [10, 7] to interpret free-hand gestures as continuous controllers. Here we discuss some issues that arise when using this type of device for 3D navigation, particularly addressing the question of what it means for a gestural interface to feel "natural".

1 Introduction

In the context of the current workshop, we need to distinguish our approach from that of standard gestural interfaces to computers. The most common approach is to design a *language* of user gestures, and to develop recognition algorithms that interpret (some) hand movements as valid examples of commands in our language. There are then at least three distinct sub-problems:

1. choosing a set of primitives for the gestural language which is appropriate for the given task domain
2. given a particular input medium (dataglove, video etc), designing syntactic recognition algorithms to appropriately identify user gestures in terms of the language chosen
3. once particular gestural statements have been recognised, performing an unambiguous semantic mapping from these statements to domain referents (both this and the preceding problem may involve considering multiple input modes simultaneously; see for example [3]).

In contrast, we have addressed a rather different problem:

1. we have not implemented a "language" as such, but instead have mapped continuous movements of the users hands in three dimensions onto continuous movements of a virtual 3D joystick.

2. given the physical properties of Electric Field Sensing that we have described elsewhere [2, 10, 7], it is relatively straightforward to design a virtual joystick which passively senses the presence of a user's hands in front of the screen, and uses this to control 3 dimensions of movement simultaneously, without the need for wearing gloves etc. Adding a simple foot-pedal gives both the ability to have continuously variable gain on our navigational controller (like a car's gas pedal), and to have an easy means of switching our controller on and off.

3. The semantic mapping problem is therefore reduced to the apparently trivial questions like "If I move my hands to the left, should the objects on the screen move left or right?". However, we argue that this is not so trivial. For each dimension we sense, there are two choices of "direction" of mapping, but we then have a further choice for each dimension of whether to map this onto translational or rotational movement in 3D space, which gives us twelve possible configurations. As we show in Section 2 below, for 3D navigation there are then additional choices about how we conceptually model movement in the domain, in terms of movement of self, objects, or some intermediary.

We are interested in what makes a particular configuration of a free-hand 3D gestural input device feel "natural" as an interface to navigation in a particular 3D computer application. We suggest the use of "invisible metaphors" to describe the different ways that we can experience navigational interactions in 3D virtual worlds, when the user interface contains no graphical display of an analogue of the control device. We analyse naturalness in human-computer interfaces in terms of a number of interacting factors:

- application task
- physical properties of the input device
- functional mappings from the input device to movements in the domain
- formal representation of the object space
- visible and invisible metaphors
- user preferences

The following sections describe how these factors apply to our work with the Flying Fish.

2 Conceptualising the 3D navigation task

In a navigational interaction, where we do not see one object moving with respect to a background of other fixed objects, but rather we see all objects moving, there are several possible physical models of what could be moving:

- all the objects in the world
- the position (and/or orientation) of the self

- a vehicle mediating between self and objects - here there may be an additional level of indirection, as when I *rotate* a car's steering wheel anti-clockwise, the car *translates* towards the left, and objects seen through the windscreen translate rightwards.

- a viewer mediating between self and objects - again there may be an additional level of indirection, as when we move the end of a camera or telescope mounted on a tripod upwards, and objects seen through the camera lens appear to move *up*, versus raising hand-held binoculars, where objects in the field of vision move *down*

No matter how we interpret the navigation task, the visual feedback given by the movement itself is sufficient to accomplish it successfully, *no matter what kind of input device one is using*. This is unlike the task of on-screen target-acquisition, where for some input devices (like touch-screens), it is sufficient to give feedback about when the target has been acquired, whereas for others (such as mice, joysticks etc) it is necessary to have a tracking symbol such as cursor, or some other form of feedback about the difference between one's current state and the goal.

Each different way of conceptualising the navigation task has different implications for user expectations about the types of movement that can occur. If the user feels "outside" the objects of the virtual world, it may feel natural to rotate the world in its entirety around the notional "center of the world" (which may be some distance in front of the user), whereas if a user feels "inside" the virtual world (moving the self through it, possibly within some sort of vehicle), it will feel natural for rotational movements to occur with respect to the user's current position in the virtual world (cf. [9]).

It is possible to influence user expectations directly by using explicit graphical representations of a particular movement metaphor, for example by including in the virtual scene a car's dashboard, steering wheel and windscreen through which the world is viewed. But as we discuss in Section 6 below, we have not concentrated upon how best to force a particular interpretation of the task, so much as investigating how the combinations of the other factors we have identified can lead to a strong sense naturalness for each different interpretation of the navigational task, even without using explicit visual metaphors.

3 Physical properties of the Flying Fish

We have given a detailed description of our input device elsewhere [2]. It effectively measures the distances of one or two hands from the four corners of a computer screen, by comparing the amounts of electric field sensed by the wing-shaped receiver electrodes around the monitor. These measurements are converted to a measure of the amount of body-mass displacement in three dimensions from a virtual center, which lies approximately half-way between the user and the monitor, on an axis running through the middle of the screen. The device therefore makes no explicit distinction between one-handed and two-handed gestures.

Therefore all three Figures below (1a–c) illustrate what is, from the point of view of the physics of the input device, the "same" gesture. However, the hand-drawn annota-

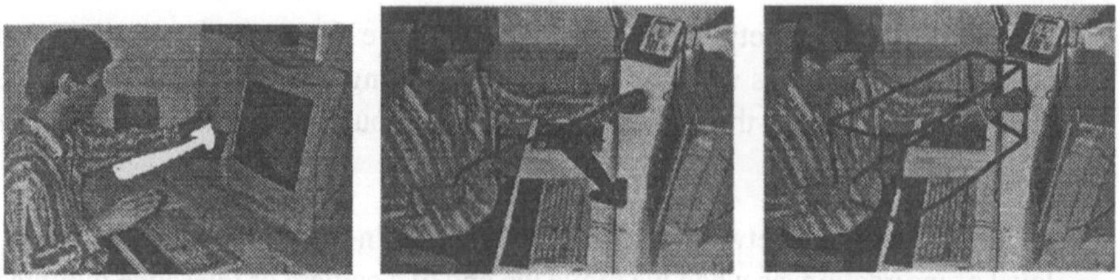

(a) Translate left. (b) Rotate right. (c) Rotate clockwise.

Figure 1: Examples of the "same" gesture.

tions on the photographs attempt to show some different, equally "natural", interpretations of this gesture from the point of view of the user. In the first case (Figure 1a) the user is thinking of the gesture as meaning "move to the left". He will expect objects on the screen to move right. Next (Figure 1b), he is interpreting his movements as controlling the handlebars of a virtual bicycle, and he will expect this "rotate right" gesture to result in a movement of objects on the screen to the left, rotating around a center corresponding to his own point-of-view.

In the third case (Figure 1c) the user is interacting with a single virtual object on the screen which rotates around its own center, and so it feels natural to think of this gesture as grabbing the virtual object between his hands and rotating it clockwise (as seen from above) around the vertical axis. This illusion could also be achieved with devices like the Polhemus or DataGlove which allow similar large-scale physical gestures, but would be difficult if not impossible to achieve with a mouse, joystick, spaceball etc.

Another effect of the input device's physical properties is that, when using indirect devices like mice, it is easy for us to experience our navigation as if we are in a vehicle, using the vehicle's controllers to move through the world. But with completely free-hand interfaces like the Flying Fish, it is also especially easy to feel that it is our self that is moving directly through the environment.

4 Functional mappings from input device to domain movements

The Flying Fish implements isotonic rate control, with a control gain that is varied by the foot pedal. In other words, for a given displacement of the user's hands from a position of being balanced around the center, we get a corresponding velocity of movement, which is then scaled by the gas pedal setting (which may be zero). Our device is sensitive to movements of a few millimeters, and produces eight bits of resolution in the 3D control measurement.

Whilst it would be theoretically possible to implement a 3D virtual mouse (displacement $\rightarrow$ displacement mapping) with the same sensing mechanism, this would not be convenient for the 3D navigation task. This is because typically the part of the space that is visible to the user at any one time is small compared to the size of the virtual world to be explored, and we need to avoid a constant "nulling problem" [4].

5 Formal representations of virtual spaces

As reported in [1], we have used the Flying Fish to move through several different types of virtual space. The Financial Viewpoints space [9] is formally a Euclidean 3D space, but it contains a single virtual structure that either rotates around its own center or else moves closer or father away in response to input controls. This can strongly suggest that one is holding it as a virtual object between one's hands, as shown in (Figure 1c). Interestingly, it is not necessary for this interaction to have a complete physical analogue in order for it to feel natural. In the physical world, static gestures such as those in (Figure 1c) do not cause continuous motion, even though a movement from a position with hands parallel to the position of (Figure 1c) can easily be experienced as an analogue of setting a pivoted object spinning, after which it will continue to spin with its own momentum. This analogy breaks down, however, when we move our hands slightly back from the position of (Figure 1c) towards the center; our virtual object continues to spin (because as we discussed above (Section 4) our device maps position $\rightarrow$ rate). However, there is still some resemblance here to the effect of slowing down a spinning object by applying slight friction to its sides, so the lack of complete correspondence to interactions with the physical world does not cause our interaction here to feel unnatural.

In contrast, the Galaxy of News space [8] is non-Euclidean; it has depth, but with an orthogonal rather than perspective projection, and it dynamically reconfigures itself as the user moves through it. Visually there are some similarities with the way that we see more detail in natural scenes as we move closer towards the focus of our attention, but in the Galaxy of News space there is also an effect that we never experience in the physical world: the textual objects re-arrange themselves as more detail appears, in order to maintain legibility of as much of the visible information as possible. However, there is still sufficient correspondence with some aspects of our movement through the physical world that we can provide a natural and intuitive gestural interface using the Flying Fish. Neither of the rotational interpretations of (Figure 1b) or (Figure 1c) make sense in this domain, since the application's camera is constrained to always view text in an "upright, straight ahead" orientation which precludes rotational movement, but the feeling of zooming in and out as one's hands move forwards and backwards, or translating left,right or up and down as one's hands move parallel to the screen (as in (Figure 1a)), gives rise to a feeling of natural interaction with an unnatural world.

We have also experimented with the Flying Fish as an interface to standard Euclidean 3D "virtual worlds", of the kind found in contemporary VRML[1] scenes. The formal representation of these space, and the types of motion possible in them, allow navigation through it to be naturally be interpreted in any of the ways listed in Section 2 above.

6 Visible and invisible metaphors

As Gaver has pointed out [6], graphical computer interface metaphors such as "windows" differ considerably from everyday metaphors; instead of highlighting similar-

[1] cf. `http://vrml.wired.com/vrml.tech/vrmlspec.html`

ities between existing objects in the world, they create new (graphical) objects, where the *conceptual* mapping of the interface metaphor differs from the *perceptual* mapping used to express it. Thus the ways in which computer windows are conceptually similar or dissimilar to physical-world windows (for example, similarly, they may provide partial views into larger spaces; dissimilarly, they may be moved around and re-sized at will) are distinct from the ways in which their graphical counterparts are perceptually similar or dissimilar (for example, similarly, they are normally rectangular in shape; dissimilarly, they have a scrollbar and buttons as decoration instead of curtains or blinds).

Many discussions of computer interface metaphors have blurred this distinction, and as Buxton has argued [5, 4], there has been an exaggerated emphasis on the visual aspects of computer interfaces, at the expense of the tactile, sonic and other aspects. We would go further and suggest that, even for interactions with 3D graphics, sometimes the visual aspects of the interface are the least important. Given the separability of conceptual metaphors and perceptual metaphors, along with the ability of direct input devices like the Flying Fish to support 3D navigation tasks without visual feedback (cf. Section 2 above), it is possible to employ conceptual interface metaphors that have no graphical representation. These are what we have called "invisible metaphors": the only *perceptual* expression of the metaphor lies in the dynamic functional mapping of hand-movements to movements of the objects on the screen (eg. the movement metaphors which support the interactions shown in Figures 1).

In addition, since the Flying Fish is used with relatively large-scale hand gestures, *proprioception* also plays a large role in our experience of the human-computer interaction. Everyone has a strong internal sense of what it feels like to make certain movements of our limbs, and we are accustomed to associating these proprioceptions with the motion of our bodies through the world. The Flying Fish interface can take advantage of this fact to suggest invisible metaphors, which arise out of *the experience of the interaction itself*, and are a result of the way that certain kinds of gestural navigation *feel*. And since there is no graphical interface object mediating the interaction, we claim that contrary to conventional usage, what should really be called "direct manipulation" are interactions such as those illustrated in (Figure 1c) above.

7 User preferences

What an individual user experiences as a "natural" interaction is, we believe, constrained by the combination of personal preferences with the other factors we have outlined above: the application task, the physical properties of the input device, the functional mappings from the input device to movements in the domain, the formal representation of the object space, and interface metaphors both visible and invisible. In each case, a user may have special experience or abilities, for example as a result of having spent a lot of time playing a particular computer game which implements a particular model of 3D motion, or using a particular input device. Individuals may also have varying degrees of experience with special types of 3D motion in the real world, such as flying planes, scuba-diving, riding bicycles, playing musical instruments etc, and hence the ways in which their sense of proprioception relates to their concepts of 3D motion may be developed in special ways.

8 Conclusions and further work

We believe that navigation in large multidimensional spaces will be increasingly important, especially now that 3D browsers for the World-Wide Web are becoming available. Our experience with the Flying Fish shows that Electric Field sensing can provide a very intuitive and natural gestural interface that is fun to interact with.

There are a very large number of different ways in which we can map a 3DOF device onto a 6DOF movement, and it is clear that there is no single "best way" to do this, but we have explored a number of different parameters that affect how natural a given mapping feels. Recent technological developments have given rise to the possibility of very cheap, convenient 3DOF sensors using Electric Fields, as well as bringing down the price (and size) of more traditional sensors using gyroscopes, accelerometers, radar etc. There is now a huge range of possibilities for creating new input devices that allow far greater expressive power at drastically reduced cost, and there is a need for both qualitative and quantitative research on the effectiveness of these new designs for user input.

Much of the work in user interfaces for 3D navigation to date has emphasised how graphical interface metaphors can reinforce mappings to known types of motion in the physical world (eg providing virtual cockpits, etc). However, our work has shown that it is not always necessary to have a direct physical analogue to a "natural" 3D interaction, and we can use our sense of proprioception along with invisible metaphors to provide a sense of natural movement even when we are moving in unnatural worlds.

Acknowledgements

I would like to thank Joe Paradiso, Tom Zimmerman and all the other members of the MIT Media Lab's Physics and Media group for their work on the original "fish" hardware and software, and Lisa Strausfeld, Earl Rennison and Yin Yin Wong for their discussions on scale, movement and metaphor in 3D representations.

References

[1] D. Allport, E. Rennison, and L. Strausfeld. Issues of gestural navigation in abstract information spaces. In *CHI 95 Human Factors in Computing Systems*, pages 206–207, Denver, Co, 1995. ACM Press.

[2] D. Allport, T. G. Zimmerman, J. A. Paradiso, J. R. Smith, and N. Gershenfeld. Electric field sensing and the "Flying Fish". *ACM Special Issue on Multimedia Systems and Multisensory Virtual Worlds (in press)*, 1996.

[3] R. A. Bolt and E. Herranz. Two-handed gesture in multi-modal natural dialog. In *Proceedings of UIST 92*, pages 7–14. ACM Press, November 1992.

[4] W. Buxton. There's more to interaction than meets the eye: Some issues in manual input. In D. A. Norman and S. W. Draper, editors, *User-centered Design: New Perspectives on Human-Computer Interaction*. Lawrence Erlbaum Associates, Hillsdale, N.J, 1986.

[5] W. Buxton. The three mirrors of interaction: a holistic approach to user interfaces. In L. W. MacDonald and J. Vince, editors, *Interacting with virtual environments*. Wiley, New York, 1994.

[6] W. W. Gaver. Oh what a tangled web we weave: Metaphor and mapping in graphical interfaces. In *CHI 95 Human Factors in Computing Systems*, pages 270–271, Denver, Co, 1995. ACM Press.

[7] J. A. Paradiso and N. Gershenfeld. Musical applications of electric field sensing. article submitted to Computer Music Journal, June 1995.

[8] E. Rennison. Galaxy of news: An approach to visualizing and understanding expansive news landscapes. In *Proceedings of UIST 94*, November 1994.

[9] L. Strausfeld. Financial viewpoints: Using point-of-view to enable understanding of information. In *CHI 95 Human Factors in Computing Systems*, pages 208–209, Denver, Co, 1995. ACM Press.

[10] T. G. Zimmerman, J. R. Smith, J. A. Paradiso, D. Allport, and N. Gershenfeld. Applying electric field sensing to human-computer interfaces. In *CHI 95 Human Factors in Computing Systems*, pages 280–287, Denver, Co, 1995. ACM Press.

Feeling It as well as Seeing It – Haptic Display within Gestural HCI for Multimedia Telematics Services

A. Hardwick, J. Rush, S. Furner and J. Seton

BT Laboratories, Martlesham Heath, Ipswich, IP5 7RE, UK.

E-mail: {andrew.hardwick, jim.rush, stephen.furner, john.seton}@bt-sys.bt.co.uk

Abstract

Typically, the mechanical feedback that a user obtains during a gesture is simply the mechanical weight and friction of the specific input device being employed. This is very different from everyday experience. Here mechanical feedback to the hand and arm results from the manual manipulation of tools and other objects. This paper reports preliminary research to provide tactile feedback within gestural human computer interaction (HCI) at the users desktop. It discusses our preliminary ideas on the use of force display within gestural HCI for broadband telematics applications.

1 Introduction

Future communications systems are expected to carry many of the current activities of daily life. In the presentation of these services analogy and metaphor to real world objects will be necessary to provide easy command and control of technology being used. Typically, this is expected to be via virtual objects within virtual worlds. In this context haptic display has a vital role to play as a component of the sense of presence that the customer will have. This will be particularly important for training and education in high skill subjects that demand sophisticated manual skills or for decisions that require a knowledge of the tactile properties of real world objects.

Within BT Labs we are investigating the integration of computer generated tactile information within telematics services to enable people to feel the objects they are interacting with on the display screen. The user receives computer generated tactile information during the operation of a gestural input device. The gestural input device produces forces under the control of the computer to create a haptic image at the users hand. In this research a commercial force feedback device is being used. It is intended that a user be able to control a pointer seen on a display screen and feel, through the input device, tactile properties of the objects he or she can see the pointer touching.

We are using three dimensional force-feedback to create a collection of simulated textured objects. This is both for quantitative controlled psychological studies and for a technical demonstration of a potential telematics service concept. The investigation reported in this paper is in its early stages.

2 Touch and Gesture in the User Interface

Gestural interaction with computer based information systems has traditionally consisted of recognising human physical movement as commands. A light pen or mouse can be used to translate a human arm movement into a command to move a graphical object on a display screen. Typically, the mechanical feedback that a user obtains during a gesture is simply the mechanical weight and friction of the specific input device being employed.

When reaching to touch a virtual object, the user is performing a gesture. The history of actions that results in the touching is the gesture. The gesture and the haptic sensations will be intertwined. Unlike in the real world, the recognition of a gesture and its properties could therefore contribute to the generation of an appropriate haptic response from a virtual object.

2.1 Tactile feedback for manual manipulation

Integrating force display into gestural input devices increases the information available to a user. This increase can yield greater interaction speed [2] and fewer input errors. The user receives feedback that directly guides the hand during the manual operation of the gesture rather than having to make fine corrections based on changes seen on the computer screen.

To manipulate simulated objects with subtlety and skill it is anticipated that visual feedback will need supporting with haptic feedback. This will not only be for training hand-to-eye co-ordination skills, but also for manipulating tools and controlling dialogues in computer based applications. In conventional 'WIMP' graphical user interfaces, as well as three dimensional simulations, tactile feedback can improve human machine communication.

2.2 Desktop force display technology

Virtual reality systems do not always need to immerse the user in technology. A conventional visual display can be used to provide a window through which a virtual world can be viewed. For commercial or domestic applications it is possible to use this as a component of a conventional workstation. This 'fish tank' approach to virtual reality offers the advantage of a robust display technology that fits easily into the current work or home environment.

The development of desktop virtual reality applications is being accompanied by the development of simple mechanical haptic display devices [1]. Some of these are being used to improved access to computer systems for people with visual disabilities

[1]See `http://intron.kz.tsukuba.ac.jp/`

[2]. Tactile images have been created to enable blind people to feel more sophisticated images than that available from tactile codes such as Braille.

2.2.1 *Computational haptics*

The physiology of tactile perception reveals a complex interaction of sensory mechanisms. In the skin there are mechanical and temperature sensors and within the muscles and joints there are force and position sensors. The sensory information is combined to form familiar meaningful experiences of shapes and textures. Tactile perception is not simply the sensory detection of pressure on the surface of the skin. The computer controlled tactile images will need to take account of the psychological processes.

The creation of a stable tactile image will require a complex manual display that is, in many cases, integrated into a manual gesture as the user feels or manipulates an object.

3 Modelling texture and shape

3.1 The Hardware

The force-feedback we are using device is an Impulse 3000 probe[3] manufactured by the Immersion Corporation. The probe is a metal rod that can tilt about two axes perpendicular to its length in the manner of a joystick and slide in-and-out along its length. The probe's tip, held by the user, can thus be moved in three dimensional space. Figure 1 shows the possible motions in a simplified sketch. The actual mechanism consists of three identical sets of motors and encoders. The encoders measure the position of the probe's tip in space and the motors allow forces to be applied to the user. Its three axes of force-feedback give it a 13 x 23 x 23 cm^3 working volume with 23 μm spatial resolution, forces up to 9 N in 5 mN steps, less than 0.14 N intrinsic friction, and a 650 Hz bandwidth.

3.2 Coordinate Transformations

The commercial software 3000 treats the coordinates (α, β, L) as (x, y, z) which is sufficient to represent objects and textures but the resulting curved planes and cubes with sloping sides are not ideal so the transformation,

$$x = L\sin\alpha\cos\beta - (\text{x-axis Origin}) \quad (1)$$
$$y = L\cos\alpha\sin\beta - (\text{y-axis Origin}) \quad (2)$$
$$z = L\cos\alpha\cos\beta - (\text{z-axis Origin}) \quad (3)$$

was used instead. That gave a true Cartesian coordinate system. Similarly the two torques (T_α and T_β about the α and β axes and the force (Φ_L along the L axis) need to be calculated from the required force vector (Φ_x, Φ_y, Φ_z). The original version had

[2]See http://ccrma-www.stanford.edu/CCRMA/Overview/node37.html

[3]The Impulse 3000 probe was supplied with a pen-like handle attached to the probe via a universal joint. Slack in the joint reduced the tactile fidelity so the attachment was removed.

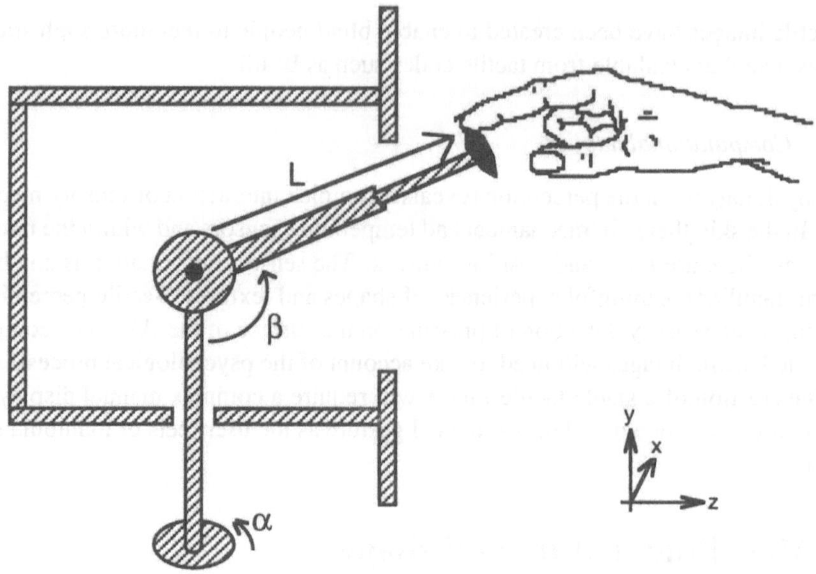

Figure 1: A simplified didactic sketch of the probe showing the coordinate systems.

simply $T_\alpha \propto \Phi_x$, $T_\beta \propto \Phi_y$ and $\Phi_L \propto \Phi_z$. The more accurate version based on Equations 1 to 3 works out as

$$T_\alpha = LA^{3/2}\left(\frac{\Phi_x \cos\alpha - \Phi_z \sin\beta}{(\cos^2\alpha + \sin^2\alpha\cos^2\beta)\cos\beta}\right) \quad (4)$$

$$T_y = LA^{3/2}\left(\frac{\Phi_y \cos\beta - \Phi_z \sin\alpha}{(\cos^2\beta + \sin^2\beta\cos^2\alpha)\cos\alpha}\right) \quad (5)$$

$$\Phi_L = LA^{1/2}\left(\frac{\Phi_x \cos\beta\sin\alpha}{\cos^2\alpha + \sin^2\alpha\cos^2\beta} + \frac{\Phi_y \cos\alpha\sin\beta}{\cos^2\beta + sin^2\beta\cos^2\alpha} + \right.$$

$$\left. \frac{\Phi_z A cos\alpha cos\beta}{(\cos^2\alpha + sin^2\alpha\cos^2\beta)(\cos^2\beta + sin^2\beta + cos^2\alpha)}\right) \quad (6)$$

where $A = 1 - \sin^2\alpha\sin^2\beta$.

3.3 Simulation of Flat Textured Planes

For simplicity, the flat textured planes were simulated by a force-field. The force that the probe feeds back to the user depends solely upon the position of the probe, not its velocity, its acceleration, its history or the time. To simulate a smooth textureless planar surface of a solid, there must be a normal force towards the surface when the probe tip is in a position corresponding to being inside the solid. When outside the solid, the force is zero. The transition between the non-zero force inside and the zero force outside

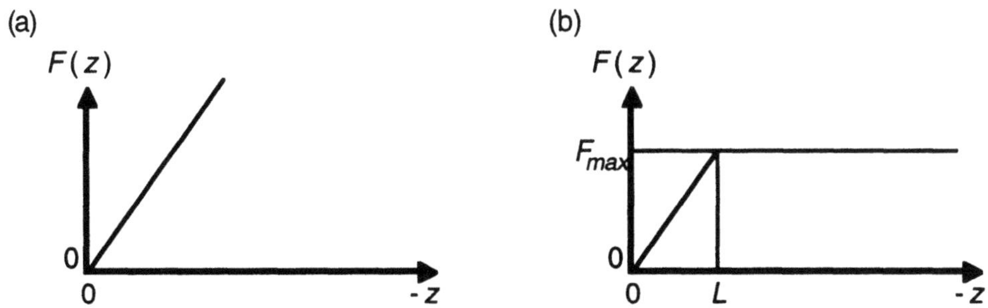

Figure 2: Force profiles. (a) Hooke's, (b) Used in this simulation. *F* is the reaction force and z is the displacement from the plane (negative values of z represent positions inside the object).

must be smooth to prevent the probe being oscillated in and out of the surface when the user tries to gently touch the surface.

A sensible dependence of the reaction force, $F(z)$, on the displacement of the probe tip from the simulated surface, z, had to be chosen. The obvious simple realistic force profile would be to follow Hooke's Law and have the reaction force proportional to depth of the probe below the surface (Figure 2a), but the 9 N limit to the force feedback makes this infeasible for all but the softest objects. Instead, the surfaces were given a simulated elastic skin layer of thickness L beyond which the reaction force is a constant value F_{max} (Figure 2b). This was mechanically equivalent to not having a plane with a simple spring beneath it (Figure 3a) but instead a weight linked to the plane by a spring (Figure 3b). After a certain amount of compression of the spring, the weight lifts from the floor and the force no longer increases. This gave a convincing haptic impression of a smooth surface. F_{max} or L could be varied to change the object's apparent hardness.

The best way of simulating texture was found to be simply to represented it as a local displacement of the surface that locally varies across the surface, $s(x,y)$ where x and y are co-ordinates on the plane. The direction of the reaction force is first calculated if the surface were smooth. When calculating the distance to the surface to work out the reaction force's magnitude, the texture is taken into account by using $F(z-s(x,y))$ instead of $F(z)$. Forces in the plane of the surface are then added so that the resultant force is normal to the local surface of the texture (Figure 4). The expression for the resultant force vector, $\underline{R}$, is therefore simply (Equation 7):

$$\underline{R}(x,y,z) = F(z-s(x,y))\left(-\frac{\delta s(x,y)}{\delta x}\underline{\hat{x}} - \frac{\delta s(x,y)}{\delta y}\underline{\hat{y}} + \underline{\hat{z}}\right) \qquad (7)$$

Fortunately, this force field is not only usually smooth but is always conservative so the chances for feedback instabilities in the simulation are minimised. The texture is varied by specifying different displacement functions (e.g. sinusoidal ridges, grids of lumps, random surfaces etc.), amplitudes and periodicities. Unlike the textures simulated by the 'Sandpaper System' [3], which used two dimensions of force-feedback, these textures have a forces normal to the plane as well as in it and allow the user

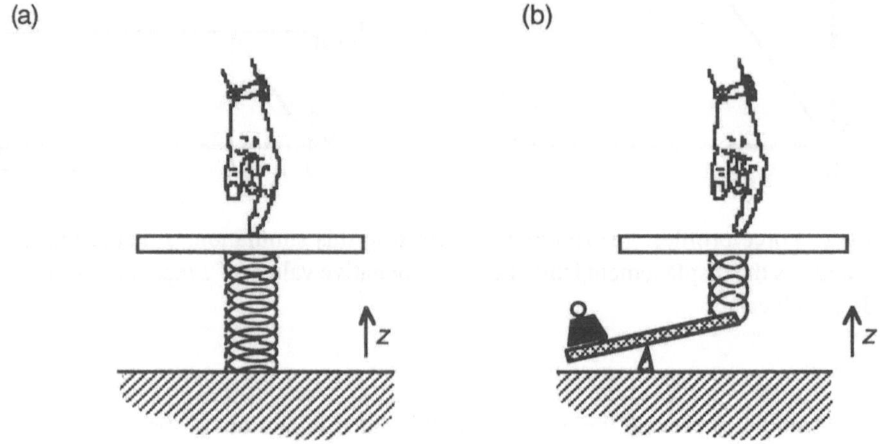

Figure 3: Simple mechanical models for the force profiles of Figure 2

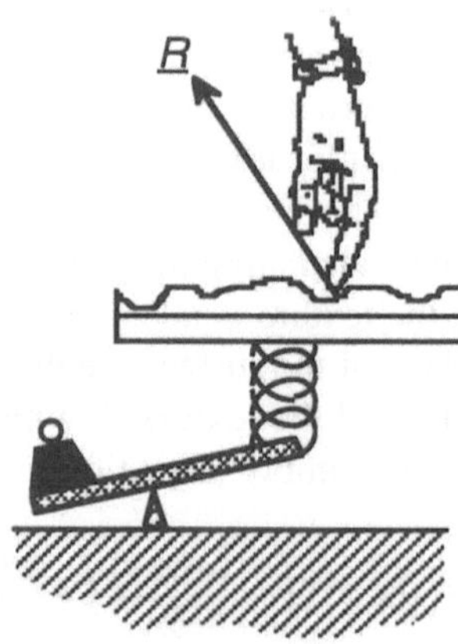

Figure 4: Simple mechanical model for texture simulation scheme showing the direction of the resultant force when feeling a part of the texture.

to move off the plane. The method of texture reproduction used here mathematically reduces to that used in the 'Sandpaper System' in the two dimensional limit where $F(z)$ is a constant.

It is intended to just have flat representations of the textures in windows on the monitor and the texture in the currently selected window is the one that will be simulated by the probe. There will be options in the application program for the users to alter the parameters of the displayed textures.

3.4 Simulation of Solid Textured Objects

For stereohaptic simulation of three dimensional objects, similar methods to the above are used for representing surfaces and textures but spatial regions other than those bounded by infinite planes are used. The part of the simulated object's surface nearest to the position of the probe tip is the one that determines the force. For example, a smooth solid sphere simulation always has forces directed out radially. A textured solid cube has been simulated by considering it to be composed of six square-based pyramids with their tips together at the centre of the cube and their bases acting as the cube faces. Reaction forces act towards the base of the pyramid that the probe tip is in and textures are applied in exactly the same way as for an infinite planar surface.

It is hoped that it will be able to have a visual simulation of the solid objects displayed on the monitor whilst the corresponding haptic simulation is displayed on the probe. The plan for co-ordinating the two aspects of the simulation is to have them running essentially independently with each notifying the other of position changes. The visual simulation routines would tell the haptic ones of the current position and orientation of the viewpoint which the haptic routines would then use as an offset for its position calculations. Likewise the haptic simulation routines would tell the visual ones of the position of the probe tip so that a cursor can be drawn in the correct place in the visual simulation. This should allow the two parts to be updated at different rates: the force-feedback must be updated frequently ($\sim 10^3$ Hz according to [3]) but the visual simulation can be slower (and often is, because of processing power limitations).

4 Initial Human Factors Observations

The effective integration of haptics into human machine communication will require an understanding of the perceptual systems being used. The construction of haptic images and their roll within a human computer dialogue will need to take account of the ways in which haptic data is used within human information processing.

Basic psychophysical processes will govern the sensory stimulation required to create a haptic image. The form and content of a sequence of haptic events will require an understanding of higher level processes. The memorability of physical gesture may be based in the storage of a repertoire of "action primitives" [1], thus training or haptic memory tasks may need to segment around these primitives for efficient human machine communication to take place.

The following are some of the examples that were found when various people felt a simulation of a 40 mm wide cube fixed to a hard plane with a sinusoidal texture on its front face. In the Figures, the cube is shown in vertical front-to-back cross-section through its centre and the arrows show the direction of the normal forces in each region.

4.1 Distracting Visual Information

Though the haptic information the user gets corresponds to a cube, visually, it is still just a steel rod connected to some pivots and motors. One result of this is that a simulated coarse texture can, instead of giving the impression of roughness, create the impression of grating in the probe's bearings. These two situations would, of course, feel the same. Hopefully this distraction will be lessened when the mechanics of the probe are hidden and the subject is provided with a visual simulation on a monitor that matches what they are feeling.

4.2 Differing Mental Models

Asking different people to touch the front, top, back etc. faces of the simulated cube unexpectedly revealed that, though they all felt the cube, their mental images of it varied. For example, one can imagine the cube to be at one's finger tip where it touches the probe (Figure 5a). Alternatively, one can imagine the cube to be inverted at the other end of the probe to where it is being held and that the probe is a rod that pivots about its midpoint to touch the cube. (Figure 5b).

4.3 The Force Limit

The 9 N force limit means that one can put one's finger into supposedly rigid objects fairly easily. The simulation must provide some sensible response when the user performs actions that would be impossible in reality, such as feeling inside an unopened box. The force limitation does have advantages though. For example, a system capable of feeding back realistically strong forces could potentially injure a user whereas this the Impulse 3000 is unlikely to do so.

4.4 Unrealistic Modelling

The simple force-fields used are not completely realistic, especially near cube diagonals where the direction of the reaction force changes abruptly. A more realistic force-field could be calculated by taking into account non-local deformations in an elastic cube, but that would require substantially more computation and the simplified force-field modelled a cube convincingly.

4.5 Feeling with a Point Contact

The simulation models the cube being touched by a single point of contact at the probe's tip (where the user's finger is assumed to be), so feeling a texture is more like rubbing it with one's fingernail than with the ball of one's finger, which is what people usually expect unless they have been forewarned.

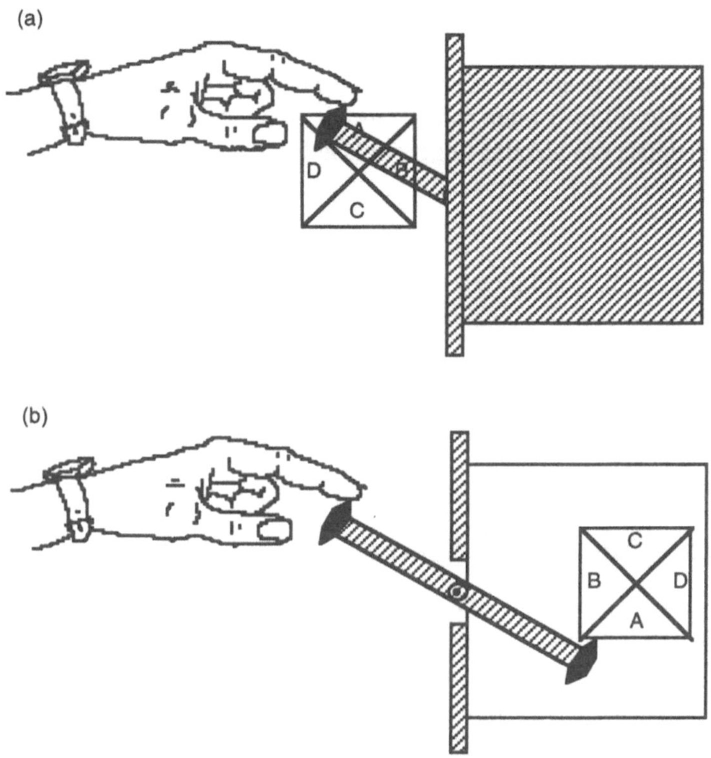

Figure 5: Two possible mental models of a cube ABCD that fit the same haptic model. In both cases the user is really touching the tip of the probe which simulates the feeling of a cube. In (a) the user imagines the cube at their finger tip whereas in (b) the user imagines the probe to be a lever with the cube at the other end.

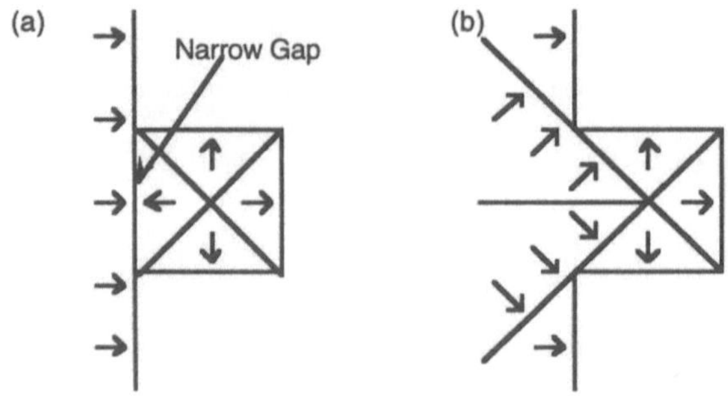

Figure 6: Two force-fields that can represent a cube fixed to a plane. (a) is closer to the real situation but (b) feels more natural since it eliminates the narrow gap into which the point of contact can go but a finger could not.

Figure 7: The path of a contact point (a) following the surface of a texture and (b) skimming across it.

4.6 Getting into Narrow Spaces

Another problem connected with simulating a contact point instead of a contact region is that it can slip into crevices in the haptic model where a human finger would not fit. An example is slipping between a cube and an attached back plane when both are simulated realistically as in Figure 6a. Replacing the simulated point contact with, for example, a small spherical simulated contact and calculating the force feedback for that situation would solve the problem but it would increase the complexity of computation, especially when the point contact has been pushed inside a solid. It would also reduce the resolution available to the user for feeling fine textures. An easier solution is to design model to give the right haptic response even if that entails making the geometry less realistic; Figure 6d shows a solution for a cube on a back plane.

4.7 Skimming The Textures

When a texture is being felt, the point of contact does not necessarily follow the surface texture (Figure 7a) but often slips from peak to peak across it (Figure 7b). This is most likely to happen when the local surface gradients are large and the motion across the surface is rapid. Though this is exactly what happens in reality when one rubs a fingernail across a rough surface, in the simulation it gives an impression of extremely rough texture or an instability in the feedback loop. It could be that the audio feedback for the equipment reinforces this impression.

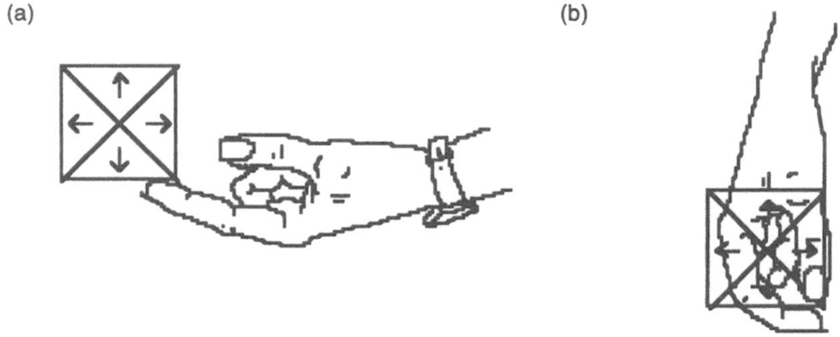

Figure 8: Two ways of touching the same point on the bottom of a simulated cube with a forefinger. The probe has no way of telling the realistic case (a) from the unrealistic case (b).

4.8 The Lack of Friction

It was at first thought that friction need not be explicitly put into the haptic simulation since the texture would provide sufficient resistance to motion on the surfaces; real friction is mainly caused by small projections on the moving surfaces. In practice, the textures, though feeling rough, did not feel fricative so a separate friction force may need to be added later.

4.9 Impossible Reaching

There is no way for the simulation to know where any part of the user is. It just knows where the tip of the probe is and assumes the user is holding it. Therefore the user can put their hand through some parts of the simulated object whilst feeling other parts (e.g. Figure 8), which can seem rather counter-intuitive.

5 Conclusions

We have successfully been able to combine force display and gesture to demonstrate the creation of simple three dimensional haptic images. This work has raised some interesting issues in computational haptics and allowed us to observe some aspects of human interaction with the three dimensional tactile images. Clearly, there is a great deal of further research that needs to be carried out in this area. Desktop force display has the potential to be used within gestural input so that users can feel the content of virtual worlds provided via networked multimedia telecommunications services.

References

[1] J. Annett. Imagery and motor processes: Editorial overview. *British Journal of Psychology*, 86(2):161–167, 1995.

[2] F. L. Engel, P. Goossens, and R. Haakma. Improved efficiency through I- and E-feedback: a trackball with contextual force feedback. *International Journal of Human-Computer Studies*, 6(41):949–974, 1994.

[3] D. Minsky. *Computational Haptics: The Sandpaper System for Synthesizing Texture for a Force-Feedback Display*. PhD thesis, MIT, 1995.

Real Time Hand Tracking and Gesture Recognition as a 3D Input Device for Graphical Applications

R. Bowden, T. Heap and D. Hogg

School of Computer Studies, University of Leeds, Leeds, LS2 9JT, UK.

E-mail: {richard, ajh, dch}@dcre.leeds.ac.uk

Abstract

This paper outlines a system design and implementation of a 3D input device for graphical applications which uses real time hand tracking and gesture recognition to provide the user with an intuitive interface for tomorrow's applications. Point Distribution Models (PDMs) have been shown to be successful at tracking deformable objects. This system demonstrates how these 'smart snakes' can be used in real time with a real world problem. The system is based upon Open Inventor[1] and designed for use with Silicon Graphics Indy Workstations, but provisions have been make for the move to other platforms and applications. We demonstrate how PDMs provide the ideal feature vector for model classification. It is shown how computer vision can provide a low cost, intuitive interface that has few hardware constraints. We also give the reader an insight into the next generation of HCI and Multimedia, providing a 3D scene viewer and VRML browser based upon the handtracker. Further allowances have been made to facilitate the inclusion of the handtracker within third party Inventor applications. All source code, libraries and applications can be downloaded for free from the above web addresses. This paper demonstrates how computer vision and computer graphics can work together providing an interdisciplinary approach to problem solving.

1 Introduction

For many years the prevalent input device has been the QWERTY keyboard, a device that was specifically designed to slow user input. However, as times progress new forms of interaction with computers have been developed. The advent of the mouse changed the face of computing applications and the 'window' was born. It was this simple input device, within the price range of the masses, that revolutionised the computer industry. Applications are changing and with the move to 3D graphics, Virtual

[1]Open Inventor, OpenGL are registered trademarks of Silicon Graphics Inc.

Environments and the introduction of world wide standards such as VRML the computer industry is being forced to rethink the user interface that was once a cold ASCII based system.

New input devices are appearing, from the low cost 3D mouse to the dataglove and datasuit. Devices such as these either lack usability, or are out priced by the technology. Multimedia is here; soon every terminal will have its own camera. The use of a camera as an input device provides the possibility to introduce the ultimate in computer interaction to the user. Real world events in 3D can be converted directly into meaningful interaction. Imagine reaching into your VDU, grasping a file and dropping it into a bin or virtual directory structure. What could be more intuitive for the user, than an interface that mimics the real world. This paper is not intended to provide all the solutions, but to investigate the possibilities of such a technology.

2 The Handtracker

The hand tracker code, developed at the University of Leeds [4], uses a 2D deformable Active Shape Model (smart snakes [2]) to produce a generic and flexible model that can be used to track any 2D deformable object. To locate an object, a contour which has a similar shape is applied to an image close, or near to a desired feature. The process is an iterative one, where by the contour makes small steps within the image to find a natural resting place. The model uses suggested movements from control points (using edge detection or grey level matching). Movement of the model is then allowed through the relocation of the model within the image, and deformation of the model within the bounds of the of the shape deviation gained from the training set.

The handtracker uses a Point Distribution Model (PDM) [2] to describe the shape of the deformable contour. The model is described by a vector $\mathbf{x_e} = (x_1, y_1, \ldots, x_N, y_N)$, representing a set of points specifying the outline of an object. A training set of these vectors is assembled for a particular model class, in this case the hand in its various different poses. The training process is outlined in Figure 1. The training set is then aligned (using translation, rotation and scaling) and the mean shape calculated by finding the average vector. To represent the deviation within the shape of the training set Principle Component Analysis (PCA) [5] is performed on the deviation of the example vectors from the mean. In order to do this the covariance matrix $\mathbf{S}$ of the deviation is first calculated:

$$\mathbf{S} = \frac{1}{E} \sum_{e=1}^{E} (x_e - \bar{x})(x_e - \bar{x})^T \tag{1}$$

The t unit eigenvectors of $\mathbf{S}$ corresponding to the t largest eigenvalues supply the variation modes; t will generally be much smaller than N, thus giving a very compact model. It is this dimensional reduction in the model that will enable simple gesture recognition and will be discussed later. A deformed shape x is generated by adding weighted combinations of $\mathbf{v_j}$ to the mean shape:

$$x = \bar{x} + \sum_{j=1}^{t} b_j \mathbf{v}_j \tag{2}$$

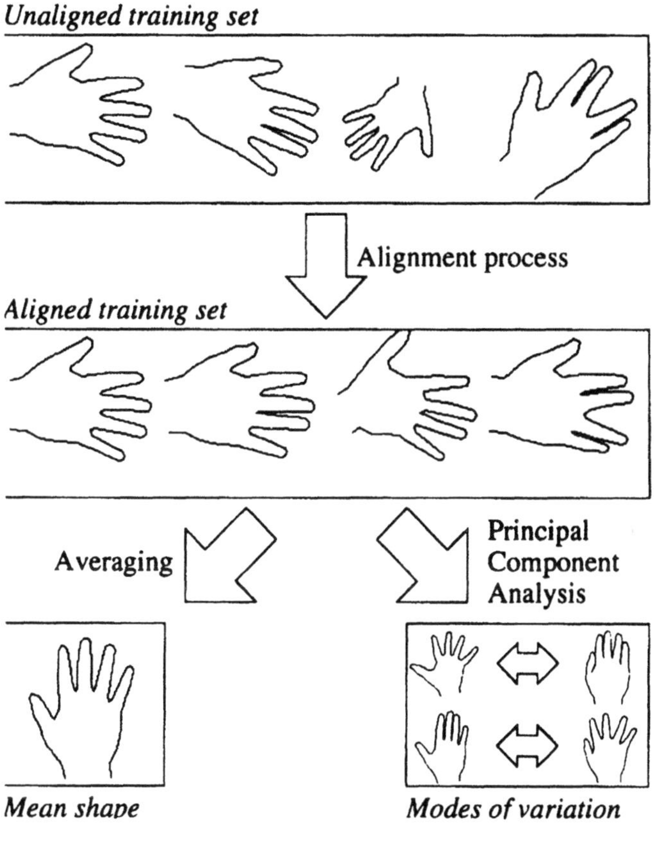

Figure 1: Training a Point Distribution Model

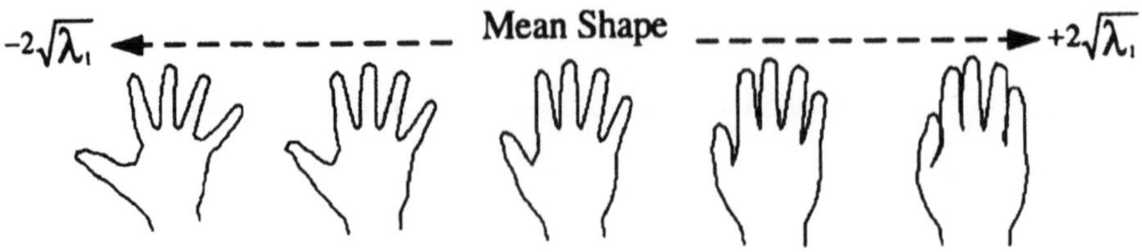

Figure 2: The major mode of Variation

where b_j is the weighting for the jth variation vector. Suitable limits for b_j are $\pm 3\sqrt{\lambda_j}$ where λ_j is the jth largest eigenvalue of **S**.

The hand model uses a mean shape that corresponds to a relaxed open pose hand and will deform and track a hand in real time using only the first four modes of variation (the four eigenvectors that correspond to the largest four eigenvalues). The model hand shape is described solely in terms of these vectors and the mean shape, these along with its position in 2D image space (x, y), its size and rotation allow the model all the flexibility needed to track a hand within an image frame. This provides a very compact mode from which to work.

Figure 2 shows the primary mode of variation of the hand model after PCA has been performed, the readers attention is brought to the movement of this primary mode which encompasses the majority of deviation within the training set. This primary mode is closely linked to the movement of the thumb, and will be of interest later.

3 Gesture Recognition

The model is a fixed 2D outline of a hand in an open pose, allowing variation of the hand under heavy constraints. These constraints provide a robust system that facilitate accurate tracking in 3D, however this limits the gestures that can be recognised. Further extensions to the basic model are under continuous development and as the model is extended more flexible gestures can be implemented.

Figure 3 shows a hand in the mean position along with some of the gestures the system recognises. The model provides a distinct pose that reduces the opportunity for misclassification of intensity edges which occur in noisy and cluttered backgrounds.

Each shape of the model is represented by the values of the four weights along the four primary modes of variation. Each shape therefore produces a distinct 4D feature vector that can be used for pattern recognition. PDMs allow considerable dimensional reduction, the model consisting of 61 points generating a 122 dimensional shape vector can be reduced to 4 dimensions through PCA while retaining the information needed to classify types of shape deformation within a specific class of shape. It is primarily for this reason that PDMs lend themselves so well to this application.

Gestures were selected so as to be as intuitive as possible whilst attempting to separate individual gestures into distinct clusters within the *4D Gesture Space*. A **positive** training set was produced directly from running the handtracker that consisted of the gestures to be recognised. Deviation from specific gestures (noise) was introduced to

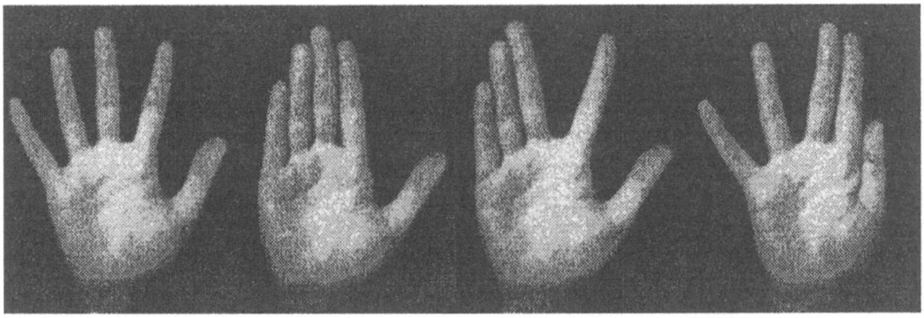

Figure 3: Some of the Gestures that the System Recognises. (a) The normal hand pose i.e. mean shape. (b) Flat hand pose with thumb out. (c) Pointing gesture. (d) Grouped finger gesture.

allow generalisation to be possible during pattern recognition. The final training set contained approximately 2,500 4D feature vectors. Due to the positive training set and similar model poses corresponding directly to similar feature vectors it would therefore be expected that each gesture would occupy a distinct, finite, cluster in *Gesture Space*. Working on this assumption it is possible to introduce linear separators in order to segment the *Gesture Space* into the designated gestures.

Many approaches are applicable to this problem from simple thresholding to those of neural networks. All techniques rely upon the same basic principles and the appropriate technique is denoted by the dimensionality of the problem. As static gestures are of primary concern, the clusters can simply be approximated and extracted through the use of k-means cluster analysis without any prior knowledge of their nature. This enables much larger dimensional problems to be solved for complex models and therefore lends itself directly to 3D PDMs (see Future Work). As the move to dynamic gestures is considered, it is the authors' opinion that neural networks would provide a more suitable solution. It has already been shown that American Sign Language (ASL) can successfully be recognised through the use of a data glove and a neural network [3]. Working with a PDM provides a significantly smaller dimensional problem than that of a data glove with its multiple flexation sensors and therefore again demonstrates the beauty/simplicity of the PDM.

4 K-means Cluster Analysis

K-means is a cluster based technique. It attempts to find the exemplars (centre points) of a specified number of clusters (see Figure 4) within a data set by minimising the cost function:

$$\text{Cost} = \sum_{i=0}^{n} D(x_i, z_i) \tag{3}$$

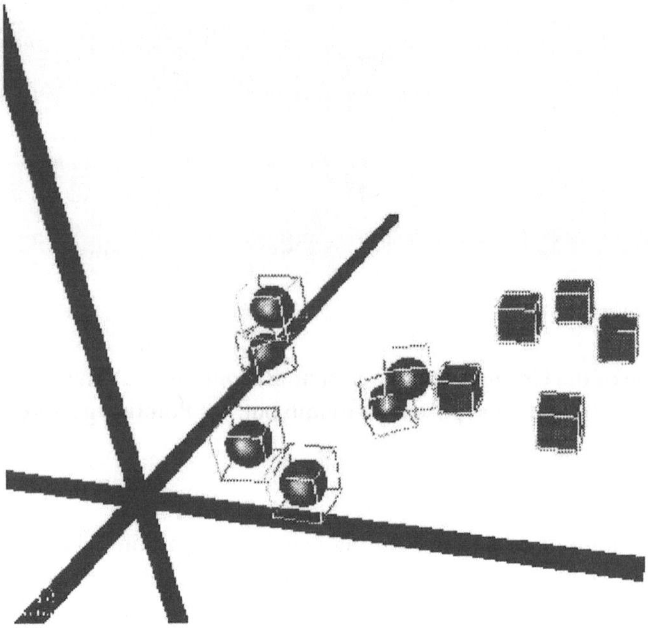

Figure 4: K-means

where n = number of clusters, x_i = set of points that belong to the exemplar z_i and D = User defined distance function.

K-means minimises this cost function through the iterative refinement of cluster centers. It will always converge on a low cost solution but because the energy surface that it traverses is full of local minima, it will not necessarily find the global solution. The solution it finds depends upon the initialisation of the exemplar positions and the number of clusters to be found. To obtain a good solution it is necessary to run the algorithm many times choosing the lowest cost obtained [1].

The number of gestures within the training set is known and k-means allows us to locate approximate positions and sizes for these clusters through the minimisation of the cost function (Equation 3) which is the total distance of poses from their respective cluster centres. When the analysis was performed for the four expected clusters only three distinct solutions were generated with one of these providing the best cost.

It would be expected that the lowest cost solution would provide the best solution for recognition, however the slightly higher cost solutions in practice provided more robust recognition. This suggested that the training set may contain noisy data or irregularly shaped clusters. By looking for the natural number (see below) of clusters it would be expected that noisy vectors would generate separate clusters and irregular clusters may be separated into multiple smaller clusters that better describe their shape.

When the number of clusters is one the resulting cost will be the high. When the number of clusters is equal to the number of points within the data set (N) then the cost solution will be zero. As the number of clusters increases from 1 to N, so the over-

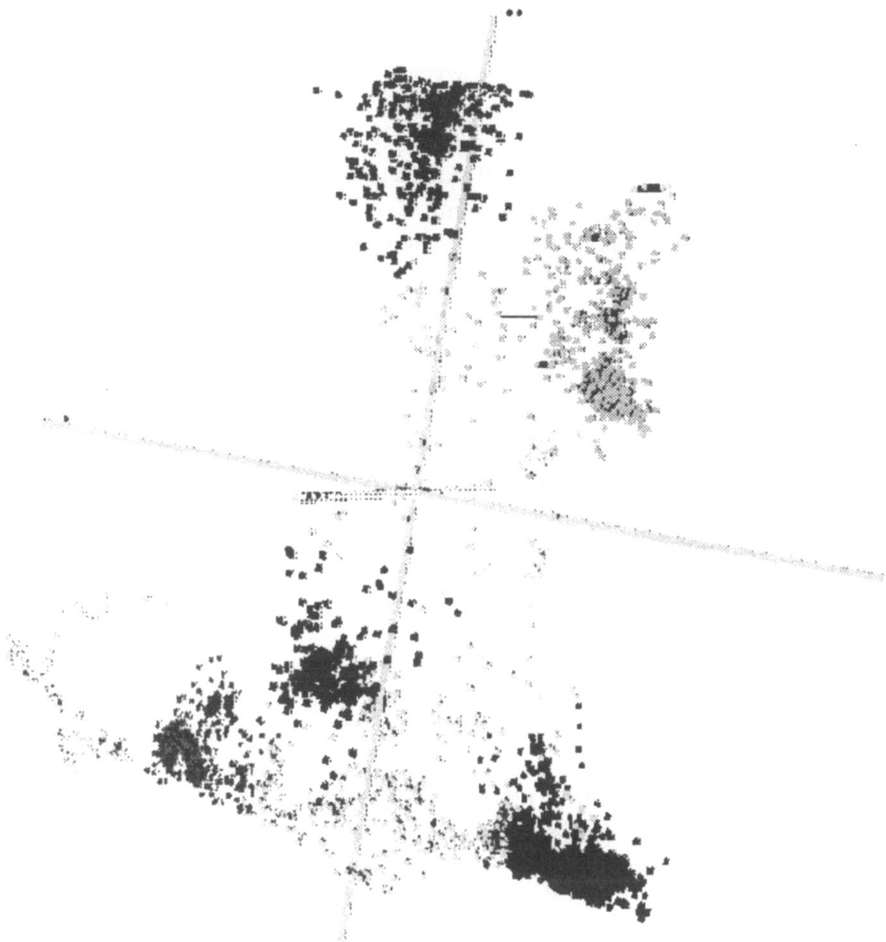

Figure 5: Clusters in Gesture Space

all cost will decrease. There will however be a point at which increasing the number of clusters further results in little benefit of cost. This can be said to be the **natural number** of clusters within the data set. On investigation, our *Gesture Space* suggested eight natural clusters existed, twice what was originally expected. Again performing cluster analysis for eight clusters, a global cost solution was obtained that performed well on recognition. Out of the eight clusters, two provided little or no recognition purpose. These can be said to be noise within the training set which although introduced to provide generalisation also resulted in unnecessarily large clusters and therefore misclassification. All the original gestures were recognised by a single cluster except one which had been broken into two clusters suggesting an non-hyperspherical cluster. The remaining cluster detected a gesture that was not intentionally present within the training set.

The original training set had a flat hand pose (Figure 3b) but due to the aforementioned reasons of generalisation the training set contained the flat hand with both the thumb flush and extended. As the movement of the thumb is closely related to the primary mode of variation (See Section 2 of [4]) this has been sufficient to separate the gesture into two different clusters enabling the handtracker to be capable of recognising five gestures.

Figure 5 shows the 4D *Gesture Space* projected into 3 dimensions, the differently shaded clusters correspond to the five detected gestures. Note the elongation of the Thumb cluster which uses two separate clusters to better model the gesture. It can also clearly be seen that even in 3 dimensions each gesture is a unique separable cluster. This suggests that even though the 4 largest eigenvectors are needed to best model the hand, only the primary three are needed to perform pattern recognition on the designated gestures, this is a total dimension reduction of 122 to 3 ($\approx 41 : 1$).

5 Camera Calibration

In order for the output from the handtracker to be of any use to an application, it is important to calibrate the camera to provide meaningful communication between applications. The intrinsic and extrinsic parameters of the IndyCam[2] were determined using a weak perspective model (scaled orthographic). This is possible due to the nature of the model being primarily 2 dimensional. Using this model results in a direct relationship between image size in pixels and real world object size/position in meters. The system is designed to work in an operational spatial cube of $0.5 \times 0.5 \times 0.5$ metres. The movement of the hand within this space is normalised to the range $(-1, 1)$ in the x, y and z directions. This allows simple use of the handtracker in applications where an appropriate scaling can be used.

6 Open Inventor

Open Inventor is a library of objects and methods used to create interactive 3D graphics applications. It is a set of building blocks that enables the application programmer to

[2] IndyCam - Silicon Graphics multimedia workstation digital colour camera.

take advantage of the powerful Silicon Graphics hardware features with minimal programming effort. Inventor focuses on creating 3D objects. All information about these objects; their shape, size, colouring, surface texture, location in 3D space, is stored in a scene database. This information can be used in a variety of ways. The most common use is to display, or render, an image of the 3D objects on the screen [6].

The basic model behind Inventor is that of the scene graph. This is a tree structure that allows the entire scene to be represented within one hierarchical design, allowing complex objects to be assembled from simple primitives. As well as the existence of the scene graph it is necessary for the reader be familiar with the idea of a viewer and camera. Cameras in Inventor are nodes within scene graphs that tell the hardware how to render the graph (they specify the users view of the scene). Viewers are used as the user interface to applications and translate events generated by mouse movement into events that control the camera position, orientation, state of the graph and interaction with objects.

Inventor uses a window -based system and allows interaction with the scene graph primarily through the use of a mouse, but also devices such as the space ball. It is important that the existing user interface not be compromised by the inclusion of the handtracker. The handtracker is therefore designed to work with the existing user interface, duplicating many of its features, and using automatic re-calibration.

7 System Overview

Figure 6 shows the system overview for the handtracker. The PDM is contained within a separate executable that uses the IndyCam to track the movement of a user's hand through 4 degrees of freedom (x, y, z, and rotation about z). The image from the hand tracker is displayed within a small window with the PDM overlaid to allow the user to monitor its progress. Fast inter-process communications are provided through a shared memory segment that allows the information from the handtracker to be incorporated within the Inventor application.

Communication between applications through the shared memory segment is handled through a shared memory class that provides both guaranteed and un-guaranteed transmission of data structures. For this application the current location of the hand in normalised 3D space is constantly written to the memory structure with no guarantee of data transmission. As the nature of Inventor applications means that the application will only look at the memory segment when needed, this ensures that information read from the memory segment is always up to date. When a gesture is detected within the PDM a guaranteed data transmission is required to ensure that the application acts upon it if necessary. In this instance the data within the shared memory is locked until acknowledged from the application. For completeness the shared memory class uses a fixed size buffer to buffer information in the event of multiple consecutive gestures occurring.

The handtracker base class contains the shared memory class and handles the basic communications between the applications providing an easily interface to the handtracker for any application. The handtracker Inventor class provides higher level functions and will automatically alter the viewer, camera and scene graph depending upon

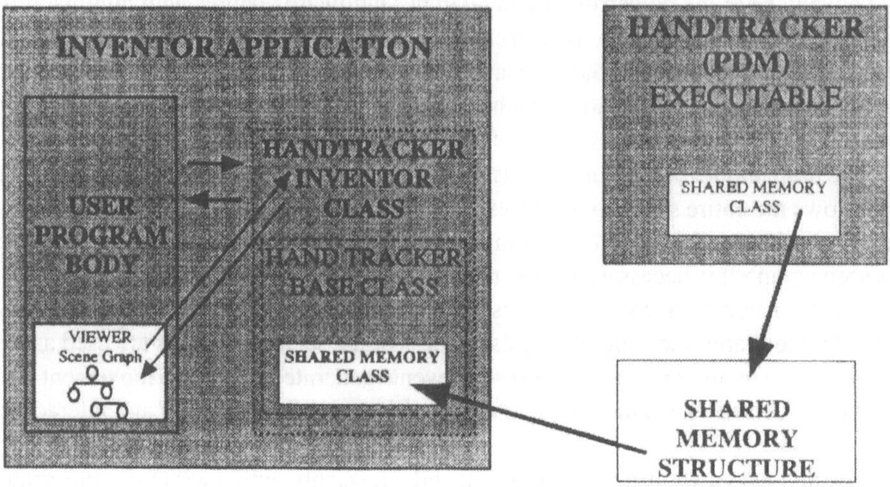

Figure 6: The System Overview

the users actions and the present mode of operation.

7.1 Modes of Operation

There are three basic modes of operation, each performing a specific function:

- Hand Mouse Mode
- Walk Viewer Mode
- Examiner Mode

In *Hand Mouse* mode the movement of the users hand is tracked and mimicked exactly within the environment by a virtual hand modelled out of basic shape primitives. This allows the user a virtual presence within the environment and a 3D pointer with which to interact with objects. The movement of the thumb makes a grasping action where the function of this action is user definable. In many cases it selects an object or 'picks up' that object. The hand changes both shape and colour at each issued gesture to illustrate the present state of the system and provide user feedback.

In *Walk Viewer* mode the user's movement controls the movement of the camera and allows the illusion of walking through an environment. Movement in the x, y and z direction move the camera respectively and rotation of the hand rotates the camera about its own y axis giving the illusion of turning.

In *Examiner Viewer* mode the user's movement moves the camera on the surface of an imaginary sphere. Movement in the x and y direction moves the camera on the surface of this sphere respectively. Movement in the z direction changes the radius of the sphere and gives the illusion of zooming in and out and rotation of the scene.

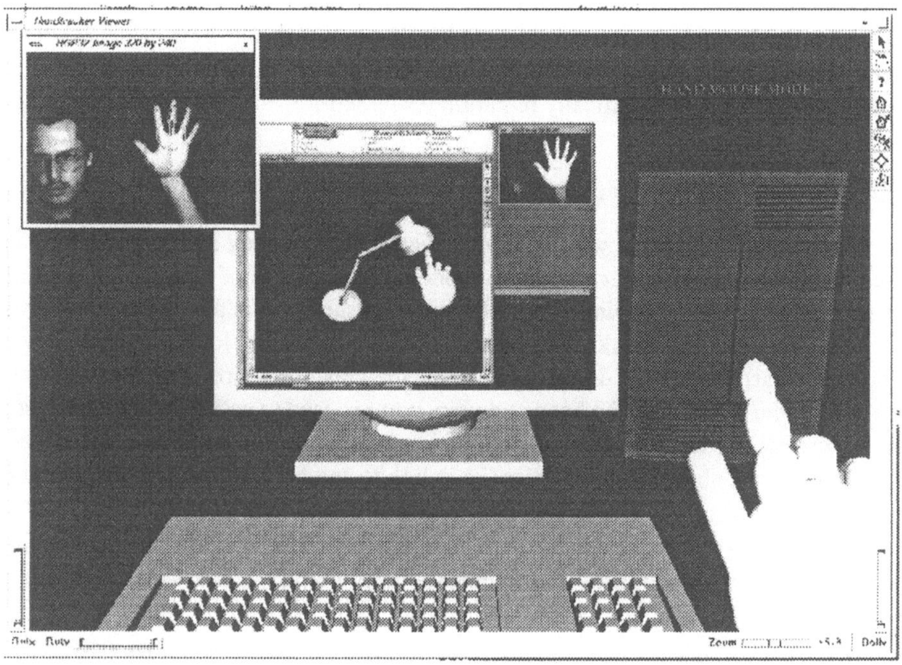

Figure 7: The Handtracker in Operation

In all modes the issue of the *flat hand with thumb in* gesture resets the camera to its home position duplicating the function of the **HOME** widget on the viewer area.

The transition between modes of operation is also done through the use of gestures. The nature of the modes of operation allow the user to interact in real time with applications/environments of different types. A virtual environment can be navigated in Walk Viewer mode until a particular area of the environment is located. This can then be examined further using the Examiner Mode and interaction is facilitated with the environment and objects in 3D through the use of the Hand Mouse Mode.

Gestures are fixed to that of these basic tasks except the movement of the thumb which is user-definable allowing the application programmer to provide the interaction required for specific applications. All other gestures are reported to the application and allow further extension to their function. At the level of the handtracker base class all recognised gestures perform no specific function but are reported to the user interface to provide as generic an input device as possible.

Figure 7 shows the handtracker in operation. The small window in the top left is the view from the camera, with the PDM overlay. The larger window contains the Inventor application. The scene is of a modelled terminal and is in Hand Mouse Mode. As the user moves the hand in x, y and z so the virtual hand will move within the scene. Note the widgets on the inventor application. these are the standard user interface to Inventor and are accessed through the use of the mouse. These work with the handtracker and allow either or both user interfaces to be used. The handtracker is based upon the base viewer, so any user defined viewer will work with the handtracker providing it has been built upon the base class viewer. The handtracker monitors the state of the Inventor application and if any changes are made within the scene graph that were not performed by the handtracker it automatically re-calibrates its self.

7.2 Applications

The handtracker is available with a 'Simple Viewer' for viewing .iv (Inventor format) object files. Here it works in its default mode with all modes of operation turned on but no function to the grasping action (thumb in gesture). It is also available within a 'VRML Viewer[3]' that works with Mosaic (NCSA) accepting local and remote .wrl (VRML format) object files. In this application the grasping action is defined as a user pick action, the position of the hand and view point is used to cast a ray into the scene and select objects. On selection the application communicates to mosaic and can act accordingly if the object has properties (i.e. a link to another html page or another .wrl file).

The handtracker is also available in its development form, with this the input device can be included within any Inventor application providing the IndyCam hardware is available on the system. The system uses 'macro' type functions to enable simple inclusion in applications. In its base form only 5 lines of code need be included within an application in order for the handtracker to be used. This simple user interface can then be extended upon by call-back functions that use information from the handtracker class to further update the scene. New classes can also be written that inherit the handtracker class to provide more functionality for specific applications.

All the development files, sample viewer and VRML viewer can be obtained for free from the web addresses:

- `http://dream1.leeds.ac.uk/~richard`
- `http://http1.brunel.ac.uk:8080/~empgrrb/`

8 Future Work

The handtracker is an ongoing project with constant updates and new developments, the latest addition is an automated training procedure for lighting calibration and will be included in the next release. Future work includes optimisation of the base code and the move to OpenInventor 2.1 for increased speed. An intended extension to the handtracker is the addition of a headtracker. Here the camera would move within the scene from left to right as the head moves respectively. This could be invaluable in giving additional 3D cues to the user and is akin to the way a chameleon sways its head before making a strike in order to more accurately estimate the distance of its prey.

Much work is being done on 3D and Non-linear PDMs in order that a more complete model can be used to provide a full 6 DOF. This will also facilitate the inclusion of more complex and intuitive gestures for use with the system.

[3] See Acknowledgements

The applications of such an input device are endless, limited only by the developers imagination. As the system becomes more robust it is hoped that more complicated applications can be driven by the handtracker. A example of such an application would be a video phone for the deaf/blind that incorporates the handtracker to provide automated sign language to speech decoding.

Acknowledgements

The authors would like to thank Craig Hart for access to the pre-release version of the VRML viewer 'RENAISSANCE'.

References

[1] R. Beale and T. Jackson. *Pattern Recognition*, pages 15–37. IOP Publishing Ltd., 1990.

[2] T. F. Cootes, C. F. Taylor, D. H. Cooper, and J.Graham. Active shape models - their training and application. *Computer Vision and Image Understanding*, 61(1):38–59, 1995.

[3] S. S. Fels and G. E. Hinton. Building adaptive interfaces with neural networks: The Glove-Talk pilot study. In D. Diaper et al., editors, *Human-Computer Interaction — INTERACT '90*, pages 683–688. Elsevier Science Publishers, 1990.

[4] A. J. Heap. Real-time handtracking and gesture recognition using smart snakes. In *Interface to Human and Virtual Worlds*, 1995 1995.

[5] M. Kendall. *Multivariate Analysis*. Charles Griffin and Company Ltd., 1980.

[6] J. Wernecke. *The Inventor Mentor*. Addison-Weslet Publishing Company, 1994.

3D Deformable Hand Models

T. Heap and D. Hogg
School of Computer Studies, University of Leeds, Leeds LS2 9JT, UK.

E-mail: ajh@scs.leeds.ac.uk
Telephone: +44 113 233 5430 Fax: +44 113 233 5468

Abstract

We are interested in producing a 3D deformable model of the human hand, for use in a tracking application. Statistical methods can be used to build such a model from a set of training examples; however, a key requirement for this is the collection of landmark coordinate data from these training examples. To produce a good model, hundreds of landmarks are required from each example; collecting this data manually is infeasible. We present a method for capturing landmark data which makes use of standard physically-based models. The process is semi-automatic; key features are located by hand, and a physical model is deformed under the action of various forces to fit the image data. We demonstrate how the technique can be used to build a 3D Point Distribution Model from 3D MRI data, using a Simplex Mesh.

1 Introduction

Statistical shape models have already proved useful in many computer vision tasks involving the location and tracking of deformable objects, including our own work on hand tracking [6]. A key requirement for building such a model is the collection of training data. Essentially, this involves finding the coordinates of perhaps several hundred *landmarks* over a range of training images of the object being modelled. This process is often performed by hand, with the aid of some visualization tool; it is time consuming and laborious, and inevitably leads to inaccuracy and error. Gathering landmark data for 3D models is near-impossible due both to the problem of image visualization and the sheer quantity of data involved.

There are, of course, many established methods for capturing the positions of image features automatically. Edge detectors such as Canny are of limited use in this context, but more applicable are corner detectors, such as the Plessey algorithm; however, the results can often be susceptible to noise, with background detail causing confusion. In the 3D domain, another option is mesh building. [10] describes a "Marching Cubes" algorithm which triangulates a surface from 3D voxel data. More recently, work on physically-based deformable meshes [5, 2] provides more robust methods of capturing surface information.

However, for the purposes of building statistical models there must be a direct correspondence between similar landmarks across the whole training set (ie. a particular landmark must mark the *same* feature on each training example), so applying any of the above techniques independently to each training example is unlikely to be of any use.

Attempts have been made to address this problem. [8] and [1] both describe methods for 2D models which work in the case where it is possible to obtain a single clean pixelated boundary from each training image. Hill applies a pairwise corresponder in a hierarchical fashion to find approximate matches between training boundaries, whereas Baumberg constrains the problem by assuming constant object orientation. Both employ some form of iterative optimization to improve the models produced. [9] shows how to capture 3D data by way of 2D slice contours; however it is still necessary to find these contours.

We present a more general, semi-automated methodology based on the use of 2D or 3D physically-based modelling techniques. A two-stage process is used; firstly a physical model of the object is constructed – this can be done manually or automatically with the aid of one of the training examples. Following this, the model is deformed to fit each training example – a few key features are located manually, and various forces are applied to drive the model into position. Internal forces keep the model smooth and even, and image forces help to give an accurate fit.

This idea is not entirely new; [3] describes how to combine physical and statistical shape models in such a way as to rely initially on physical modelling but to place emphasis more on statistical modelling as the number of training examples increases, demonstrating how such a system can be used to 'bootstrap' a statistical model. [12] develops this idea into a more robust and practical tool by allowing *guided* model fitting, whereby key features are located by hand. We also make use of guided fitting, but we adopt a slightly different approach to modelling by drawing a separation between the physical and statistical domains; this allows us to use *any* physical modelling technique, not just the Finite Element Method used by Cootes and Syn.

The remainder of this paper gives more details on the processes involved. There is an overview of physically-based models, and we describe how to apply them to this task. Results are given for the case of a 3D hand model, for which a Simplex Mesh [5] was used to extract 3D landmark data from MRI volumetric images, and a Point Distribution Model [4] was subsequently constructed.

2 Physically-Based Models

Physically-based models come in a variety of different forms. They all have in common the ability to deform under the action of various forces. When applied to feature location/tracking, a physical model is usually considered as a system of N point masses whose motion over time is governed by standard Newtonian dynamics. Two types of force are generally applied:

- *Internal Forces*: the point masses interact with one another to hold the model in shape. These are usually elastic forces tending to drive the model towards a stable rest configuration.

- *External Forces*: the point masses are 'attracted' towards particular image features in order to fit the model to the image data. These forces might be applied manually (in a guided system) or via some sort of feature detection (eg. edge detection).

By allowing these forces to act over time it is hoped that the model will deform to fit the image data. We can describe the dynamics of the system with the following Newtonian law of motion:

$$m_i \frac{d^2 P_i}{dt^2} = F_{int} + F_{ext} - \gamma \frac{dP_i}{dt} \tag{1}$$

where P_i is the instantaneous position of point i, F_{int} and F_{ext} are the instantaneous internal and external forces on point i, m is its mass and γ is a damping factor. If we make time discrete in even steps and assume unit mass, integrating (1) with respect to time gives the following:

$$P_i^{t+1} = P_i^t + F_{int} + F_{ext} + (1-\gamma).(P_i^t - P_i^{t-1}) \tag{2}$$

where P_i^t is the position of point i at discrete time interval t. We can use this equation to calculate the new position of the model given its previous two positions. Deformation of such a physical model thus progresses iteratively.

2.1 Simplex Meshes

The physical model used in our system is a basic version of the Simplex Mesh as described in [5]. Simplex meshes are surface meshes existing in 3D, consisting of a number of vertices (of unit 'mass'), each connected to exactly three neighbouring vertices. It is possible to model any conceivable topology in this way. Delingette describes many properties of Simplex Meshes; the most useful for our purposes is the concept of the simplex angle - this is measured as shown in Figure 1.

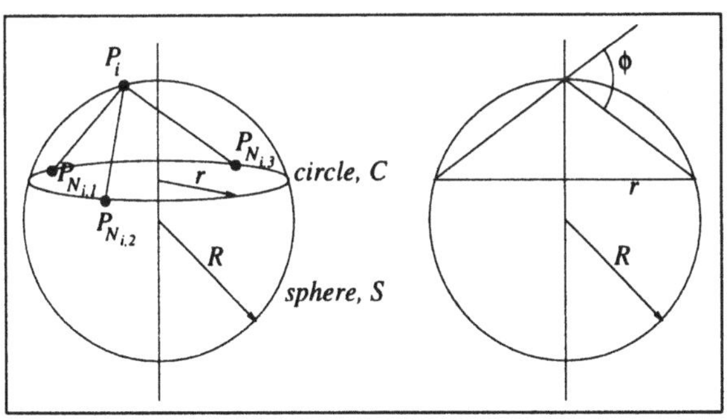

Figure 1: The Simplex Angle ϕ_i at vertex P_i with neighbours $P_{N_{i,1}}$, $P_{N_{i,2}}$, $P_{N_{i,3}}$.

The simplex angle ϕ_i for a vertex P_i has the good properties that it is invariant to scale, to the positions of its neighbours $P_{N_{i,1}}$, $P_{N_{i,2}}$ and $P_{N_{i,3}}$ on the circle C, and to the position of P on the sphere S. In other words, it describes the curvature of the surface at vertex P without constraining the actual coordinates of the vertices. This can be put to good use when generating the model's internal forces. For vertex P_i, an elastic force is constructed which drives the point towards a position such that:

- The simplex angle subtended is some specific angle Φ_i, and
- P_i is equidistant from $P_{N_{i,1}}$, $P_{N_{i,2}}$ and $P_{N_{i,3}}$.

Full details are given in [5]. The choice of the Φ_i alters the 'stable' shape of the mesh. For example, choosing $\forall i.\Phi_i = 0$ encourages continuity over the surface of the mesh. Using $\forall i.\Phi_i = \phi_i^t$ sets the stable shape as the shape at time t. We make use of both of these settings at various stages of the model fitting process.

3 Model Definition

Before we can deform a physical model to fit training images, it is necessary to define the model structure; ie. how many vertices are required, which part of the object each one represents, and how they connect together.

For models of a few hundred vertices or less, it is possible to define the structure by hand. However, this is very time consuming and involves a great deal of pencil-and-paper work. It is also error-prone, although errors are usually easy to spot.

Alternatively, any of the mesh-fitting algorithms described in [10], [5] and [2] can be used to generate an initial structure for the model automatically by applying them to one of the training images. However, it is not guaranteed that particular object features will be landmarked and for more complex objects some guidance may be required (particularly for Simplex Meshes).

The automatic mesh-fitting algorithms also provide an initial *shape* for the model, but for manual construction it is necessary to find initial coordinates for each vertex. We choose to place each vertex randomly within a unit cube. This is sufficient as we can use *guided* deformation, along with the mesh connectivity to 'pull' the model into shape, as described below.

4 Model Deformation

Once a physical model has been constructed, it is deformed under the action of various forces in order to fit each training example, using (2). Internal forces are as described for the Simplex Mesh above, using various simplex angle constraints as detailed below. External forces come from two sources:

- *Guiding forces.* These are set up manually and are used to help the model find its approximate destination. The coordinates of prominent object features are located in the training image by hand, and virtual 'springs' are attached between these positions and the corresponding model vertices. The stiffness of the springs can be altered to strengthen or weaken the forces. The force S_i on vertex i is given by:

$$S_i = k_i(D_i - P_i) \tag{3}$$

where P_i is the vertex's current position, D_i is the ideal position and k_i is the spring stiffness coefficient.

- *Image forces.* These are forces exerted on vertices due to the 3D image data itself. The aim is to drive each vertex towards a 'good' position locally with respect to the image data. In the simple case we look for edges or surfaces in the image data close to the vertex. The current implementation looks at pixels along a normal to the model surface at each vertex (defined as the normal to the plane containing the vertex's three neighbours), finds the strongest edge (intensity change) within a fixed distance, and forces the vertex towards that edge.

For best results, careful use of these forces is required. We have adopted a three-stage deformation as follows.

1. Gross Location using Guiding Forces

   The initial model is deformed under the action of guiding forces alone to move it into roughly the right position This can be a trial-and-error process; if the fit obtained is not close enough (as decided by the human eye) then more guiding forces may be needed. This is especially the case when the vertices are initially randomly positioned as described above. The model's 'stable' position is fixed as the *initial* model position using $\forall i.\Phi_i = 0$, as described above, thus keeping unguided vertices in a sensible configuration with respect to the guided ones. This is no use in the case where the initial position is random, and we must opt instead for the maximum continuity constraint ($\forall i.\Phi_i = \phi_i^t$).

2. Refinement using Image Forces

   Image forces are introduced to drive every vertex into its ideal position. Vertices which find no sufficient image data are hopefully pulled into position by their neighbours. The guiding forces are kept in place during this stage to maintain stability, and the maximum continuity constraint is used to ensure maximum smoothness.

3. Fine Tuning

   The guiding forces are removed so that previously guided vertices can adjust to their ideal location. This increases the tolerance for slightly misplaced guiding forces.

5 Results

The technique was applied to 3D volume data of human hands, obtained via Magnetic Resonance Imaging. A Simplex Mesh with 498 vertices was constructed by drawing a mesh on a surgical rubber glove stuffed with tissue paper, labelling each vertex, then entering the connectivity data by manual inspection. The coordinates of each point were initialized randomly.

The processes detailed above were applied to each of 8 training images. For the first image, the mesh was deformed from an initially random position (see Figure 2). Manually-located guiding forces were required for 80 vertices in order to 'untangle' the mesh. After 200 iterations, image forces were introduced at *all* vertices to draw the mesh towards edge data, and after 400 iterations the original guiding forces were removed to allow guided points to equilibrate (this is most noticeable around the wrist).

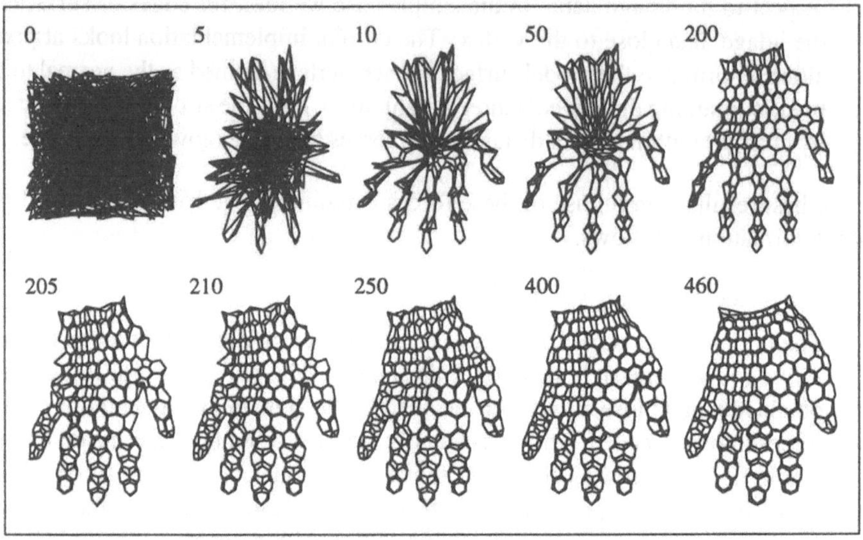

Figure 2: Deforming a Simplex Mesh from an initially random position to fit MRI data of a human hand (numbers show iterations).

The resulting model is used as a starting position, and stable shape, for fitting the mesh to subsequent training images; consequently, fewer guiding forces are needed (roughly 25 per example), and convergence is quicker (125 iterations as opposed to 460). Figure 3 shows fitting to an image where the thumb has moved. After 50 iterations (3rd frame) image forces are applied and after 100 iterations (4th frame) the guiding forces are removed.

The eight meshes thus produced were used to construct a Point Distribution Model; this is a statistical deformable model first described in [4]. For each training mesh, the coordinates of the vertices are collated into an n-vector (here, n = 498 vertices × 3 dimensions = 1494) and the mesh is considered as a point in n-dimensional space. A *Principal Component Analysis* is applied to these points in n-space to find 'modes of variation' of the model. The result is a mean shape (from the mean position in n-space) and a set of 'sensible' orthogonal deformations which can be combined to give a range of valid hand shapes. Figure 4 shows the two most significant 'modes' of deformation. The results appear to be realistic, despite the small number of training examples, suggesting that the meshes are fairly noise-free.

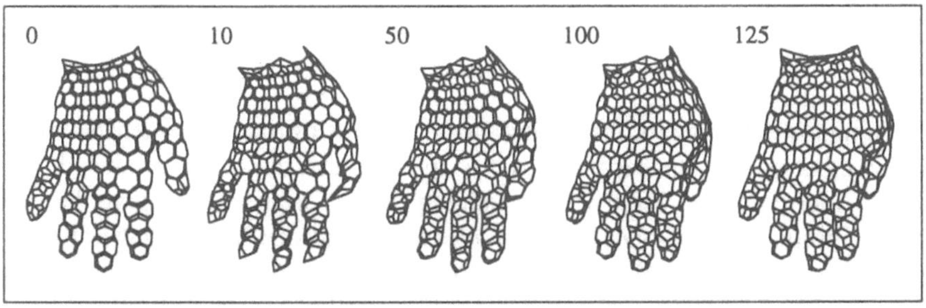

Figure 3: Deforming the first model to fit a second training image.

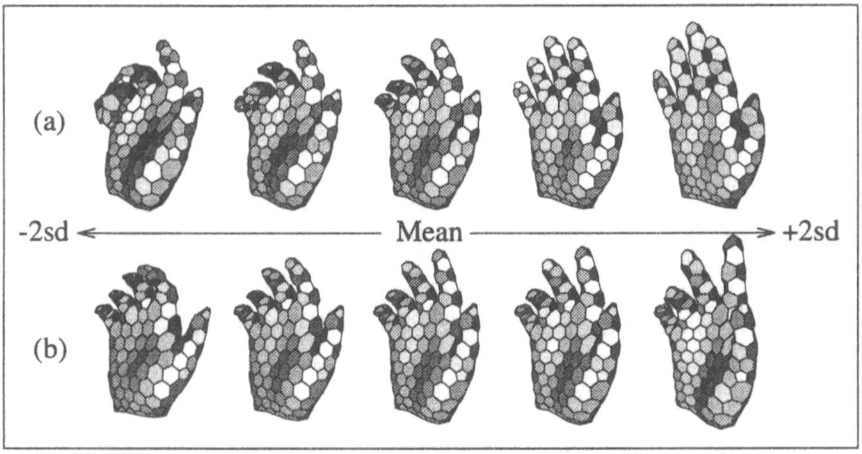

Figure 4: The first (a) and second (b) modes of variation of the Point Distribution Model produced.

6 Discussion and Conclusions

We have shown how one can construct a complex 3D Point Distribution Model from 3D volumetric training images via the use of physically-based models. The technique is not fully automatic but *guided*; with a well-designed interface, user effort would be minimal.

We have described a specific procedure using a Simplex Mesh in 3D. Some obvious generalizations apply:

- The physical model used does not have to be a Simplex Mesh. Any physical modelling technique could be used, for example the less constrained meshes used in [2], or the Finite Element Method as used in [11].
- The technique can be applied in a 2D situation using a 2D physical model such as a Snake.
- Where MRI data is not available it may be possible to use a sparser input source eg. range data, since internal model forces keep non-visible vertices in position

(and in any case, statistical models are fairly robust to small errors in point position). However there is still the question of how to obtain an initial shape.

Preliminary experiments on tracking a hand in 3D using a single camera have proved promising, but even at the early stages it is apparent that the model produced suffers from two shortcomings. Firstly, more training images are needed to give the model more variability. Secondly the model's modes of variation are bound by their linearity; that is, for a particular mode of variation, every model point can only vary along a straight line. Non-linear variation is achieved by combining two or more modes. We have developed a non-linear PDM which allows points to move along arcs [7] and we intend to apply this technique to the 3D hand example.

References

[1] A. Baumberg and D. Hogg. Learning flexible models from image sequences. In *Proc. 3rd ECCV*, pages 299–308, Stockholm, Sweden, 1993. Springer-Verlag.

[2] A. Bulpitt and N. Efford. An efficient 3D deformable model with a self-optimising topology. In *Proc. BMVC*, Birmingham, UK, September 1995.

[3] T. Cootes and C. Taylor. Combining point distribution models with shape models based on finite element analysis. In *Proc. BMVC*, pages 419–428, York, UK, 1994. BMVA Press.

[4] T. Cootes, C. Taylor, D. Cooper, and J. Graham. Active Shape Models - their training and applications. *Computer Vision and Image Understanding*, 61(2), January 1995.

[5] H. Delingette. Simplex Meshes: a general representation for 3D shape reconstruction. Technical Report 2214, INRIA, 1994.

[6] A. Heap. Real-time hand tracking and gesture recognition using Smart Snakes. In *Proc. Interface to Human and Virtual Worlds*, Montpellier, France, June 1995. Also available as ftp://agora.leeds.ac.uk/ scs/doc/reports/1995/95_5.ps.Z.

[7] A. Heap and D. Hogg. Automatic pivot location for the Cartesian-Polar Hybrid Point Distribution Model. In *Proc. BMVC*, Birmingham, UK, September 1995.

[8] A. Hill and C. Taylor. Automatic landmark generation for point distribution models. In *Proc. BMVC*, pages 429–438, York, UK, 1994. BMVA Press.

[9] A. Hill, A. Thornham, and C. Taylor. Model-based interpretation of 3D medical images. In *Proc. BMVC*, pages 339–348, Guildford, UK, 1993. BMVA Press.

[10] W. E. Lorensen and H. E. Cline. Marching cubes: a high resolutions 3D surface construction algorithm. *Computer Graphics*, 21(4):163–169, 1987.

[11] A. Pentland and S. Sclaroff. Closed-form solutions for physically based shape modelling and recognition. *IEEE Transactions on Pattern Analysis and Machine Intelligence*, 13(7):715–729, 1991.

[12] M. Syn and R. Prager. A model based approach to 3D freehand ultrasound imaging. In Y. Bizais, C. Barillot, and R. Di Paola, editors, *Information Processing in Medical Imaging*, Computational Imaging and Vision, pages 361–362. Kluwer Academic, 1995.

Structural Analysis of Co-verbal Deictic Gesture in Multimodal Dialogue Systems

N. Bellalem and L. Romary
CRIN-CNRS & INRIA Lorraine, Bâtiment LORIA – BP 239
54506 Vandœuvre-lès-Nancy, France

E-mail: {nbell, romary}@loria.fr
Telephone: +33 83 59 20 33 Fax: +44 113 233 5468

Abstract

From the time it is decided to develop communication between man and machine which essentially relies on spoken (natural) language, it seems reasonable to take gesture into account as a possible complement to voice. As a matter of fact, many gestures have a semiotic function which facilitate the communication act, especially in its referential component. Among the roles played by semiotic gesture, the deictic function is undoubtedly a major one when considering graphical units of human computer dialogues. The study we present can be situated in the framework of the interpretation of deictic gesture as a complement of a spoken utterance. We have identified three parts in the shape of an elementary designation gesture: the first part corresponds to hand or device positioning (preliminary phase), the second one corresponds to the designation act (effective phase) and the last one to the hand backward movement (final phase). Not surprisingly, when several designation acts appear in one single gesture, co-articulation phenomena can be observed. This consists in a combination of final phases with preliminary phases of the consecutive elementary designations. Among these three parts, only the second one is informative in the sense that it gives some information about the spatial location of the referent. The difficulty is to isolate this meaningful part. In order to resolve this problem, we have developed a method to analyse gestural trajectories provided by a 2D or 3D device, which allows us to identify the effective phase. This analysis is based on the notion of singularity which consists in studying different parameters of the trajectory (speed, curvature etc.) so as to establish the presence of relevant segmentation clues.

1 Introduction

The proposed study should be considered within the general framework of the design of multimodal dialogue systems where speech is the user's main communication channel. These systems, which are usually dedicated to such application as process control or information retrieval, are mainly intended to take full advantage of the spontaneous communicative abilities of the user/speaker. In this perspective, the kind of gestures that we consider are essentially co-verbal ones which relate to the content of the associated spoken part of discourse, see [4] and [2]. More precisely, the study we have conducted has addressed the problem of designation gesture, which means any gesture which — in a way or another — allows to designate a referent in the communication context, in combination with a referring linguistic expression. Such a gesture can thus refer to a visual object, as well as to one of its intrinsic properties (size, shape, colour, etc.).

Three main reasons at least may justify this choice. First, it is clear that gesture can convey some information which is not part of that carried by the linguistic message. Second, this communication means is particularly adapted to the control of applications where objects are being represented graphically, for it simplifies and shortens any reference to objects in the visual environment [5]. A last reason is related to the level of adaptation that is required from the user. Indeed, such as it is the case for language, using gesture — and especially co-verbal gesture — does not imply any learning period since it is part of a man's spontaneous communication abilities.

Our study of gesture is based on a contextual analysis which aims at interpreting it taking into account any relevant element in the production environment, either visual or linguistic. We thus reject the idea that the meaning of gesture can be established on the sole basis of its shape (e.g. a hand configuration or a specific trajectory) but to consider the different components which are part of the communicative situation: the ongoing dialogue, task constraints, the scene being represented on the screen etc. [5] thus remarks that there is a major chance of failure for the gestural reference if the corresponding discourse context is ignored. To take this into consideration, we will propose an analysis of gesture which will integrate the different steps from the capture of an elementary signal up to the ultimate interpretation in context.

2 Difficulties of gesture interpretation in multimodal dialogue

To illustrate the complexity of the subject (even under the strong restrictions that we have put forth), we can take a glance at a specific example which presents some of the problems involved in gesture understanding. Let us consider an application of furnishing which consists in arranging some pieces of furniture within a flat. We consider that the user of such a system has uttered the following orders:

- *Take an armchair*
- *Put it in the living-room* [1]

in association with a gesture, the trajectory of which is being observed (thick line) in Figure 1 (this trace is supposed to have been captured by some designation device).

---

[1] The utterances we have chosen are only examples. In fact, designation gesture is often associated with demonstrative expression. It is interesting to remark that the type of the referring expression influences the interpretation process, see [1] and [3].

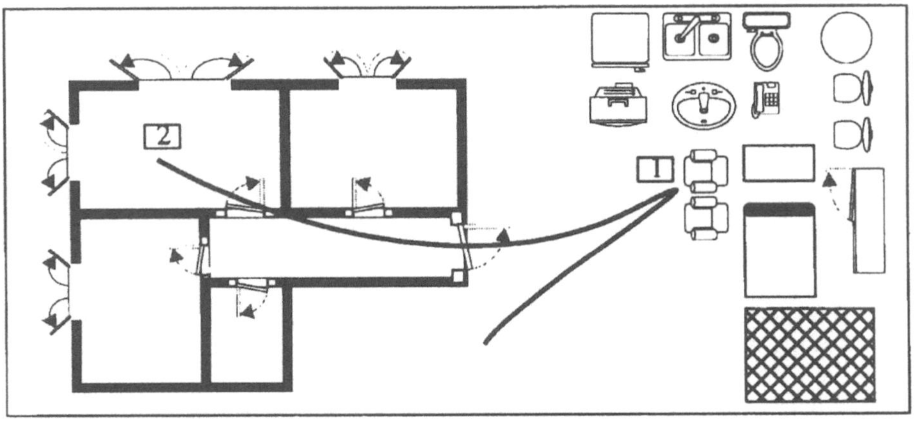

Figure 1: Some difficulties related to the interpretation of gesture.

We will suppose here that the sentences have been construed and reach the "multimodal analyser" in a form reflecting their content, that is:

- predicate,
- referring expression composed of:
  - determiner (type: demonstrative, definite, ...),
  - type,
  - number (when a numeral adjective is encountered),
  - deictic adverbial (e.g. here, there),
  - pronoun (definite, demonstrative, ... , singular, plural).

The joint interpretation of the sentence which has been uttered and gesture might be seen as achieving the request which has been intended by the user, which implies proper determination of the different references, the action to be executed, but also to infer some of the related information concerning the ongoing task. As a matter of fact, the following questions are raised at the different levels of gesture analysis:

1. It may be observed that a gestural trajectory presents some meaningful parts as well as non meaningful ones. How can they be distinguished?

2. If we assume that there exist some features allowing one to recognize the meaningful sections, what are these and how should we interpret them?

3. A meaningful section of a gestural trajectory points to one or several elements in the visual space (as exemplified by numbers 1 and 2 in Figure 1). How these elements can be searched for in the visual space?

4. If we speak of a "visual space" where objects are being searched, this implies that the system bears a representation compatible with the user's visual perception. How can such a representation be built?

5. If we want a system to make a joint interpretation of the verbal and gestural messages, it is necessary to synchronize the two sources of information. What are the features which will allow a proper synchronization?

6. A designation gesture is not necessarily accurate and the angle point 1 on the trajectory (See Figure 1) may not — from a pure geometrical point of view — be associated to any object on the screen. Still, a human interlocutor would have no difficulty in relating it to the armchairs which are close to it.

7. Is it relevant to choose among the two armchairs in Figure 1? It certainly is not for a human interlocutor since the speaker actually asked for an armchair, which implies that he has not a specific uttered preference for one or the other.

8. What would have happened if instead of speaking of an armchair — a term which can be supposed as known by the system — the speaker had uttered seat, a more general noun? A human interlocutor would have had no difficulty in associating this description with one of the two armchairs, and he would have even rejected the two alternatives on the top right of the figure, on the basis of the gestural message1.

9. Does the second meaningful part of the gestural trajectory in Figure 1 indicate the precise destination of the armchair in the flat or does it just point to the corresponding room, thus assuming that it is named as the living-room? In other terms, does the designation refer to a specific location, an englobing locus which is being categorized or maybe to both? In a man to man communication, the addressee would have certainly placed the armchair close to the extremity of the trajectory, even if he assumes that this might not be its final position, and at any case, would infer that the room is the living-room.

The different problems associated with these questions are connected with different levels in the process of gesture analysis. Some have to do with the problem of the recognition of the meaningful parts within a trajectory. Others concern the different mechanisms by which the two component of a multimodal message can be associated. Finally, several questions relate to interpretation: interpretation of the trajectory shape in relation to the scene, interpretation in relation to the linguistic message and more precisely to the type of the referring expression, interpretation within the task context. Analysing this simple example allows us to draw an overall sketch of what may be involved in a proper understanding of gesture.

Two main trends seem to emerged so far:

- a gestural trajectory correspond to a dynamic shape. This shape contains meaningful and non-meaningful parts the boundaries of which are not made explicit by the trajectory as such;

- the meaningful part and thus the meaning of gesture is closely related to the context in which it has been produced, associating task and dialogue.

This leads us to consider two levels of treatment for the analysis of gesture in a task oriented man-machine dialogue. The first one consists in recognizing the shape of gesture and in proposing a possible division where the meaningful parts are clearly identified. Since we have no specific clue which might make us distinguish between a designation gesture from any other co-verbal gesture, we make the hypothesis that any gestural activity corresponds to designation acts. The contextual interpretation of the different meaningful elements — which corresponds to the second step we distinguish — will choose among the different possibilities by combining the available hypotheses with the linguistic message (and the contextual information that we have signalled below). The first step above may be called structural analysis and is close to the syntactic and semantic levels which are put forward in natural language processing. The second one — named contextual interpretation — is more related to a pragmatic analysis of a sentence within its uttering context. This analogy we make here, even if it only corresponds to the overall structure of the processing steps, may denote some strong similitudes corresponding to the fact that both language and gesture are instances of more fundamental cognitive processes.

3 Basic aspects of the structural analysis

The study we propose here for gesture consists in analysing a gestural signal independently of the actual transducer from which it has been acquired. As a matter of fact, each transducer has its own particularities which one has to take into account but as a whole, we can draw a line between two main categories of transducers. The first one tracks gesture on a 2D plane, as for example a mouse, a pen or a touch screen. The second one corresponds to devices which not only provide some information concerning the 3D position of the hand, but also about the hand configuration. External devices such as the numeric gloves are part of this second category. In the following section, we try to define in more details the nature of a gestural signal before tackling the problem of its analysis.

3.1 Gestural signal

The gestural signal is the whole set of information which a transducer provides during an actual gesture (See Figure 2). As mentioned before, a two dimensional device essentially brings a series of positions on the screen. In the particular case of a mouse, the signal is a series of events associated with elementary motions to which specific events concerning buttons may be added. In the case of three dimensional gestural devices, the gestural signal is made of a series of positions in the euclidian space, relatively to a reference point, together with the successive hand configurations. In the case of the numeric glove for instance, these corresponds to the different angles between hand phalanges. It should be noted here that the accuracy and reliability of this information are highly variable and dependant upon the kind of technology which is being used.

3.2 The purpose and difficulties of a structural analysis

Understanding a gesture which has been made by the user of a dialogue system implies that it is possible to analyse the gestural signal coming from the transducer and

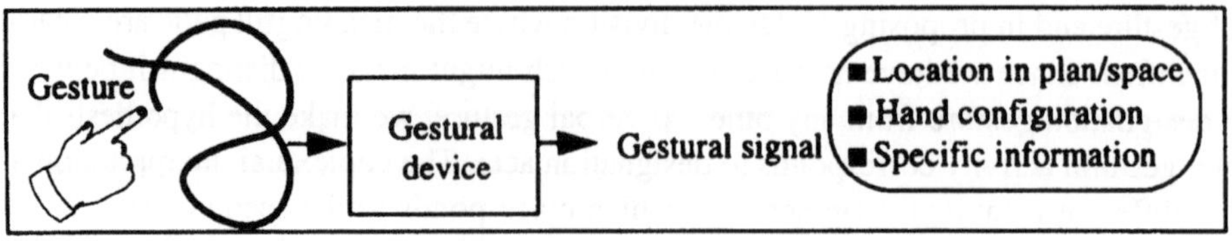

Figure 2: Capture of the gesture.

to isolate the meaningful part of it, that is that corresponding to a real communicative intention. For such an analysis, three main levels of difficulty can be put forward.

Distinguishing the different gestures. When looking at the hand activity, one may observe phases of quietness as well as phases during which the hand is in motion. Since all motions are not intended to designate something, it is necessary to make a distinction between this type of gestures and other motion events. This distinction can be based on several types of features:

- linguistic features: that is when, within the linguistic message, there occurs a referring expression which is likely to have a deictic value (demonstrative NP, "pure" deictic etc.)
- gesture specific features:
  - the beginning of a movement after a phase of quietness;
  - a specific hand configuration such as a pointing finger;
  - the observation of a motion of the hand towards the space of designation (e.g. the screen).

Extracting the meaningful parts. This second difficulty is centred on the designation gesture itself. It consists of the extraction of the parts of the signal which actually designate a specific element. The question which is raised here is what characterizes the useful information within a designation signal? Some transducers such as the mouse or numeric gloves do not always allow a user to indicate precisely where he intends to designate something within a given trajectory. For instance, when the interface does not constrain the semantics related to the usage of the buttons of a mouse, the user has a complete freedom to indicate or not the beginning/end of his designation act, either through clicking or dragging acts. In the same way, and even more convincingly, using a dataglove to designate an object on a computer screen provides the system with a gestural signal where there is no clear-cut boundaries associated with the beginning and end of a given designation act, since the screen may not be even touched. To the contrary, the necessity to be in contact with the screen in the case of a pen or a touch-screen provides real limits within which the useful information is to be found. It may be possible to consider that the two "seats" in the upper right part of the figure are better candidate than the two armchairs, since they are closer to what might be thought of as the prototype of a seat. In that case a sub-dialogue would have to be generated to ensure that there is no ambiguity (e.g. Do you mean one of the two armchairs?).

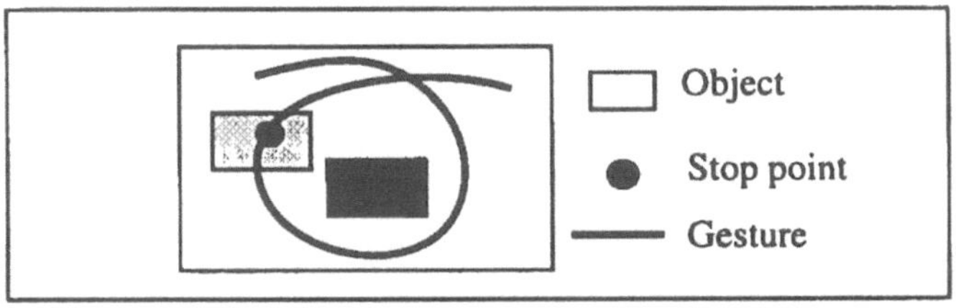

Figure 3: Ambiguous cases of gesture interpretation.

Existence of ambiguities. Another difficulty presented by this analysis is related to the ambiguous nature of the trajectory shape. This may be observed in Figure 3 where it is not possible to know whether the designation act corresponds to the stop point or to the circling shape. This may of course have some immediate consequences upon the targeted object. If the meaningful part of the gesture is the stop point, then the referred object will be the light-grey object. To the contrary, if the trajectory is seen as a circling event then the referred object is more likely the black one.

Before proposing a solution to these different problems (associated with the analysis of designation gesture), let us summarize our terminology:

- by designation gesture we mean the whole motion which has been observed for the hand, comprising phases where the hand is getting close to the targeted locus, is actually designating and is moving away;
- the gestural signal corresponds to the information that is provided by the gestural transducer;
- the designation or meaningful part corresponds to the portion of the gestural signal which identifies the object which is being aimed at by the user.

4 The three phases of designation gesture

The observation of the shape of a designation gesture as produced by a user (See Figure 4) shows that there exists three main phases (See Figure 5):

- a preparatory phase which corresponds to the hand (or the transducer) being positioned in the right direction;
- an active phase which corresponds to the actual designation of the object — what we called the meaningful part of gesture;
- a final phase, where the hand usually moves backward or the transducer released.

Among these three phases, only the second one really carries useful information in the perspective of a designation act. As a matter of fact, the first or the second phase may not necessarily be present since this depends upon the transducer which is being used, the actual gesture that has been produced by the user, but also, upon possible "co-articulation" phenomena within a sequence of designation acts. In particular, between

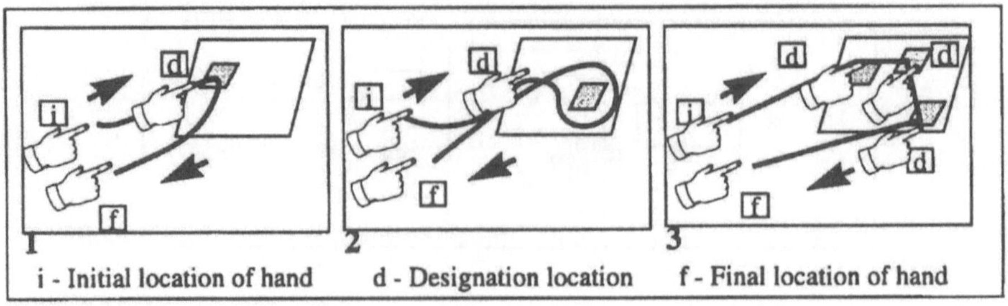

Figure 4: Gesture to designate: (1) an object, (2) an area, (3) a set.

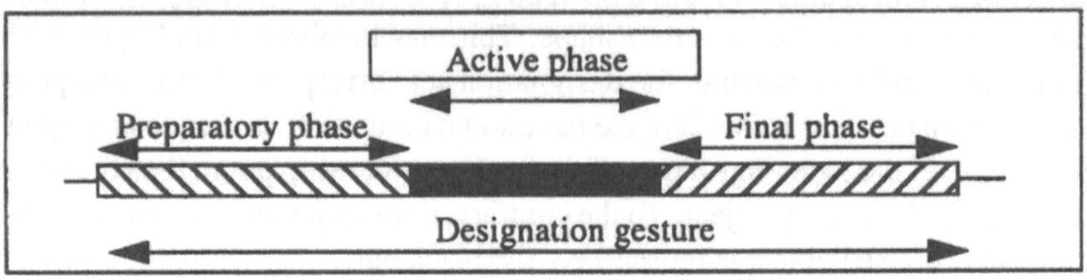

Figure 5: Three phases of designation gesture.

two successive designations, the ending phase of the first one may be merged with the preparatory phase of the second one if it is ever to be observed. The intermediate motion may just be a short move between two positions (See part 3 of Figure 4).

The preceding examples of gesture show that the useful stretch is characterized by the appearance of a structure which, in a way or another, is different from the preparatory and closing phases. The designation gesture may thus comprise as its meaningful part a click, a stopping point, an angle point, a closed or semi closed loop etc. Of course, these are not the only possibilities to express a designation. For instance, a zig-zagging gesture can correspond to the designation of a section of a text in a word processing context. Our aim is not to make a complete inventory of all the different possibilities, but rather to propose a theoretical framework from which it can be possible to derive most of those which might be observed.

5 A possible solution

In the previous section, we have put forth the existence, within a given gesture, of a meaningful part corresponding to a real designation act. This one can be characterized by:

- from the point of view of its shape, by a specific structure which we call singularity;
- from the point of view of meaning, by the possibility to be associated with the semantic content of a designation act.

The idea that we want to advocate is to construct a symbolic representation of the gestural shape from which some singularities will be detected on the basis that no singularity is purely accidental but comes from the underlying intention of the user to communicate something: in particular to designate something. The specific case of purely accidental singularities (i.e. not related to a communicative intention) will be eliminated at the interpretation level, either because no referring expression can be associated with it, or because no final object can be interpreted as a possible referent. In the following sections, we will try to clarify this notion of singularity by first giving a few definitions and notations.

5.1 Some definitions

- The gestural signal, which is the initial object of our analysis, can be seen as a trajectory $T(x,y,z,t)$ where (x,y,z) indicates a position in the 3D space and t the time associated to this position.

  This trajectory can be studied from different points of view such as the curvature and its variations, the motion speed etc. For each point in the trajectory, it is possible to associate a set $\mathcal{P}$ representing the different values of these parameters. These values can be seen as a set of properties associated with the points in the trajectory. These properties can then be extended to segments of the trajectory by computing the average value of their values along the different points of the segment.

- An element corresponds to either a point or a segment in a given trajectory.

- Two elements are said to be stable or homogeneous relatively to a set of properties P *if they are either identical (for discrete properties) or close in a given distance space (for continuous ones);*

- Segments within a trajectory are built by aggregating adjacent points which are stable in relation to a given set of properties.

5.2 Singularity: a definition

As a consequence of what we have said so far, we can define a singularity as an element of a trajectory which corresponds to a break along a property relatively the adjacent neighbouring elements. In other terms, a singularity is detected upon an element of a trajectory and relatively to a property P if it can be observe that the property P has changed on this element and that P can be considered as stable on the adjacent elements (See Figure 6).

5.3 Different kinds of singularities

From the preceding definition of a singularity and depending upon the nature of the element concerned by such a characteristic (either a point, a segment or even a combination of these), it is possible to make a distinction between three types of singularities:

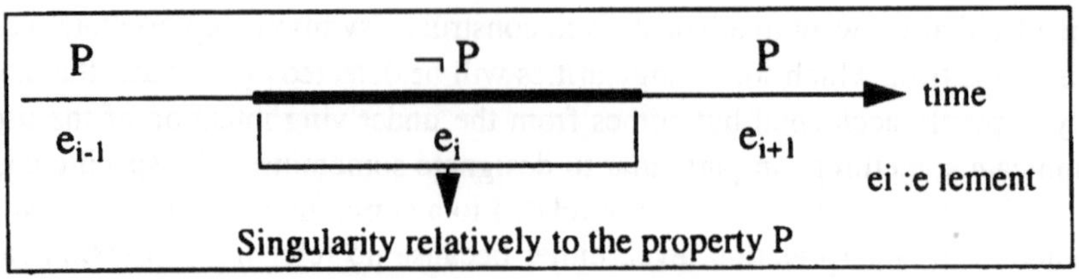

Figure 6: Definition of singularity

1. *Punctual singularity*

   Punctual singularities are bound to a given point in the gestural trajectory. This non-homogeneous points as regards its neighbouring elements present a discontinuity along one of the properties associated with the trajectory.

   Example: *A point within a trajectory where a user has stopped for a while can be considered as a punctual singularity in relation to the property of motion speed and relatively to adjacent segments characterized by a non-zero acceleration.*

   As a matter of fact, a punctual singularity is often associated with a break along several properties at the same time. An angle point is thus characterized by a change in curvature and in speed.

   From a semantic point of view, a punctual singularity aims at designating a subregion — grossly centred upon the corresponding point — of the visual space. Consequently, it may be used to refer to the object or the locus associated with this point.

2. *Simple trajectory singularity*

   A segmental singularity corresponds to a stretch of the trajectory which is non-homogeneous regarding the adjacent segments, relatively to a set of properties.

   Example: *A semi-closed loop closed by straight lines constitutes a singularity along the property of curvature*

3. *Repetitive singularity*

   These singularities corresponds to the repetition of a pattern made of punctual singularities for a set of properties P1 intermingled with segmental singularities for a set of properties P2. A repetitive singularity results from a combination of these elements. For instance, a zig-zagging trajectory combining angle points and line segments is a good illustration of such a singularity.

From a semantic point of view, both segmental singularities and repetitive ones aim at putting to the fore an extended region of the visual space. These singularities point to spaces which, even if their extensions are not necessarily larger then those of punctual singularities, presents boundaries which are made more explicit by the user. It generally corresponds to the designation of objects which are spatially included within the associated region.

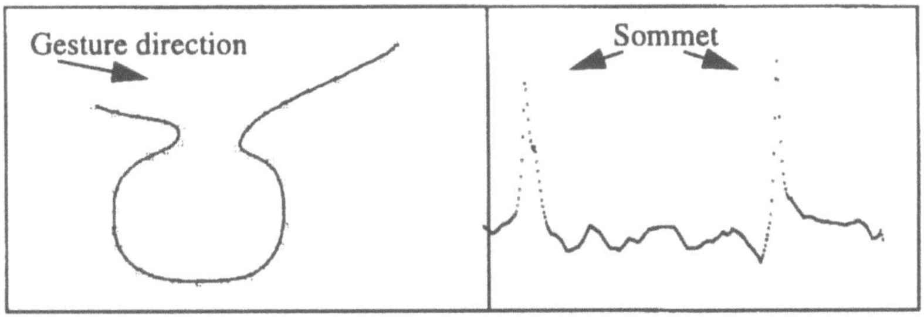

Figure 7: Gesture and the corresponding curvature

6 Implementing the structural analysis

The gestural signal which is delivered by the transducer cannot be used immediately. Indeed, it does not allow the kind of computation which is necessary to detect the gestural singularities which we have defined above. This is why it is necessary to build an intermediate representation of the trajectory from which the observation of singularities will be made possible.

6.1 Modelling the gestural trajectory

This step consists in finding a representation of the gestural shape in terms of elementary syntactic elements corresponding to primitive shapes or specific features. It is possible to consider the following criteria:

1. Curvature: The study of the function associated to the curvature value at each point of the trajectory allows us to detect variations in its shape: a line, a curved arc, an corner point, an inflexion point.

2. The motion speed: This feature is first important to detect the general phases preparatory or closing the designation gesture, since these are usually faster and second, it is part of the detection of stop points (among which are angle points), which either correspond to designations or to hesitations.

3. Crossing points: These are essential to detect loops within a trajectory, which are usually non-ambiguous indicators of region designations.

4. Stable segments as regards curvature: they are quite useful to detect portions of the trajectory which, even if they are not closed, can be interpreted as being a loop designating a region.

5. Device specific features: These generally correspond to events associated with the buttons of a mouse and are interpreted as punctual singularities.

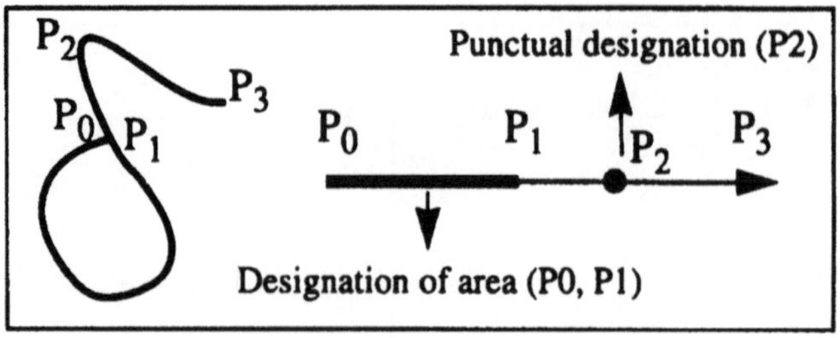

Figure 8: Gesture example with disjoint singularities.

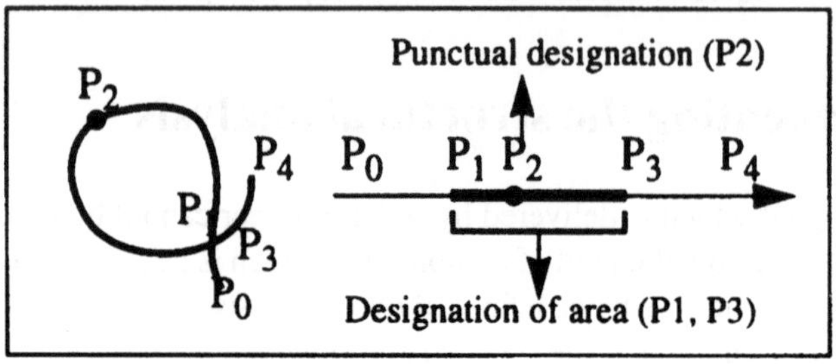

Figure 9: Ambiguous case.

6.2 Interpreting the different elements

The study of the different properties which can be observed upon a trajectory leads to a representation which, for a same gesture, combines a whole set of singularities at different places along the trajectory. The problem is then to combine these different knowledge sources in order to propose a global semantics for the gesture. Several cases can be encountered:

1. In the case of disjoint singularities, for which there is no overlapping of the time interval where they appear, the global meaning is determined by considering the different singularities one after the other: punctual singularities for the designation of non-bound regions and segmental singularities for closed regions (See Figure 8).

2. The association of a punctual and a segmental singularity — e.g. a stop point within a closed loop. At this stage, it is usually difficult to make a real choice between both hypotheses. This case can be managed by preserving two hypotheses for the meaning of the corresponding gesture: the designation of a delimited region on the one hand and a punctual designation on the other hand (See Figure 9).

3. The association of two segmental singularities, an example of which could be a closed loop made in combination of a mouse down event. In this case, the interpretation will privilege a possible combination of the two events, event if hypotheses corresponding to a specific and independent interpretation of the two singularities have to be kept.

7 Conclusion

In this paper, we have presented a possible model for the detection of meaningful parts of a gestural signal. It is clear that we have not provided a hundred percent safe criteria which may allow us to state for each singularity that it actually corresponds to a designation act. It is thus necessary to carry on the research in this domain in order to take into account of the visual context, the task which is addressed by the dialogue, the history of the preceding interactions between the user and the system, and before all the specificities of the linguistic utterance which has been uttered in combination with the gesture. As a matter of fact, it can be considered that the user has produced his gesture while having in mind, at least unconsciously, these different pieces of information. This second step of our research will allow us to identify precisely the meaningful part of a gesture and consequently to identify even more accurately the designated referents. It should be noted that such a research is impeded by the lack of clear knowledge that you may have concerning the basic cognitive and perceptual mechanisms which are at the root of the construction of multimodal utterances in a communicative perspective.

References

[1] B. Gaiffe and L. Romary. Ce matin, il pleuvait, ou la référence à l'épreuve du temps. *Langages, Temps, Référence et Inférence par Jacques Moeschler*, 112, December 1993.

[2] D. McNeill. *Hand and Mind: What gestures reveal about thought*. University of Chicago Press, 1992.

[3] C. Mignot, C. Valot, and N. Carbonell. An experimental study of future "natural" multimodal human-computer interaction. In *INTERCHI '93*, April 1993.

[4] B. Rimé and L. Schiaratura. Gesture and speech. In R. S. Feldman and B. Rimé, editors, *Fundamentals of nonverbal behavior*. Cambridge University Press, 1991.

[5] W. Wahlster. User and discourse models for multimodal communication. In J. Sullivan and S. Tymler, editors, *Intelligent user interface*. Addison-Wesley, 1991.

A Hand Data Model for Gesture Recognition

S. Ben Salem and R. B. Yates
Department of Electronic and Electrical Engineering
University of Sheffield, Mappin Street, Sheffield, S1 3JD, UK.

E-mail: s.a.bensalem@sheffield.ac.uk
Telephone: +44 114 282 5181 Fax: +44 114 272 6391

Abstract

This paper describes a novel hand data model as a system evaluator that defines the minimum requirements for a robust recognition system. Interface devices for the user's hand can be as simple as a switch to highly complex multi sensor gloves. A model is required that can cope with both diversity of the input devices and the rich variety of gesture based sign languages and user interfaces. We adopt an estimation of the Bayes error by calculating the classification error using distribution characteristics of the patterns, and this estimation is useful in classifying the gestures, evaluating the gesture input system, and specifying the gesture vocabulary.

1 Introduction

Despite the increasing achievements in the field of hand gestures recognition and interpretation, the task of tracking and recognising a hand gesture, particularly in real time, is still a difficult one. Early work done on gestures recognition focused on written gestures [5], and on sign language recognition applied to speech synthesis [3].

Ideally we should soon witness the replacement of the Window Icon Menu Pointer (WIMP) paradigm of the user interface, by a multimodal interface including hand gesture, gaze, facial expression, speech and conventional channels such as a keyboard and a mouse. Our work currently focuses on the recognition of hand performed gestures as part of a multimodal user interface.

Because the requirements of such a user interface are difficult to meet, we subdivide the hand actions into several categories each for particular interaction tasks.

- Hand Manipulation is mainly used in applications such as object manipulations in a virtual environment.

- Hand written gesture or pen based gestures are particularly suitable for document editing and Computer Supported Co-operative Work.

- A vocabulary of gestures can be part of a comprehensive sign language (like British Sign Language, BSL) or part of a multimodal user interface.

This work deals with the recognition and the correct classification of hand performed static gestures. We also find the minimum set of channels to track and define a device dependant set of gestures. It is our intention to extend the results of this project into the recognition of dynamic gestures.

The recognition procedure will be dependant on the problem domain, that is, it would be expected that hand performed recognition would require different classification techniques from hand written gestures. In fact the whole classification process depends not only on the type of gestures but also on the characteristics of the hand tracking system such as noise, frequency and number of channels. We have formed a model which represents the relation between all these variations in the hand data and the recognition performance. The consistency of the error classification is to be used as an indication of the robustness of the system, that is the dependence of output on the variation in the data characteristics. The magnitude of the error classification is a clear indication of the reliability and quality of the system.

A device independent Hand Data Model is advantageous because it allows us:

- To evaluate the maximum acceptable level of noise in the signal without information loss.
- To define the maximum possible number of recognisable gestures.
- To reduce the number of data channels to monitor (feature extraction, and selection)
- To select the right measurement metrics.
- Indirectly to assess the most efficient classification method (discriminate functions, nearest neighbour classifier ...)

Most important the Hand Data Model allows us to make informed decisions about the system components and to estimate the expected consequences of such a decision. This is important since the trade off between data collection and data classification is generally made without a full knowledge of the characteristics of the data and their role in the classification process.

The evaluation and prediction of a pattern classifier performance is essential if it is to be implemented as part of an user interface.

2 Gesture classification

From a pattern classification point of view, a hand static gesture may be regarded as a point lying in the pattern space of dimension N, where N corresponds to the number of channels being monitored. The Nearest Neighbour Rule (NNR) stipulates that the closer patterns are together in the feature space the more likely they are to belong to the same class. By calculating the distance between a pattern and a know class and compare it with distances between the same pattern and other classes it is possible

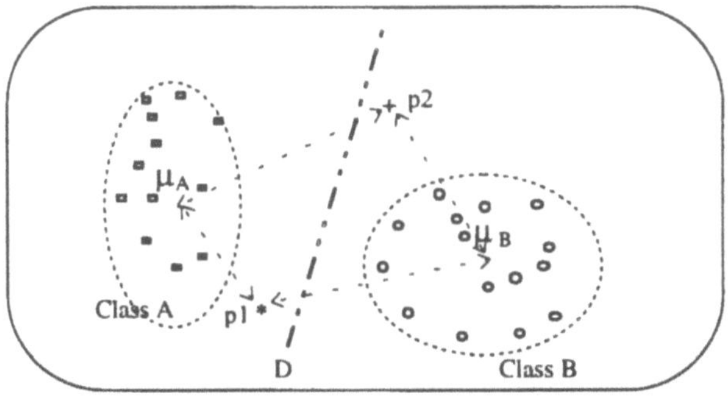

Figure 1: Nearest neighbour classification (μ is the mean of the class).

to estimate the most likely class that the pattern belong to. In Figure 1, $d(p_1, \mu_A)$ is smaller than $d(p_1, \mu_B)$, p_1 belong then to class A, the same rule is applied to pattern p_2 and a decision boundary D can be drawn in the feature space.

2.1 Source of errors in gesture classification

Patterns that possess a high number of common features (characteristics) have the tendency to cluster in the pattern space. These clusters of patterns (classes) are distributed over the pattern space. The overlap of such cluster/classes is the main cause of misclassification. Another source of misclassification is noise which added to the underlying signal can potentially shift the pattern point away from the cluster/class to which it belongs, and erroneously closer to other classes.

Given the high probability of class overlap, it is likely that imperfect classification will occur.

We can summarise the sources of error in gesture classification as being one or the combination of the following:

- The complexity of the vocabulary and the number and type of gestures.
- The noise level in the signal which is generally due to the hardware
- The irregularities and variations in the performance of the gestures.

Resulting in alteration of the:

1. Compactness of the classes or intraclass distribution of the patterns.
2. Distribution of the classes in the pattern space or the similarity between different gestures.

2.2 Gesture feature selection

The purpose of feature selection is to select the appropriate data channels from the whole set available, which carry information comprehensive enough about the pattern

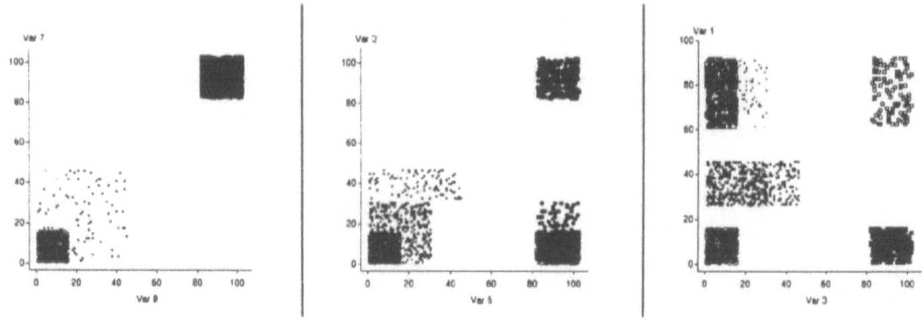

Figure 2: From left to right: Ring/Little, Index/Middle and Thumb/Index Interphalangeal joints channels.

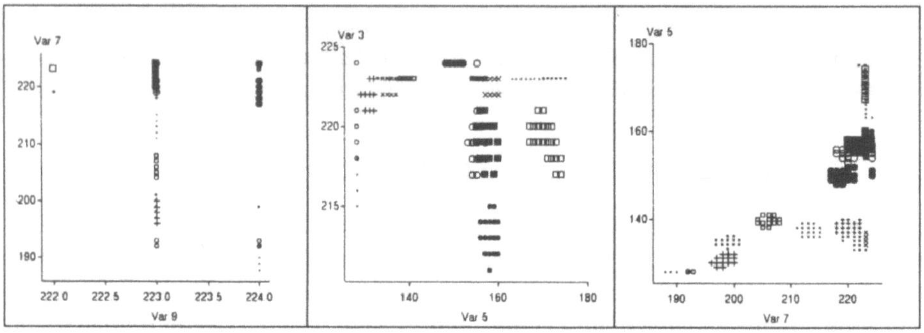

Figure 3: From left to right: Ring/Little, Index/Middle and Middle/Ring Interphalangeal joints channels.

instance so that the new set of data represents merely a reduction of dimensionally without loss of the most significant aspects of the pattern [2]. Feature selection is very useful when the data acquisition is costly, by reducing the number of channels to track it is possible to reduce dramatically the time-lag when tracking in real-time. Additionally feature selection eliminate irrelevant information and redundancy, potentially improving the probability of correct classification.

We then generated a vocabulary of 18 simulated gestures and visualised them using X-Gobi, a multidimensional data visualisation tool. Figure 2 shows the results, when using the ring and little finger joints, the clusters are not well separated, there is an important improvement when using the thumb and the index. So even with these sample data, selecting the right channels can increase dramatically the chances of correct classification.

The experiment was then done using the same vocabulary but performing the gestures using the glove device developed in house. Figure 3 shows the results. Please note that the thumb channels were not working properly at the time of the experiment, so the thumb/Index distribution was not available. Nevertheless, this second set of results illustrate furthermore the need of feature selection to filter out redundant channels.

2.3 Gesture noise and data quality

We adopted an empirical approach to the noise analysis, which was based on the distribution of the pattern data. After having generated simulated hand gesture data the clustering of the data was estimated visually using X-Gobi.

All the gestures were performed using an in house developed glove device. The glove fabrication process contributes additional noise, and can perturb the output signal. We have managed to improve the manufacturing of the glove and we are currently undergoing the manufacturing of the fifth generation prototype using transducers designed and manufactured in-house. This should reduce dramatically the imperfection in the circuitry.

Another source of inconsistency is derived from the variation between users performing the gestures. Gestures are rarely performed twice the same way and there is a noticeable difference in the way the gestures are performed depending on the user involved. Not only does the size of the hand affect the data characteristics, but the dexterity and the cultural background of the user are also relevant factors.

3 Calculating the hand data error

To calculate the hand data error, an empirical approach has been adopted. This is derived from a method used to evaluate a technique for classifying shapes in images [1]. The method includes the following steps:

1. Extract the data.
2. Calculate the Interclass frequency (f_{inter}) which is the normalised PDF of the interclass distances.
3. Calculate the Intraclass frequency (f_{intra}) which is the normalised PDF of the intraclass distance measured between pairs of patterns of the same class.
4. Qualitative evaluation of the Hand Data Error ε by comparing the values of α and β.
5. Estimation of the Hand Data Error ε.
6. Use the value of ε for nearest neighbour classification.

This method has the advantage of being independent of the classes distribution

3.1 Selection of measurement metrics

Several measure metrics exist when considering the distances between patterns. The most common ones derive from the Minkowski metric and those are the ones that we have implemented. In our case we will use the different metrics and have an opportunistic approach by choosing the metrics giving the most accurate evaluation of the classification error ε.

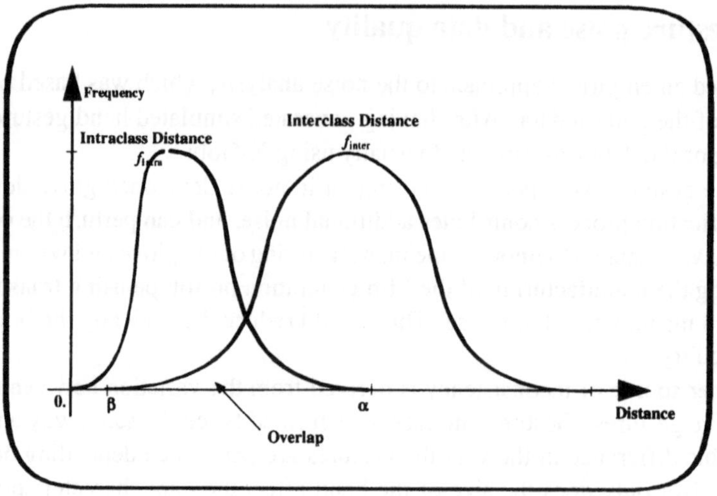

Figure 4: The Frequency Distribution of the Intraclass and Interclass Distances.

Minkowski metric of order s is given by:

$$\delta_M(\underline{x}_k, \underline{x}_1) = \left(\sum_{j=1}^{n} \left| x_{kj} - x_{ij} \right|^s \right)^{\frac{1}{s}} \tag{1}$$

where s is the order of the metric, x_{kj} is the co-ordinate of pattern x_k in the jth dimension and x_{ij} is the co-ordinate of pattern x_i in the $j^t h$ dimension.

There is no golden rule for the selection the right metrics, when the distribution of the data is unknown.

3.2 Frequency distribution of the interclass distance

In the pattern space the pairwise distance between clusters/classes of patterns is a good indication of the difficulty of the classification process, together with the intraclass distance (see next section). If different clusters/classes tend to be close to one another in the pattern space the classification process will increase in difficulty.

3.3 Frequency distribution of the intraclass distance

The intraclass distribution is a good indicator of the compactness of the cluster/classes in the pattern space. If the patterns belonging to the same clusters/classes tend to be close to each other they are less likely to be closer to the centre of gravity/means of neighbouring cluster/classes. The pairwise intraclass distance is calculated from the distance between two patterns known to belong to the same class.

We then as for the interclass distance, calculate the frequency distribution of the intraclass distances and normalise the results into unity.

β and α are defined as the distance where the interclass and the intraclass distance frequency distribution respectively fall below some defined threshold values. The distance between α and β gives us a qualitative evaluation the classification error ε.

The interclass distances and the intraclass distances both are determinant in the evaluation of the probability of misclassification. As a rule of thumb, if the interclass distances are large and the intraclass distances small then the misclassification error is reduced to a minimum, but in the other case the value of ε increases.

3.4 Estimating the Bayes error with the classification error ε

Evaluating the classification error is a way of measuring the effectiveness of a pattern classifier. However using the Bayes error is often computationally complex particularly for multidimensional patterns. We have to rely on other measures of class separability such as comparing the frequency distribution of the interclass distances f_{inter} and the frequency distribution of the intraclass distances f_{intra}. These measurements give an approximation of the Bayes error, and are a compromising trade off between the accuracy of the measurement and the processing time required.

The Bayes error can be resumed as being the optimal decision rule which minimise the average likelihood of misclassifying a vector pattern [4].

The probability of misclassification P_r of a pattern x can be derived from f_{inter} and f_{intra} (where $\gamma = x$):

$$P_r = \int_{\gamma-\delta_\gamma}^{\gamma+\delta_\gamma} f_{intra}(x) \int_{\beta}^{\alpha} f_{intra}(y)\, dy\, dx \qquad (2)$$

The probability of misclassification ε (or Hand Data Error) can be determined from P_r as being:

$$\varepsilon = \int_{\beta}^{\alpha} P_r(x)\, dx \qquad (3)$$

4 Using the hand data model for system evaluation

Having obtained an estimated value of the classification error ε, which is the main feature of our method, the overall performance of the hand tracking and recognition system can be measured. By a trial and error approach the number of channels to track can be reduced and those which carry the most significant information can be prioritised in the tracking process.

In fact, the hand data model should help through the following:

- **Feature Selection:** We can reduce the number of data channels to track, thus the amount of data to process without any loss of information about the hand actions.
- **System Evaluation:** the value of the classification error ε, can be used to evaluate both the robustness and the reliability of the system.
- **Gesture Classification:** The classification error ε calculation is part of a nearest neighbour classifier.

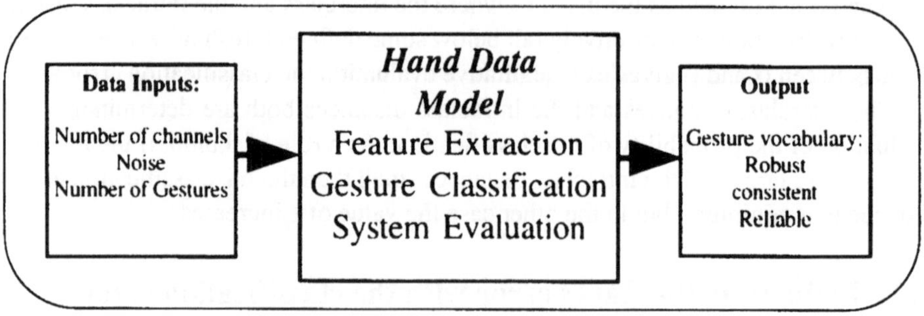

Figure 5: The Hand Data Model

The consistency of the misclassification error ε, indicates an invariance in the system performance independently of the variation in the parameters describing the data such as noise level and number of channels. Such an invariance corresponds thus to the robustness and consistency of the hand tracking and recognition system.

The value of the misclassification error ε is a accurate measurement of the performance of the hand tracking and recognition system.

5 Conclusion

We have designed and are implementing a robust hand tracking and recognition system evaluation that is platform independent and helps to pre-process the data by eliminating redundant and irrelevant data channels as well as estimate the minimal requirements of the gesture vocabulary, the hardware performance and the classification method.

The Hand Data Model allows us to evaluate of the tracking and recognition system that will help measure and compare the efficiency of different tracking technologies such as glove input devices, video tracking and silhouette tracking.

Within a multimodal User Interface, different sets of hand gestures can be used, and a decision about which set is to be used depends not only on the application but also on how tractable and recognisable the gestures are. The Hand Data Model provide an elegant way of quantifying the characteristics of each set to help the interface designer select the best set of hand functions. We hope to extend this model to dynamic performed hand gestures, and other hand functions.

A third advantage of the Hand Data Model is in the evaluation of the classification method. By comparing the misclassification error ε of different methods we have a better means of selecting the most efficient, reliable and robust classifier.

We intend to further use the results from Section 3 to evaluate threshold values of α and β which would increase the efficiency of our method. Experiments are needed to determine the value of ε for a useful hand gesture recognition system. Then a comparison of this method with conventional nearest neighbour classifiers is required to evaluate its efficiency and reliability as a gesture classifier.

We would like also to investigate the Hand Data Model as a generic model for multimodal interface, where each interaction method could be evaluated and the most suitable one for a particular task chosen.

Acknowledgement

The authors acknowledge the important help of Dr. D.Prendergast as well as discussions with Mr. A. Ashbrook. The authors wish also to thank Dr. N. Thacker for his criticisms. All trademarks are acknowledged.

Appendix

List of gestures performed and generated: Agree, Attention, Deep, Down, High, I, Left, No, Nothing, Pointing, Object, OK, Right, Rude, Scissors, Stop, Two, Walk. These gestures are described in [6].

References

[1] A. Ashbrook. *Geometric Histograms for Object Recognition: Developments and Analysis*. PhD thesis, University of Sheffield (to be submitted), 1996.

[2] P. A. Devijver and J. Kittler. *Pattern Recognition, A Statistical Approach*. Prentice-Hall International, 1982.

[3] S. S. Fels. *Building Adaptive Interfaces with Neural Networks: The Glove-Talk Pilot Study*. PhD thesis, University of Toronto, 1990.

[4] K. S. Fu. *Applications of pattern recognition*. CRC Press Inc., 1982.

[5] J. Rhyne. Dialogue management for gestural interfaces. *Computer Graphics*, 21:137–141, 1987.

[6] M. Skelly. *Amer-Ind gestural code based on universal American Indian hand talk*. Elsevier, 1979.

Non-Emblematic Gestures for Estimating Mood

A. Stove
Philips Research Laboratories, Cross Oak Lane, Redhill, Surrey, RH1 5HA, UK

E-mail: stove@prl.research.philips.com
Telephone: +44 114 282 5181 Fax: +44 114 272 6391

Abstract

This paper discusses work which is currently taking place within Philips Research Laboratories to study the use of gestural information to provide information about a person's mood so as to enhance their interaction with computer-based equipment.

1 Introduction

A core motivation for studying the capabilities of gestural inputs arises from consideration of the relative poverty of human-machine interaction compared with human-human interaction, as discussed, for example in [4]. The effects of this poverty have become even more widespread since that book was written. Since then the capabilities of low-cost digital computers have increased very greatly and they have become embedded in all manner of everyday devices. Improved forms of interaction could realise the potential benefits available from this technology in two major ways: Interaction with existing devices could be improved, and completely new ways of interaction can lead to new devices and to new applications for existing devices.

This paper will discuss ways of allowing computers to share in the non-verbal interactions which take place between people when they converse. This ability can be used to estimate something of the user's mood, which may then be expected to be able help in both of the areas mentioned above - both to provide exciting new capabilities for existing products, and also to foster the development of radically new applications for generic, computer-based education and entertainment systems.

The paper includes a description of an experimental and demonstration system which is currently being built, and will discuss what it is hoped to be able to learn from it.

2 Improved Interaction

Even a toaster may now contain a microcontroller, but the most technically literate can still have problems programming something which is as near-universal as a video recorder. The microcontrollers within such devices can offer such a wide array of functionality that few of the users understand, let alone use, all the functionality which is provided. The customer often finds that the controls do not actually provide quite what is wanted. Although adding extra functionality into the microcontroller would be relatively easy, bringing it out so that the user can communicate with it is less so - there is no space for extra buttons on either the front panel or on the remote control, and the additional functionality will be lost amidst other functions which this customer does not want, although other customers do.

One part of the solution to this lies in the growing use of various products in conjunction with computers. This is sometimes in the form of physical union, such as combined computers and televisions, sometimes in the form of overlapping functionality, such as a CDi player, for example, which is somewhere between a computer and a television, and sometimes this integration may arise when one device can control another, which is another emerging trend. Many people are already familiar with the 'virtual' CD player controls which allow the CD-ROM and sound card on a Personal Computer (PC), or a CDi player, to act as a CD player. Besides imitating the conventional controls, these systems would allow other sorts of options, for example to select a CD track by title, using a pointer, rather than by number. There is thus more 'space' for the interface. This is an important advance, but is not sufficient on its own. One further requirement is for the machine to be able help the user to make the best use of the functionality.

A fuller knowledge of the particular users, such as that which can be gained from attempting to estimate something of their underlying mental state can improve the way in which the machine tries to interact with these users. The ideal will be to enable the machine to appear to the user as though it could read their minds and could respond to their needs and wishes. An important part of any programme to implement this idea must be to find out how well the system needs to work in order to maintain enough of this illusion and for the user to feel happy cooperating with the machine on this basis.

3 Novelty

The above discussion has focused on how the understanding of mood might help make existing devices easier to use. As mentioned in the introduction, however, the ability to make estimates of the user's mental and emotional state is expected also to have a much more fundamental impact on the way people interact with machines.

It may be observed that almost all of current input from humans to computers, either explicitly or when the computer are embedded within other devices, is concerned either with intellectual activities (such as work or solving puzzles) or with action games which require rapid reactions. There is no effective way to convey any of our other feelings to the computer. The machine can try to affect these other parts of our nature, for example our sense of beauty or wonder, but at the moment it cannot do this very well, and certainly not in any way which can respond to how we are actually feeling.

Seen in this light, it is clear that computers have only affected two aspects of what it is to be human. It is clear that there must be scope for introducing computers into the stimulation of other fields of human sensibility, such as emotions or of spirituality, if the machine can understand some of these aspects of the user's feelings.

4 Gestures

It is well known that human beings communicate with one another in many other ways in addition to the speaking of words. Ekman and [1] described five categories of verbal behaviour: Emblems, which replace words; Illustrators, which supplement words; Affect Displays, which indicate emotions; Regulators, to manage the interaction, for example to indicate "I don't understand, please repeat" and Adapters, which help the Affect Displays and the Regulators. An important distinction for this work is seen to be that between emblems, which replace verbal statements and are conscious, and non-emblematic signals which comprise the ways in which human unconsciously communicate with one another. Of course the actual boundary between emblematic and non-emblematic behaviour is less well defined than is implied above - there is a continuum between unconsciously turning one's eyes in the direction of something which is being talked about, half consciously using a pointing gesture when saying "look over there," and deliberately replacing the words by a gesture.

Unconscious behaviour is also seen in animals, of course, and some of their actions are recognisably the same as those of humans (cats yawn and chimpanzees scratch their heads). The aim of our work is to use these non-emblematic gestures, in conjunction, where appropriate, with whatever other information is available, to estimate something of user's mental state.

It may also be observed that there is an important non-emblematic content in speech. Changes in pitch and in the speed of speaking for example, also convey 'non emblematic' information about the speaker's thoughts, which may be recognisable if an appropriate interface is available.

It is not the intention of this work to explore emblematic gesturing, for example pointing, still less to generate an artificial 'language' of gesturing as a substitute for present-day computer interfaces. There may however be important questions about the extent to which a user might expect the machine to have an ability to understand 'emblematic' gestures, once it has been recognised that it can detect non-emblematic behaviour.

4.1 Visual Gestures

Visual gestures (predominantly hand gestures and facial expressions) are seen as the most promising mode of non-emblematic behaviour to try to understand. Whilst tactile communication may be best for some portable devices, and the hardware for detecting 'tone of voice' is less expensive, at least at the moment, visual observation of the user none the less offers the prospect of giving the most information as well as providing an important source of synergy with other applications such as video telephony, identification of the user, or the recognition of emblematic gestures, such pointing at objects in the environment.

The approach which is currently being followed is to build on existing work which had been developed for face recognition, but can also be used to recognize expressions

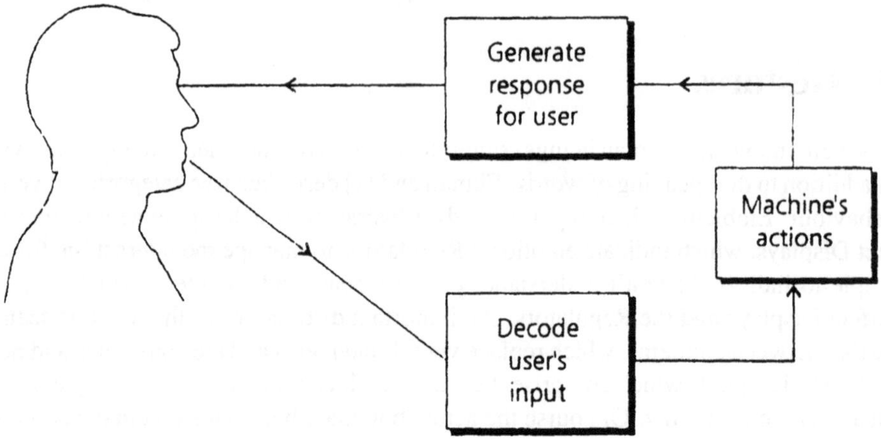

Figure 1: Conventional interaction.

[3]. In parallel with this, the system will be based on work to detect gestures which are made by moving the hands.

It is noteworthy that the facial gestures which are known to be universally recognisable [2] (happiness, sadness surprise, fear anger and disgust) are all emotional rather than intellectual. This suggests that this aspect of the work will be more suitable as a source of information about 'mood' in order to complement the 'intellectual' information which is available from more conventional sources. Other research is looking at how widely other expressions can be recognised and how far the machine can recognise gradations within these expressions (for example, looking 'rather' surprised or 'very' happy).

It is similarly expected that the most readily recognisable gestures will probably relate to aspects of mood, such as how confident a person is in the responses they are giving, rather than to adding to the semantic content of the conscious dialogue.

5 Demonstration System

Figures 1 and 2 illustrate the difference which the ability to estimate mood can make to a computer-based system. Figure 1 shows a simple model of a 'conventional' system, where the computer interprets, as best it can, the inputs which the user gives it, reacts as it thinks appropriate and presents something to the user.

If an understanding of mood is included, a sensor must be available to detect something of the user's non-emblematic behaviour. In the demonstration system this will be a video camera which will detect information both about the user's facial expression and about hand gestures. Two separate processing algorithms will extract the expression and hand-gesturing information from the images and these will be used to help to estimate the user's mood. This information can then be used to moderate the meaning

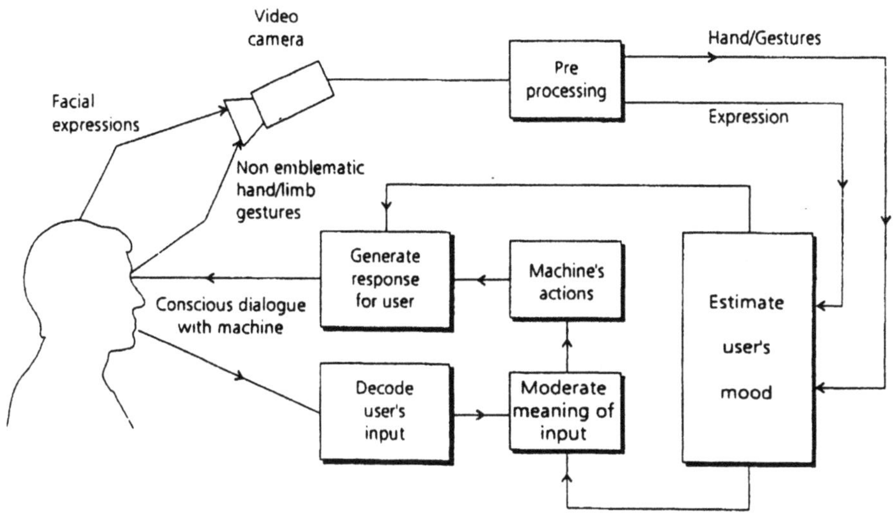

Figure 2: Interaction with machine understanding of mood.

of the conscious inputs, for example to estimate how sure the user is of what he is doing, and whether he is pleased with the way things are going. The information can also be used to moderate the outputs - to adapt the terminology or the modality to one with which the user seems happy.

Early work has suggested that useful estimates can be made of users' states based on gross observations of how their hands move. This has been deduced by tracking the areas of changing brightness in reduced-resolution video images. The areas where the brightness is changing indicate where motion is taking place, which in turn indicates where the hands are moving in the image.

Before more work is done to study this technique, we must discover how useful the estimates of mood are in a 'real' application, and then further work can be done, if necessary, to try to improve either the video processing or the mood estimations. The effectiveness of these techniques can only be determined by using the system in a realistic application. In order to be able to achieve this, a demonstration system, which can also be used for experiments, is currently being built.

The demonstration system is based on a poetry browser, which will suggest pieces of poetry or short sections of prose to the user, based on estimates of their current mood and of how it is changing. The 'intellectual' input required from the user should be minimal.

One advantage of the 'poetry browser' is that it will engage the user on an emotional level. On the other hand, because the poetry can be represented by text, it is relatively easy for the machine to analyse its content, making it easier for the machine to make a selection from its library than would alternatives which selected from amongst more visual material. However sound output can also be incorporated, i.e. the texts can be read out loud by the machine in order to enhance the user's interest and increase the sense of its being a real application.

5.1 Hardware Requirements

The system is being built in a near state of the art Personal Computer using a processor with 120MHz clock rate. It is predicted that this will be able to process the information at an adequate rate to detect the 'mood' signals and to track their changes. The continuing reduction in the cost of digital hardware means that this is not considered an important issue in the long term. The monochrome TV camera can be very simple and is also affordable. Special purpose hardware is likely to be needed to perform the digitisation of the video images. It is not unusual to find that the analogue to digital convertor is a 'bottleneck' in many systems, where its price performance ratio currently seems inferior either to the analogue circuitry before it and to the digital circuitry after it. In this case however the synergy with consumer digital video recorders will bring down the prices of this component of the system.

6 Predictability

One issue of particular experimental interest is whether the users are happy with the fact that the system chooses its responses based on behaviour of which they may not be conscious. Conventional ergonomic design suggests that the user should be able understand what the machine is doing, i.e. on what basis it is making its decisions. If users accept that the machine's decisions are based on its reading of their mood, then things will probably be all right. If they are is reduced to asking how the machine is trying to deduce their mood, then things may go wrong. It is known that if people can 'suspend their disbelief,' they are happy to credit a machine with more intelligence than it actually has [5] and they may be willing to cooperate with it, and to be less critical of its judgements than one might expect. Problems will arise if the machine begins to betray the user's trust, and breaks the illusion. The effectiveness of the system is therefore expected to be highly dependent on how the critical of the machine the user decides to be.

7 Conclusion

There is wide scope for increasing the range of communication to which computers are sensitive. Making computers sensitive to non-verbal, non-emblematic, gestures in particular gives the prospect of being able to deduce things about a user's mood which can enhance interactions with existing computer-based systems and generate wholly new modes of interaction. The current state of electronics shows good evidence that such systems can be cost effective in mass markets in a few years' time. Work is currently under way to use a vision-based approach to understanding something of a user's mental state via his gestures and facial expressions. A demonstration system which is directed towards emotional rather than intellectual interaction is being built to investigate some of the human factors issues raised. A question of particular interest is the quality of performance which is needed for such a system to be acceptable to a general user, and to find out how close we are to this point.

References

[1] P. Ekman and W. V. Friesen. The repertoire of non-verbal behaviour: Categories, origins, usage and codings. *Semiotica*, 1:49–97, 1969.

[2] P. Ekman and W. V. Friesen. *Unmasking the Face*. Prentice Hall, Englewood Cliffs, New Jersey, 1975.

[3] A. Lanitis, C. J. Taylor, and T. F. Cootes. Automatic face identification using flexible appearance models. *Image and Vision Computing*, 13:393–401, 1995.

[4] L. A. Suchman. *Plans and Situated Actions: The Problem of Human-Machine Communication*. Cambridge University Press, Cambridge, 1987.

[5] J. Weizenbaum. ELIZA – A computer program for the study of natural language communication between man and machine. *Communications of the ACM*, 9:36–45, 1966.

How Do Users Manipulate Graphical Icons? An Empirical Study

S. Robbe†, N. Carbonell† and P. Dauchy‡

†CRIN-CNRS & INRIA-Lorraine, Btiment Loria, BP 239,
F54506 Vandoeuvre-ls-Nancy Cedex, France

‡ IMASSA, Dpt. Sciences Cognitives et Ergonomie, BP 73,
F91223 Brtigny-sur-Orge Cedex, France

E-mail: {robbe, carbo}@loria.fr, pierre@cerma.fr
Telephone: +33 83 59 20 47 Fax: +33 83 41 30 79

Abstract

According to [1] pointing one's finger at a graphical object then at an empty location on the screen while saying "Put this here," are semiotic gestures, since they contribute to the meaning of the concomitant utterance. On the other hand, dragging one's fingertip on the surface of the screen may be termed an 'ergotic' gesture, inasmuch as it represents an action, namely the drawing of a 2D graphic or the moving of an icon, according to the current context.

We have conducted a Wizard of Oz experiment on the spontaneous use of speech and 2D gestures for interacting with standard graphical software. Overall results [9, 6, 2] indicate that, in such contexts, hand gestures are used either for pointing at objects and locations on the screen or for acting on a 2D representation of the application.

Our study of the subjects' multimodal expression being completed, we have now focused our analysis on their use of gestures. We aim at defining useful criteria for the design of gestural human-computer interaction. In this paper, we present user profiles that were defined from a thorough analysis of the subjects' gestures.

1 Context and motivation

Several taxonomies [7, 4, 10, 1] have been proposed for the description and interpretation of gestures. The classification conceived by C. Cadoz is particularly well suited to the analysis of nonverbal human-computer interaction (HCI), inasmuch as it takes into account the main functions that can be assigned to hand gestures in this context, that is, their semiotic, ergotic, and epistemic functions.

Writing, drawing or typing, using a sign language, manipulating a mechanical or electronic command device and playing a musical instrument involve semiotic gestures. On the other hand, ergotic gestures are used to act on the physical world, for instance to manipulate objects. Semiotic gestures partake of communication, whereas ergotic gestures are actions. C. Mignot [8] has shown that, in the context of HCI, users who resort to semiotic gestures tend to communicate with the computer system, while users who manipulate the graphical objects representing the application interact with the system.

Using one's hands for feeling objects, exploring their shape, and assessing their position are instances of epistemic gestures. But designers cannot draw upon the sense of touch of users yet, due to present technological limitations; in particular, research on "artificial skin" devices is still needed.

Then the implementation of gestural HCI raises two related issues:

- should both ergotic and semiotic gestures be made available to users simultaneously (i.e. in the same user interface)?
- if not, what criteria should motivate design choices between these two functions of gestures?

For some application domains designers have no choice. For instance, ergotic gestures are required for tele-operation environments, while interaction through a sign language should be implemented using semiotic gestures.

But they have a free choice for standard applications such as text or spreadsheet processing, especially in a multimodal environment where users can interact with the system, alternately or simultaneously, through speech (i.e. natural or pseudo-natural spoken language) and gestures.

The study presented here aims at defining criteria that may help designers meet users' preferences, expectations and requirements, as regards the integration of gestural means of expression into multimodal user interfaces for standard applications. It is based on the analysis of empirical data collected in an experimental situation.

We first describe the experimental setup. Then, results of the analysis of verbal and nonverbal protocols are presented in the form of usage profiles. Finally, we put forward user categories that may prove useful for the design of gestural or multimodal user interfaces.

2 Experimental setup

2.1 Methodology

We conducted a Wizard of Oz (WOZ) experiment on verbal and gestural HCI with ergonomists from CERMA[1].

Although human face-to-face communication often involves 3D gestures, we restricted the nonverbal expression of subjects to 2D gestures in order to offer them a realistic HCI environment. In addition, as the application objects were represented graphically on the screen, gestures in a 3D space were not needed.

[1]IMASSA-CERMA, Institut de Mdecine Arospatiale du Service de Sant des Armes - Centre d'Etudes et de Recherches de Mdecine Arospatiale, 91223 Brtigny sur Orge, France

2.2 Subjects

Eight volunteer subjects with various backgrounds and occupational activities participated in the experiment. All of them had previously used application software intended for the general public, and most of them were familiar with direct manipulation [11]. Some had programming knowledge, but no computer scientist was included in the group.

2.3 Tasks

Subjects were asked to participate in three one hour sessions, one per week. During these sessions they performed simple design tasks relating to furniture arrangement, namely: given 2D plans of furnished rooms, they had to modify initial layouts according to constraints specified in eight scenarios of increasing difficulty. A scenario is reproduced by way of example (cf. Figure 1). Subjects interacted with the application

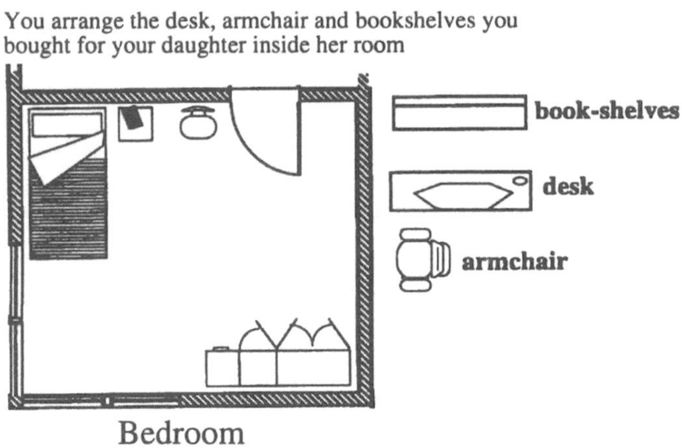

Figure 1: A scenario instance

using speech (via a microphone) and gestures (via a touch panel). Oral or gestural commands were accepted together with multimodal utterances combining both modalities. Spontaneous speech and gestures were allowed; but contact with the screen was required for gestures, so that only 2D gestures were possible. Subjects were given no instruction for the use of oral, gestural and multimodal expressions.

2.4 Implementation of the WOZ technique

We resorted to the Wizard of Oz technique for simulating the user interface functionalities. Two human operators or wizards were put in charge of the simulation. One of them interpreted incoming commands and activated relevant software functions; execution results were simultaneously displayed on the subject's and operators' screens thanks to the Shareboard collective drawing software. The other operator, in charge of dialogue management, selected and activated pre-recorded oral messages in response to incoming utterances, gestures and actions. Both operators were hidden from the subject; speech and gestures from the latter were transmitted to the formers through an audio-visual link. Figure 2 describes the experimental setup.

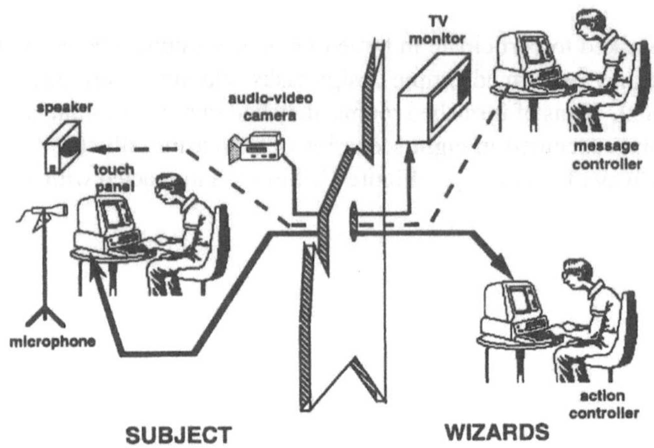

Figure 2: Experimental setup

2.5 Corpus and questionnaires

Subjects and wizards were videotaped throughout the experiment. Written descriptions of the audio-visual recordings include a transcription of utterances (from the subjects and the simulated system) together with a coarse description of the subjects' gestures and the system actions.

After the third session, subjects were asked to fill in a questionnaire which gave them the opportunity to comment on their different behaviours, strategies and preferences regarding the use of speech and gestures for interacting with standard computer applications.

3 Method

This paragraph describes the aspects of the subjects' behaviours and backgrounds on which our analysis was focused.

3.1 Analysis and labelling of gestures

Subjects' gestures were labelled as semiotic or ergotic according to the following cues:

- *the form of gestures*

  Pointing gestures (e.g. pointing at an icon or at an area on the screen) are obviously semiotic gestures, whether they occur in a multimodal context (with or without deictics) or not. On the other hand, attempts at grasping icons on the screen can be reliably interpreted as ergotic gestures. Our interpretations also take into account whether subjects touched the screen with their fingers or through a pen, as well as the hand gestures they performed in front of the screen without touching it.

- *the short-term context*

  Some gestures are ambiguous. For instance the drawing of a line on the screen cannot be classified accurately without considering the short-term context in which this gesture occurs. In particular, spoken utterances co-occurring with gestures should be analysed carefully; for instance, semiotic gestures are often accompanied by deictic phrases, while utterances beginning with phrases such as "I/We move the piano ..." accompany ergotic gestures.

3.2 Interpretation

In multimodal environments the use of gestures cannot be studied independently of the use of speech. Moreover, the way new forms of HCI are used is influenced by previous experience with computers, educational background and occupation.

To bring out the major factors capable of determining or influencing individual styles of gestural expression, and defining user profiles useful to designers, our interpretations of the subjects' forms of gestural expression take into account:

- the conclusions of a former analysis [2, 3] of the subjects' behaviours which was focused on their use of multimodality, that is: the respective functions assigned by subjects to speech and gestures, their possible preferences for one medium of expression over the other, the various forms of multimodality which they tried out, and the evolution of their use of speech and gestures in the course of the experiment.

- subjects' backgrounds and their former computer knowledge as stated in questionnaires that they filled in before the experiment.

- the short comments and remarks they expressed in the post-experiment questionnaires.

Our characterisation of the subjects' forms of multimodal expression is based on the taxonomy proposed by J. Coutaz and J. Caelen in [5]. We only mention the two most useful categories in this taxonomy:

- alternate multimodality applies to multimodal sequences of monomodal commands;

- synergic multimodality refers to the use of several modalities for stating one single command or message.

The full classification is represented in Figure 3.

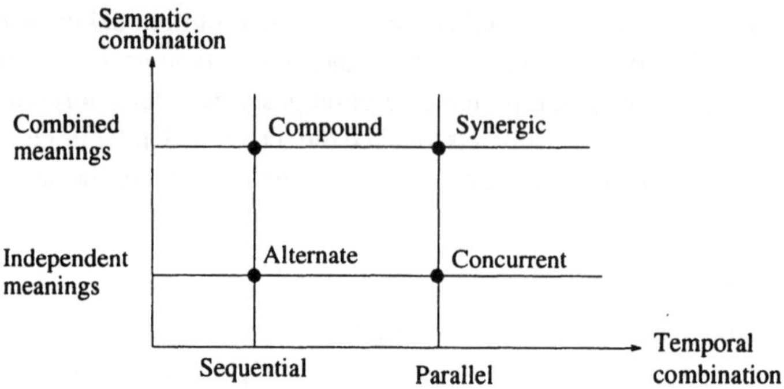

Figure 3: Classification of multimodal HCI (adapted from [5])

4 Results

This paragraph describes the different user profiles that can be inferred from the analysis of the subjects' gestures. Seven subjects only are considered, since one subject refrained from using gestural expression during the whole experiment.

4.1 Semiotic gestures for emulating human communication

Three subjects (subjects 5, 7, 8) unfailingly use pointing gestures for moving icons throughout the experiment: they first point at the graphical object they wish to move, then at the place where it should be after the displacement (cf. Figure 4, gesture 3). They often use pens as pointers to improve accuracy. On the other hand, they turn pieces of furniture through oral commands exclusively, although most of their rotation commands fail (cf. Table 2). By ANOVA, there is no significant differences between the three groups as regards failure rates ($F(2,4) = 1.40; p < 0.05$). It should be noted that while they describe rotations verbally they frequently mimic them in front of the screen but without touching it.

These subjects, who are unfamiliar with direct manipulation and are computer illiterate, favour alternate multimodality during the first session, and show a strong preference for speech over gestures. Their use of synergic multimodality progressively increases in the course of the following sessions. In multimodal contexts pointing gestures often co-occur with deictics or demonstratives.

These observations suggest that, in this new human-computer environment, subjects 5, 7 and 8 apply knowledge and skills acquired in the context of face-to-face communication. It may then be assumed that they view this HCI situation as a communication situation, because it offers them verbal and gestural expression facilities roughly similar to those they are wont to using for communicating with human interlocutors. Such transfers of knowledge, skills and experience to new activity situations are quite frequent. The fact that these subjects apply a model of human communication to HCI situations may account for their inefficient behaviours. In particular, it may explain why they have difficulty in combining speech and 2D gestures, and why they go on formulating rotations verbally despite repeated failures, instead of investigating other forms of expression and applying a trial and error strategy. One subject only (cf. subject 8 in Table 2) succeeds, during the last session, in formulating rotations accurately after numerous failed attempts: she materializes the rotation angle by drawing two segments which represent the angle edges (cf. Figure 4, gesture 7). This abstract gestural form of expression is particularly efficient, since it makes it possible to move an object and orientate it simultaneously.

The analysis of the post-experiment questionnaires confirms our interpretation of these subjects' behaviours. They are the only ones who doubt the reliability of speech recognition, whereas they are satisfied with the accuracy of the touch panel. One may assume that they ascribe their unsuccessful verbal formulations of rotations to the limited understanding capacity of the system, because in the context of a face-to-face dialogue with a human interlocutor their commands would have been interpreted correctly thanks to the contribution of nonverbal information (gaze direction, 3D gestures, etc.).

4.2 Ergotic gestures for manipulating graphical objects

Subjects 3 and 4 use speech for introducing pieces of furniture into a room, and ergotic gestures for moving them inside a room. More precisely, they point at an icon, using either their index finger or their thumb, and draw the trajectory of the intended displacement with the tip of the finger used for pointing at the icon. Trajectories bypass pieces of furniture and do not cross walls. In other words, these subjects move pieces of furniture inside the room by "dragging" the corresponding icons on the screen.

Rotations are expressed either verbally or gesturally. Both subjects simulate rotations using one of the two following types of gestures:

- pointing at an icon on the screen (with the index finger or the thumb) and rotating the finger used for pointing without moving the contact point (between the fingertip and the screen); the movement of the finger (a "screwing" gesture) simulates the intended rotation of the icon whereas the position of the fingertip on the screen materializes the centre of the 2D rotation (cf. Figure 4, gesture 4).

- attempting to grasp (or to pinch) the relevant icon (between thumb and index) and drawing a circular arc with the index finger, while the thumb stays motionless materializing the centre of the 2D rotation (cf. Figure 4, gesture 5).

In Table 2, these two forms of gestural expression are grouped in the third column entitled "Tor".

Subjects 3 and 4 favour alternate multimodality during the three sessions. Subject 4 shows a strong preference for gestures, which explains why he uses but a few

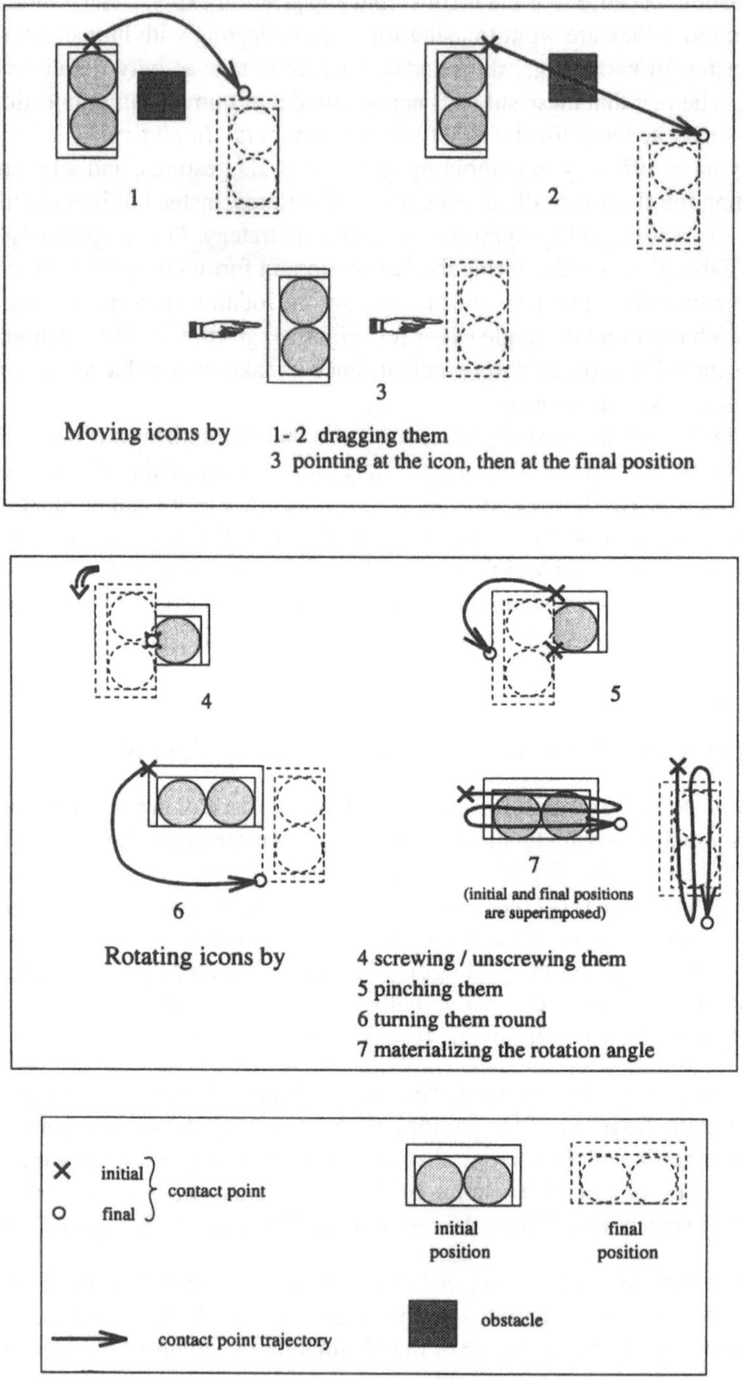

Figure 4: Gesture forms

deictics and demonstratives (cf. Table 1). Although their multimodal commands are characterised by a great inter-modality redundancy, both subjects tend to assign specific functions to speech and gestures. For instance, they use speech for introducing pieces of furniture into a room, and gestures for moving them inside a room.

As they are computer literate and use direct manipulation in the context of their everyday occupational activity, one can assume that they apply the concepts and representations they have developed through the extensive use of direct manipulation, to the new HCI environment they are offered. The influence of direct manipulation concepts on their behaviours and representations might explain why they keep to alternate multimodality, and why they seem inclined to use gestures rather than speech.

Their interaction strategies also seem influenced by their familiarity with interactive software and direct manipulation. For instance, they break down complex actions into sequences of simpler steps: pieces of furniture outside the room are first put in the centre of the room, then moved towards their final positions. Besides, they proceed by trial and error for expressing rotations (cf. Table 2); and they actively explore the functionalities and capabilities of the simulated user interface. Finally, as direct manipulation usually implies a metaphor, they develop an implicit metaphor for interpreting graphical objects and available actions on these objects: they manipulate icons as if they were stamps or labels laid on a table (cf. rotations) rather than 2D representations of pieces of furniture.

It may be that they consider the experimental user interface reliable and efficient despite the imprecision of the touch panel (cf. the post-experiment questionnaires), because they compare it with existing systems equipped with a mouse device rather than with human communication situations.

Since these subjects manipulate the graphical objects displayed on the screen, use multimodal commands where speech and gestures are largely redundant, and seem to draw upon their computer knowledge – especially the concepts and skills they acquired through the practice of direct manipulation – for controlling the simulated user interface, it is reasonable to assume that they interact with the system rather than communicate with it.

4.3 Ergotic gestures for manipulating application objects

The remaining two subjects (Subjects 1 and 2) use extensively synergic multimodality throughout the experiment. This may explain why they use deictics and demonstratives more frequently than the other subjects; this result is significant (cf. Table 1), last column, $F(2,4) = 7.62; p < 0.05$). They resort both to semiotic and ergotic gestures, but in specific contexts as follows. They use either speech or pointing (semiotic) gestures (cf. Figure 4, gesture 3) associated with a verbal command, whenever they introduce a new piece of furniture into a room. On the other hand, they move pieces of furniture inside a room using ergotic gestures similar to those of subjects 3 and 4 (cf. Figure 4, gesture 1). Their multimodal rotation commands also involve ergotic gestures: from a point on the object they draw a circular arc whose extremity indicates the final position of the selected point (cf. Figure 4, gesture 6).

These subjects are frequent, experienced computer users: they are familiar with programming and direct manipulation, and they interact with standard applications during their everyday occupational activities as well as during their leisure time. Their educational level is high, which may explain their low failure rate as regards the formulation of rotations.

A closer analysis of their ergotic gestures for expressing rotations suggests that they manipulate icons as if they were actual pieces of furniture: for instance the point they select on an icon representing a bed corresponds with the part of the bed that one should seize in order to turn the bed easily.

So, it could be assumed that these subjects, who manipulate application objects, interact rather than communicate with the system. But other observations contradict this interpretation. First, their use of semiotic gestures, then utterances like the following ones: "Now, I am going to install the desk," or "We push the bed against the wall." These data suggest two interpretations that account for the apparent contradictions in their behaviours:

- They act on the application objects together with (or with the help of) the system, and communicate with it to obtain efficient cooperation. Their representation of the system as a cooperative agent leads them to develop a complex twofold human-computer relationship: interaction with the displayed graphical representation of the application, and communication with the system manager.
- Or, more simply, they make the most of their familiarity with both programming imperative languages and direct manipulation, by using either multimodal commands or direct manipulation as appropriate; but this interpretation does not satisfactorily account for the subjects' utterances quoted above.

Further empirical and experimental studies are needed to achieve a better understanding of such behaviours.

5 Conclusions

Our study of the use of 2D gestures in a multimodal HCI environment yields results and general conclusions that may prove of some interest to designers of gestural or multimodal user interfaces, inasmuch as they give an insight into the attitudes, expectations and behaviours of potential users towards future HCI implementing new gestural expressions facilities.

Our main observations are briefly summarized in the subsequent paragraphs.

5.1 Usage profiles and user categories

Three usage profiles, which should be taken into account by designers, emerge from our analysis of empirical data.

5.1.1 Human-computer communication (cf. paragraph 4.1)

If users consider that they communicate with the system, they use semiotic gestures exclusively, and develop an abstract representation of the displayed graphical objects. Computer illiterate users belong to this category, since human communication is the only known situation to which they can compare multimodal HCI allowing verbal and gestural expression.

5.1.2 Human-computer interaction (cf. paragraph 4.2)

If users focus on the displayed graphical representation of the application, they may elaborate a metaphorical interpretation of the graphical objects that enables them to simulate interaction with 2D objects from the real world. In this context, they use ergotic gestures to the exclusion of semiotic gestures. Previous practice of direct manipulation may promote such behaviours.

5.1.3 Human-computer cooperation (cf. paragraph 4.3)

Users who resort both to semiotic and ergotic gestures view the system as a twofold component:

- a graphical representation of the application on which they perform actions that have predictable effects on the application, so that they interpret the operations they perform on the graphical interface objects in terms of actions on the application objects;
- a cooperative agent who helps them to achieve their goals.

User interface design should encourage users to develop such a twofold representation of the system, since it may increase the efficiency of gestural or multimodal HCI by promoting the use of both ergotic and semiotic gestures. Appropriate recourse to semiotic or ergotic gestures may facilitate the expression of actions and commands, and increase the accuracy of the formulation and interpretation of gestures. The fact that subjects 1 and 2 met with the lowest failure rates as regards the expression of rotations (cf. Table 2) contributes to validating this assumption.

5.2 Perspectives

Further studies are needed on the factors capable of influencing users' gestural expression. Such studies should primarily focus on factors that could promote the use of both semiotic and ergotic gestures.

The influence of previous computer knowledge on users' forms of gestural expression should also be carefully investigated. In order to determine the scope of our conclusions, we are currently working on the design of an empirical study where the task, possibly a process control task, would induce subjects to supervise the execution of complex actions by the system instead of acting themselves on the application.

	Subj.	"Here/ There"	"like this"	Dem	Total	Σcom	%
profile 1	5	39	0	6	45	283	15.8
	7	34	15	13	62	322	
	8	30	3	9	42	342	
profile 2	3	58	8	10	76	510	12.0
	4	10	1	3	14	154	
profile 3	1	61	6	20	87	373	24.6
	2	91	6	14	111	429	
	6	3	1	13	17	379	4.48

Dem : Number of demonstratives used over the three sessions
ΣCom: Sum of commands over the three sessions
%: percentage of deictics = $\frac{Total}{\Sigma com} * 100$

Table 1: Use of deictics and demonstratives over the three sessions (per subject and profile)

	Subjects	Rot G	Rot M	Tor G	Tor M	Axes M	Vocal only	Total	%
profile 1	Subject 5	0	0	0	0	0	26	26	52.0
	failure	0	0	0	0	0	16	16	
	Subject 7	0	0	0	3	0	9	12	
	failure	0	0	0	2	0	3	5	
	Subject 8	0	5	0	3	4	24	36	
	failure	0	5	0	1	0	13	19	
profile 2	Subject 3	5	2	10	4	0	27	48	43.5
	failure	2	2	5	4	0	14	27	
	Subject 4	2	0	8	0	0	3	13	
	failure	0	0	2	0	0	2	4	
profile 3	Subject 1	0	6	1	9	0	22	38	34.3
	failure	0	2	0	2	0	8	12	
	Subject 2	1	7	1	4	0	14	27	
	failure	1	1	1	2	0	5	10	

Rot : circular arc (turning a piece of furniture)
Tor : screwing or pinching/grasping stamps
Axes : drawing the edges of the rotation angle
G : Gestural formulation only
M : Multimodal formulation
% : percentage of failure

Table 2: Formulation of rotations over the three sessions (per subject and profile)

References

[1] C. Cadoz. Le geste canal de communication homme/machine. *Technique et Science Informatiques*, 13(1):31–61, 1994.

[2] N. Carbonell and C. Mignot. Natural multimodal HCI: Experimental results on the use of spontaneous speech and hand gestures. In *Multimodal Human-Computer Interaction, ERCIM Workshop Report*, pages 97–112. Rocquencourt(F) : INRIA, 1994.

[3] N. Carbonell, C. Valot, C. Mignot, and P. Dauchy. Etude empirique: usage du geste et de la parole en situation de communication homme-machine. In *Ergo-IA'94 Ergonomie et Informatique Avance*, Biarritz, 1994. Bayonne(F) : IDLS.

[4] J. Cosnier. Communications et langages gestuels. In J. Cosnier, J. Coulon, A. Berrendonner, and C. Orecchioni, editors, *Les voix du langage, communications verbales, gestuelles et animales*, chapter 4, pages 255–304. Paris : Dunod, 1982.

[5] J. Coutaz and J. Caelen. A taxonomy for multimedia and multimodal user interfaces. In *Proceedings of the ERCIM Workshop*, pages 143–148, Lisbon Portugal, November 1991.

[6] P. Dauchy, C. Mignot, and C. Valot. Joint speech and gesture analysis – some experimental results on multimodal interface. In *EUROSPEECH'93*, pages 1315–1318, Berlin, September 1993.

[7] P. Ekman and W. V. Friesen. The repertoire of nonverbal behavior: categories, origins, usage, and coding. *Semiotica*, 1(1):49–98, 1969.

[8] C. Mignot. Usage de la parole et du geste dans les interfaces multimodales – tude exprimentale et modlisation. Doctorat de l'Universit Henri Poincar, Nancy, 1995.

[9] C. Mignot, C. Valot, and N. Carbonell. An experiment study of future 'natural' multimodal human-computer interaction. In *INTERCHI'93*, pages 67–69, Amsterdam, April 1993. New York : ACM Press, Addison Wesley.

[10] B. Rim and L. Schiaratura. Gesture and speech. In R. S. Feldman and B. Rim, editors, *Fundamentals of nonverbal behavior*, chapter 7, pages 229–238. Cambridge University Press, 1991.

[11] B. Shneiderman. The future of interactive systems and the emergence of direct manipulation. *Behaviour and Information Technology*, 1(3):237–256, 1982.

GRIGRI: Gesture Recognition on Interactive Graphical Radar Image

C. P. Mertz and P. Lecoanet

Centre d'Etudes de la Navigation Aérienne, Orly Sud B.P. 205,
95542 ORLY AEROGARE cédex, France

E-mail: {mertz, lecoanet}@cena.dgac.fr
Telephone: +33 1 69 57 71 00 Fax: +33 1 60 48 70 20

Abstract

GRIGRI is a 2D gesture based HMI (Human Machine Interface) for a future air traffic controller work position. 2D gesture recognition is used to enter commands and values. To evaluate the usability and problems of such a HMI, we have experimented GRIGRI with controllers. We present results of recognition, input time and controller feelings. The experiment demonstrates the real advantages of GRIGRI compared to mouse based HMI and also its current limits. It also gives us clues for future developments.

1 Introduction

We first introduce the current air traffic controllers' tasks and work positions. Afterwards we present the goals and means of GRIGRI experiment. Then we describe the dialogues specifications of the mock-up.

1.1 The Air Traffic Controller tasks

Air traffic controllers are in charge of flight security and of ensuring a good air traffic flow. Their task is to avoid any potentially dangerous proximity between aircraft and to allow, as far as possible a steady flow of traffic. They try to allow direct routes and flight levels with low fuel consumption according to the pilots' wishes.

Controllers work in pairs in close co-operation. They are responsible for a volume of airspace, so-called sector. Present work positions are based on four main tools. A radar display gives the position of each flight and its altitude, call sign, ground speed and previous positions during the last minute. Paper strips, automatically printed 10 minutes before aircrafts enter the sector, contain flight plan information (aircraft type, requested flight level, planned route composed by a list of beacons, etc.) On these paper strips, controllers write down as a reminder the orders they give to the pilots. A radio is used by the so -called tactical controller to send orders to the pilots. A telephone is used by the other controller, the planner, to co-ordinate flight transfer with previous and next sector.

Since the middle of the 80's, air traffic has been heavily increasing. Consequently, the controllers' workload has heavily increased too. Therefore, new controllers' work positions are under design [1] or development in Europe. These new work positions will be based on large colour screens (20"×20"). Electronic strips, updated according to flight progress, will replace the current paper strips. Information displayed on radar display will be enriched. Controllers will use a mouse and a mini-keyboard to enter instructions sent orally to the pilots. These input data will then be available for other controllers and to future intelligent tools.

CENA (the French Air Traffic Research Centre) is already studying the next generation of controllers' work positions. An experiment called GRIGRI studies the recognition of written marks (2D gestures) on a touch sensitive graphic screen.

1.2 GRIGRI objectives and means

The objectives of the GRIGRI experiment (Gesture Recognition on Interactive Graphical Radar Image) was to evaluate a 2D gesture based HMI (Human Machine Interface) with professional air traffic controllers. We wanted to evaluate both the operational feasibility and usability of such a kind of interaction, the problems related to the recognition algorithm, tactile input hardware, choice of 2D gesture set, learning, memorisation and new furniture to be used.

We used a touch screen, composed of a high resolution touch sensitive layer covering the surface of a 19" colour screen. The touch screen, fitted in a specially designed table to slant the screen, was the only input device used during the experiment (Figure 1). 2D gestures are one stroke marks which can be written with either a stylus or a finger. Our touch screen main drawback is that users are not allowed to lay their hand on the screen when they are writing. So writing on such a screen is clearly not so easy and quick as on a paper sheet.

After the experiment, we also used a graphic tablet (Wakom Art Pad, A5 size) instead of the touch sensitive layer. It allows us to test GRIGRI (so-called trials below) with an enhanced input device to overcome the current limitations of the touch screen. The user has to write on the tablet and no more directly on the screen.

To classify the drawn gestures, we used Rubine gesture recognition algorithm [5] as a writer-dependant classifier, to achieve good recognition rate. So users had to go through a gesture learning phase before using GRIGRI. They completed gestures libraries to train the classifier with a gesture learning tool.

1.3 Dialogue specifications

We focused on the tactical controller's task and chose to implement a radar image, where the controller has to input, through gestures and direct interactions, the orders he sends to the pilots and information he currently writes on paper strips. We did not implement electronic strips, but a new flight is shown in a flight list element which

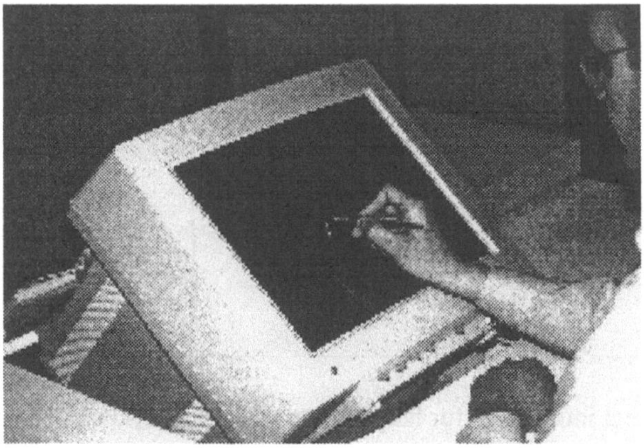

Figure 1: GRIGRI touch sensitive screen in its furniture.

disappears as soon as the controller assumed (that is, take under its responsibility and control) the flight.

Numerous dialogues [4] are possible on the radar image:

- global commands (like zooming and panning) are accessible through large buttons on the side of the tactile screen. This allows fast manipulation with fingertips. We do not develop these dialogues in this paper, as they are not gesture based.

- global commands like zooming or panning are also available with gestures. As an example, zooming starts by a Z drawn anywhere on the radar display and followed by a direct interaction. Then moving the stylus to (resp. from) the centre of the display shrinks (resp. enlarges) the radar image. The dialogue ends up at pen release.

- flight oriented commands applied to one flight, begin with a gesture (usually the first letter of a command name, e.g. S for speed instruction) drawn on the flight label. Commands are either atomic (e.g. Assuming an incoming flight) or need additional data. Values are then input either through direct interaction (for example, heading value) or numerical input (for example, speed and flight level values). All these commands may also be started by a horizontal mark drawn on specific flight label fields. This alternate way to start a command demands more pointing precision but is simpler to memorise.

- direct interaction is used for zooming as mentioned before, radar image panning, moving flights list and also for heading value selection with a rubber band indicating the value (Figure 2). These direct interactions start by a command gesture followed by a pen down, pen move and end at pen release. Another direct interaction is directly available on radar image. The controller can drag around a flight label to avoid flight label overlapping. The dialogue starts when

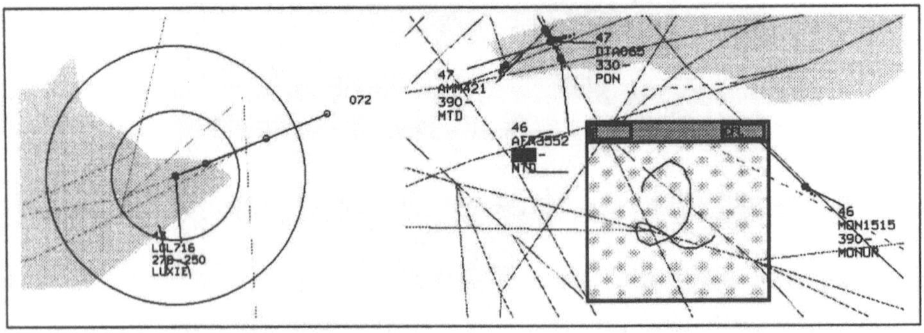

Figure 2: Direct interaction for heading input and numeric input for flight level.

the stylus touches the screen near the line joining the flight label to the current flight position. The dialogue ends at pen release.

2 Design issues

We present below clues which guided some of the design choices we made.

2.1 Gestures hot-spot

A command gesture drawn on the radar image indicates both the command and the subject or focus to which this command applies. The focus can be the full radar image (zooming or panning commands), a flight or more precisely a flight characteristic (such as speed or flight level instruction). The focus is designated by a target, and this target is pointed with the gesture hot-spot.

During the experiment we used as hot-spot of gesture, the centre of its bounding box. This seems natural for most controllers and worked fine for most command gestures which needed pointing. Yet some controllers get some trouble for large marks or unusual ones like (symbolizing a T) or even (gamma). For these marks the hot-spot is out of the desired target area in approximately 20% cases, even for a large target (approximately 8 characters long × 3 lines height).

A solution is to use the first point of the gesture as the hot-spot. This may seem unusual for some marks (for example a small horizontal mark used to point a little text field) and may need some training to be used. A consequence is that controllers do no longer have to adapt the size of gestures to the size of the target. This either enhances or lessens the recognition performance, whether the classifier use or not the gesture size as a significant feature in the gesture library. We have tried this solution with few controllers and its seems to work fine.

2.2 Gestures versus Direct Interactions

Direct interactions and gestures are interactions which can be ambiguous. In GRIGRI it is possible to use the pen for dragging a flight label around in order to avoid flight label overlapping. It is difficult to hit accurately the target due to parallax error and the lack of positioning feed-back (see below). But the main point is the ambiguity between gesture and drag. Sometimes controllers wanted to write a mark but started dragging the flight label. This is specially true if the gesture hot-spot is its bounding box centre since controllers started gestures near the sensitive field. Sometimes it happened to be the dragging line. This issue is dramatically reduced if the gesture hot-spot is the first point of the mark. In this case, the gesture first point designates either a gesture sensitive target or a direct interaction target and there is no longer ambiguity.

2.3 Choice of gestures

We tried, as far as possible, to choose natural gestures with the one stroke constraint. We used gestures like circling a text field, underlining it, and also first letter of words and acronyms that are well known by controller. As command gesture examples we used C for CFL, S for speed, h for heading.

However, some gestures were more difficult to use, so we decided before the experiment either to change them or reduce their use. Underlining a field was not really possible since they may be ambiguity when a field is just below another one. Thus we decided to strike a field instead of underlining it. In GRIGRI, circling a field is also difficult since the user could not lay his hand on the screen. So we reduced its usage. Yet, trials we did later with a graphic tablet (where the user can lay his hand on) demonstrates that circling is perfectly usable.

Less natural gestures were certainly some digits that people are used to draw in 2 or more strokes like 4, 5, 8, 9. So we forced controllers to change some of their digits drawing. A real gesture segmentation could overcome these limits, but we did not do it for this first experiment.

To reduce recognition failures, we split gestures in a command library (16 different classes of gestures) and a numeric input library (13 different classes of gestures). The latter was automatically used by the classifier during a numeric input.

3 Experiment results

The experiment [2] involved 12 volunteer air traffic controllers. Each of them spent a full day and was trained and observed by an ergonomist.

The morning was dedicated to learning and training. One hour was spent to give information and a first demonstration to the controller. Then he spent one hour and a half training the classifier with his own examples of gestures for both gestures libraries (approximately 20 examples of each of the 16+13 different classes). Training the classifier obviously helped the controller remembering gestures and dialogues. He then used GRIGRI during 1 hour with a control exercise, to learn the mock-up and the dialogues. The afternoon was dedicated to a one hour measured exercise. Then the controller answered a questionnaire and eventually he had the opportunity to comment his results and logged gestures. This gave us many explanations about difficulties faced by the controller during the experiment.

	Rate	Explanation
good recognition	80.6%	conformity to "human" choice
no recognition (technical problems)	10.3%	false touch or release, hardware of software limits, so the gesture is completely broken and "humanly" not recognisable
no recognition	7.9%	classifier does not recognise the gesture, but "human" does
false recognition	1.2%	"human" choice is different from classifier choice

Table 1: Raw recognition rates, based on every 5800 logged gestures.

	Rate	Explanation
good recognition	94.4%	conformity to "human" choice
no recognition	4.4%	classifier does not recognise the gesture, but "human" does
false recognition	1.2%	"human" choice is different from classifier choice

Table 2: Enhanced recognition rates, on every logged recognisable 5200 gestures.

We logged every gestures used for the classifier training and drawn during the measured exercises. We also recorded transactions (i.e. complete dialogues) and needed time for non atomic transactions. The ergonomist tagged recognition problems with 3 different keys of the keyboard. This helped us during logging analysis.

3.1 Recognition rates

Table 1 gives different recognition rates observed during the experiment, after a very careful analysis of every 5800 gestures logged during the 12 hours of the experiment.

Not recognised broken gestures, due to technical problems, were mainly due to the touch input layer limitations. The distance (1 to 2 cm) between the image (behind the cathode ray tube glass) and the surface of the sensitive layer makes it difficult for the controller to exactly estimate when the stylus really touches the sensitive layer. This often induces false touch and little artefacts at the beginning or end of gestures. As an example,  (alpha used as a cancel command) was sometimes written as 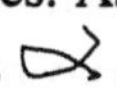 and thus could not be recognised. Input layer sensitivity defects also leads to false release of the stylus in the middle of a gesture.

After the experiment, we enhanced the classifier. On one hand we tried to cut off the artefacts occurring at the beginning and end of gesture by discarding first and last points under some angle and proximity conditions. On the other hand we filtered the points composing a gesture, by increasing the minimum allowed distance between successive points. Table 2 gives the recognition rates after applying these enhancements on every gestures logged during the experiment. However we exclude the 10.3% (600) broken gestures since they really were not recognisable.

These figures have not yet been verified through new experiments. However we have done some trials with a modified version of GRIGRI. Previous software limits have been corrected and touch input hardware limits were by-passed, by using a graphic tablet and its stylus. With these conditions, we get recognition rates very near from those given in Table 2.

3.2 Pointing precision

Command gesture designates the command subject or focus. About 20% of small horizontal marks drawn on small target (one line text fields of 3-6 characters) were wrongly positioned.

This was due to the distance between the image and the surface of the sensitive layer which caused parallax error. As the used sensitive layer is unable to detect stylus proximity we could not provide cursor position feed-back.

The graphic tablet we used for trials with GRIGRI, is able to detect stylus to tablet proximity which allows feed-back. As the graphic tablet and the screen were two completely separate devices, there was of course no parallax problem. So badly positioned gestures were reduced to 0.5% and were only due to radar update and flight label move just before the controller writes on the tablet. This gives us good clues on expected results on a perfect (no parallax, stylus proximity detection, hand lying on the screen) touch input screen.

3.3 Input duration

We measured numeric input duration. We logged the delay between opening of the numeric input tool and the end of numerical input, done by a validation mark. These delays include time really needed for numerical input, as well as time spent in possible discussion with the ergonomist (specially in case of recognition problem). As we did not video-record the experiment, it is not possible to have a good estimation of these possible additional delays. 289 such numerical input were logged during the experiment. The mean input time is around 9.5 s ($\sigma = 4.5$ s). Figure 3 gives the distribution of those numerical input times.

Table 3 gives mean delays in terms of number of errors. Number of errors in the first column is the number of unrecognised gestures and cancellation gestures. The latter were useful to cancel a wrong digit in case of false recognition. Needless cancellation gestures were often drawn by controllers in case of no recognition. In fact, the number of errors is exactly the number of gestures the controllers would not have to write with a perfect classifier.

Increase of errors logically results in increase of input duration. It is interesting to note that the appearance of a single error increases input duration by an average of 4 seconds whereas the apparition of additional errors results in input duration increases in the order of 2 seconds per error. The explanation is that the first input failure occurrence usually causes a slight surprise effect for controllers. This surprise effect is amplified by the low performance of the visual feedback (recognised numbers are displayed in a small field). After the first recognition error and first correction, subsequent recognition failure were more rapidly detected by controllers since they were already "on their guard".

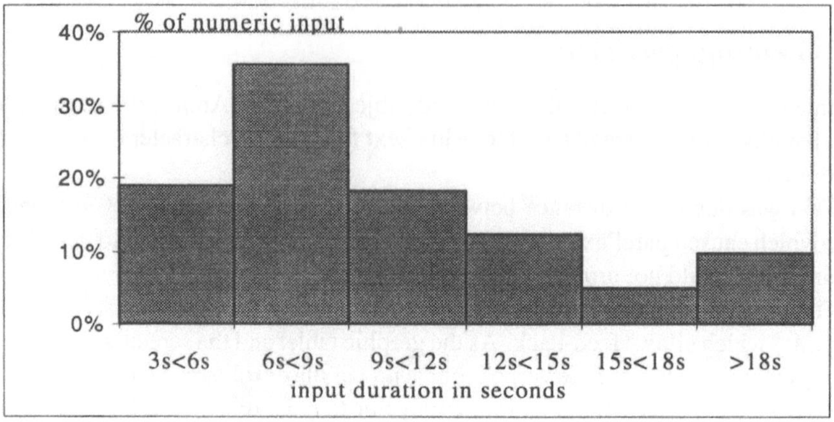

Figure 3: Numeric input delays distribution.

# errors	# inputs	mean input duration	σ
0	156	7.0 s	2.1 s
1	56	11.0 s	3.9 s
2	40	13.4 s	4.2 s
3	16	15.2 s	4.3 s
4	7	17.5 s	6.8 s
5	5	20.7 s	3.7 s
> 5	9	30.7 s	6.3 s
Total	289	9.5 s	4.5 s

Table 3: Mean numeric input duration in terms of number of errors.

3.4 Controllers qualitative perception

3.4.1 Learning curve

During the learning phase, the ergonomist instructed the controllers to write as naturally as possible. Yet all controllers were very careful and cautious during the learning phase. They wrote marks slowly, as they would do to teach a child. After using GRIGRI for 10 or 20 minutes, they became more confident in the classifier. So they began to write normally, that is more quickly than during the learning phase. Differences between learning gestures and real gestures decreased recognition rate. As a consequence, in the course of the experiment, we decided to split the learning phase in two steps. The second step was done after a first use of GRIGRI. This warranted that the classifier was fed by more natural gestures samples.

During the experiment, the gesture learning tool was a separate tool. After the experiment we decided to add a gesture learning mode to GRGRI. Easily switching between gesture learning mode and the tested HMI should dramatically reduce the delay needed by controllers to be comfortable with gesture recognition.

3.4.2 Recognition acceptability

Air traffic controllers are very sensitive to security issues. However, those who took part to the experiment, seemed to be quite confident with gesture recognition. They were aware of the experimental and long term aspect of GRIGRI. So they were less demanding than for a short term project.

Another explanation is that very few false recognitions lead to a mis-interpretation in the dialogue. False recognition of a command symbol was generally detected by GRIGRI as an "out of the context" command, that is a forbidden command due to the context. False recognition were more annoying for numeric input, even if controllers always detected the error. Syntactic verification could have been implemented, but this was deliberately not implemented for this experiment.

Controllers also felt that time and effort needed to re-write an unrecognised gesture was low enough in the context of the experiment. It seems, even if not proven, that the mental task load needed with such a gesture HMI was lower than with traditional mouse HMI.

3.5 Comparison of 2D gesture based HMI and mouse based HMI

Even if the mock-up suffers for both hardware and software limits, the experiment gave us interesting information.

3.5.1 2D gesture HMI drawbacks

Of course, the main potential weakness of a 2D gesture HMI is the recognition process. This gives the controllers the insecure feeling that the system may not understand them, or even mis-understand them (at least in some cases). Due to their high responsibility this is a real concern. Yet, mouse and keyboard are also prone to error. For example selecting a numerical value in a menu is precision demanding and may lead to pointing error.

An other drawback is the use in single-writer mode. This generally allows both better recognition rates and adaptation of the gesture library (specially digit gestures) to each controller. The problem is not that each controller has to complete a learning phase. The real difficult point appears in an operational context when we have to manage hundreds of differentcontrollers. It means that controllers have to be identified before using their tools. This is socially difficult and may be hardly applicable in every day real work for operational reasons.

Another difficult point with gesture classifiers, is to detect that a learning phase is not very good and should be extended. It is also difficult to foresee which gestures will be poorly recognised and which confusion could occur. We have not yet worked on these real problems, but we will have to prevent potential disappointing recognition rates.

3.5.2 2D gesture HMI advantages

2D gesture based HMI are very natural to controllers. It seems easier than mouse and mini-keyboard based HMI. They are many explanations.

1. The first reason is the likeness with current controllers practice. They currently write with a pencil or a pen on paper strips. They write both "standard" marks (like underlining or circling) and numeric marks. In GRIGRI, we tried to re-use, as far as possible, the same marks. Of course entering numeric value was also very similar (except for the one stroke limit). This makes the HMI more natural to controllers. Interacting directly on the image is more natural too than using an artefact like a mouse.

2. Learning new dialogues is also easier with gesture based HMI. It is obviously easier for a controller to remember that entering a CFL (cleared flight level) is started by a C mark on the flight label, rather than by simple-clicking with the mouse left button on a little field of the same flight label.

3. Writing on real paper enhances memorisation. This is a major advantage of paper strips. Even if not proven, we believe that writing electronic marks also helps the controller to remember the order he sends to a pilot. Several participants expressed this feeling too. This is very important, because it may cancel a potential drawback of electronic new HMI, that is a loss of memorisation capacity due to the use of a mouse and a mini-keyboard.

4. Gesture based HMI can appreciably decrease pointing precision requirement in comparison to mouse based HMI. To activate different commands, writing different marks on a large target like a flight label is clearly less precision demanding than mouse clicking on different smaller targets. This is a major point for air traffic controllers who work under strong time-pressure and stress.

All previous advantages (more natural dialogues, easier memorisation, less required precision) help alleviate the mental task load induced by the dialogues, in comparison to mouse based HMI.

The planner and tactical controllers of a sector work closely together. We believe that a touch input screen with gesture recognition may also enhance the collaborative work between both controllers. Such an input/output device, placed roughly between both work position may become a real shared tool. The current touch sensitive layer does not allow simultaneous impact, but it is already usable in an alternate mode by more than one user. This is a real improvement in comparison to the mouse which is impossible to be shared by two users. Such a collaborative tool also improves the awareness of each other controller activities. One controller can see, at every moment and at very little cost, what the other is doing on the screen (with his stylus or finger). This is very similar to current practice with paper strips and is quite impossible to do with a mouse based HMI. Of course such a usage of a gesture recognition based HMI needs either a multi-writer classifier or the identification of the current writer (may be through stylus identification). This is not yet implemented in GRIGRI, but it is already possible to share GRIGRI with another user, as an example of such a tool.

4 Future work

We currently plan two different evolutions of GRIGRI.

First, we want to approach a more realistic work position by using for radar image the large square (20"×20") display of next generation of controllers' work positions. With such screen the eye-to-screen distance should be around 70–80 cm [3], forbids writing on the screen. So we will use a graphic tablet for "head-up" input through both gestures and direct interaction. We will study to major points. Using a graphic tablet should facilitate easy writing by user and so gesture recognition should be better. The other issue is quick and easy pointing a flight which can be difficult because of the screen size. We will try to reduce as far as possible such precision requirement for the user.

Secondly, we also want to evaluate a 2D gesture based tool, similar to paper strips, which could be placed between two working controllers to help collaborative work. This tool will use a touch sensitive screen and will mimic the paper strips board. It should ease both electronic strips management and data input. Strip management should ideally be performed by direct interactions with the finger and data input through 2D marks written with a stylus.

Acknowledgements

GRIGRI was developed by Jean-Luc Dubocq and Frédéric Lepied. Jean-Luc also worked on logs analysis. Stephane Chatty provides ideas, help, advice and encouragements all along. Thanks to Lionel Maugis for providing helpful comments and help for English grammar.

References

[1] G. Amar. Final report. swift report. euret 1.5. Technical report, Commission of European Union, DG VII, Bruxelles, 1995.

[2] J. Garron. GRIGRI simulations results. Technical Report CENA/RR95027, CENA, Orly Sud B.P. 205, 95542 ORLY AEROGARE cédex, France, 1995.

[3] M. Giannacourou and G. Tsotsis. Rules for the anthropometric design. Swift report. euret 1.5, Commission of European Union, DG VII, Bruxelles, 1994.

[4] J. P. Labarthe. Initial integration of gesture recognition interface specifications. Technical Report CENA/R95001, CENA, Orly Sud B.P. 205, 95542 ORLYAEROGARE cédex, France, 1995.

[5] D. H. Rubine. *The automatic recognition of gestures*. PhD thesis, Carnegie Mellon University, 1991.

Semantic Representations of Situations that Fit their Description in a Sign Language

F. Forest
Language and Cognition Group, LIMSI, B.P. 133, 91403 ORSAY, France.

E-mail: forest@limsi.fr
Telephone: +33 69 85 80 58 Fax: +33 69 85 80 88

Abstract

My work addresses the problem of knowledge representation and its links to language. It is based on two hypotheses:

1. We learn by experience, that is to say we memorize a great amount of situations we have been involved in, while learning language.
2. Experience is memorized through spatio-temporal means which are nearer from the linguistic expression conveyed by sign languages (American Sign Language or French Sign Language) than from linguistic expression conveyed by the traditional linear vocal languages (English or French.)

In collaboration with A. Braffort who works on Sign Language recognition, and with a group of colleagues working on pragmatic knowledge representation based on individual experience, I propose a representation of these situations which compose the individual experience. In this approach, a situation is a set of segments in a five-dimension space. Each segment counts for an entity involved in the situation. The dimensions are three dimensions for space, one for the salience of each entity in the situation, and one for the time. Because sign languages are visual, and "draw" the situation in the space in front of the speaker, they offer an easier way of building such a representation.

Our final purpose is to be able to "understand" a sentence expressed in French Sign Language, ie to build the representation of the situation described in the sentence, using the information carried by the sentence, and also every information already memorized in the individual previous experience.

1 Introduction

We are interested in the way the gesture can enrich or transform classical knowledge representations mainly inspired by linear languages (i.e. logical representations, semantic networks, more generally symbolic approaches), and the way the gesture is bound to mental images, how its study could suggest computational models including topological and dynamic properties.

In the next section (Section 2), we shall present our approach of understanding, from an artificial intelligence point of view. Then we shall explain why gesture is so important in human communication, and how it contributes to the building of mental representations (Section 3).

In Section 4, the computational model called MoHA, in which understanding is to be simulated, will be described. The format we propose for representing the level of individual experience will then be detailed (Section 5).

After having listed the main characteristics of sign languages in Section 6, we shall describe the process of reconstruction of a situation which has been described in sign language (Section 7), and the different kinds of knowledge necessary for that reconstruction (Section 8).

2 How to model understanding?

2.1 The links between verbal information and spatio-temporal information

Our main hypothesis is that meaning is bound to the existence of an individual by whom some scene or sentence is perceived. Meaning involves several modes of representation of knowledge. Starting from perceptive information which is internalized, step by step, links are built with the words which are listened while perception is at work.

We set that perceptive information is firstly visual, and that there exists an ability to distinguish foreground from background. The links to verbal material are built all along one's individual experience, while learning and using words to explicitly verbalize what is ongoing in the scenes being observed.

2.2 The ontogenetic approach

Individual experience being central in our approach, it is of great interest to study how the notion of understanding comes to the infant. Literature proposes studies about the way infants and adults interact by tactile and vocal means, and show how, step by step, children go from designation gestures to significant ones, how the word takes place, at last, as an other mean for talking about missing entities [13]. To that point of view, pointing gestures are especially interesting ones. Following the infancy stage of communication, works of great importance have been developed about language learning by little children [10, 8]. We focussed our interest on the works carried out by Vygotsky about the links between learning and development [14].

2.3 A computational reformulation of Vygotsky's work

Vygotsky is a Russian psycholinguist who was living at the beginning of this century. He worked on the relation between thought and language, from an ontogenetic point of view. His thesis is that consciousness has social roots, and that the ability for the child to reach abstract level of thought has mainly its origin in the interaction with the adults with whom he/she interacts during his/her childhood. He showed how concepts grow, depending on their type, the spontaneous concepts emerging from the accumulation of individual experience, the scientific ones first encountered by the child through the perception of a verbal definition.

We have been especially interested in his description of the different stages through which concrete experience (what he calls the *complexes*) transforms to abstract notions (namely the mature concepts).

3 The original contribution of gestural expression

3.1 The importance of gesture in communication: diachronic versus synchronic aspects

Diachronic studies have shown the importance of gesture in the infant communication [13], as well as synchronic studies have shown it in adult communication [4, 3]. We shall now detail these two aspects.

3.2 The place of gesture in the infant's communication

It has been observed that gesture has, at first, no intentional meaning for the infant. But the reaction of the adult, little by little, gives rise to its usefulness in a given situation. It becomes, for the infant, a way of being understood and obey by the adult, that is to say "a sign" for communication. So we can say that a sound becomes a sign when a link is created by the infant between its utterance and a given state of the environment (present or becoming).

3.3 Coverbal gesture

Everyday interindividual communication gives lots of examples of the importance of coverbal gesture in a conversation. It can reinforce the verbal message, or deny it, it can gives information about the locutor's feelings. The most interesting aspect is for us its capacity of drawing part of the information, reinforcing what the verbal message was already saying, or adding some information to this message. For instance, when you talk about "a little boy", you may show his height with your hand.

3.4 Sign language gesture

The most attained communicative gesture is the gesture of the sign languages. Without any support from verbal information, it draws in space the message to be communicated. Such a possibility is for us its very interest. Because it exposes the situation from the "predicate" point of view, that is to say that it precisely situates in the space the participants of the process and the way they interact, it allows us to give a spatio-temporal representation of a situation almost naturally.

4 The framework of MoHA

MoHA (Modèle Hybride d'Apprentissage) is an hybrid model for learning knowledge through the learning of language. It can be divided into four levels. After having described rapidly the four of them, we shall focus on the basic one which is the one in which the perceptive experience is represented [1].

4.1 Four levels of representation

From perception of situations to integration of prototypic frames, the internal knowledge base is built step by step, new information being interpreted via the use of previous knowledge, and new knowledge contributing to the enrichment of previous one.

The experience level is represented by a net of situations, each situation or part of situation being linked to one or several words of the upper level, the words naming the entities and interactions involved in that situation. The semantic level emerges from the two lower ones by means of graph condensation which stands for emergence of adult concepts. The pragmatic level groups the prototypical situations which have emerged from the individual experience.

4.2 The situations viewed as the atomic parts in the individual experience

The perceived situations are the basic material from which the whole knowledge is to be built. What we know about infant acquisition of experience in interaction with the adults weighs in favour of a progression in the complexity of those situations [10]. At the beginning, the events only concern concrete objects, and the sentences are limited to isolated words. The way adults synchronize the saying of the word and the showing of the thing helps the baby to link both perceptions [13]. Our purpose is to represent a many of these situations, so that we can obtain a net of sufficient size to be able to operate significative condensation. We shall later give more detail about which representation we choose for the situations.

4.3 From the experience level to the semantic level, the central position of the word

The place of the word is central. If we leave apart the preceptive characteristics of the entity being observed, it is because of the use by the adult of the same word to designate different entities that the child builds what Vygotsky calls complexes. The complexes are sets of situations all refering to the same word, for instance the word "dog". They stand for concepts in the child's mind as long as he/she has not reached the level of adult concepts.

5 A spatio-temporal representation of the situations

5.1 Static versus dynamic situations

A situation is to be represented in two different formats, one of them is verbal, the other one has to be visual. Here is an example of a dynamic situation. We have drawn explicitly the different entities and their interaction.

A static situation is a situation in which no change is observed in the interaction of the different entities involved. It can be seen as a photograph. On the contrary, a dynamic situation can be viewed as a moving film. But both of them are built around a given number of entities which interact. A spatio-temporal representation of the entities and their interactions makes possible a survey of the different possible interactions, what Thom calls the archetypical morphologies.

5.2 The semiophysic hypothesis, cognitive archetypes

The cognitive archetypes are the different possible interactions between entities, from a topological point of view.

For instance, "to give" is viewed as the situation with three entities E1, E2 and E3 in the topological relations described in the figure. E1 and E2 keep separate during all the process. At first, E3 is in E1. At last, it is in E2.

5.3 A spatio-temporal representation of the situations

We propose to represent a situation as a set of points in a 5 dimensions space, as illustrated by the next example.

For concrete situations, the three first dimensions are spatial ones, the fourth is expressing the salience of each entity in the individual's mind, and the last is for time.

We think that this type of representation is also well fit for the non concrete situations. The dimensions count then for abstract ones, depending on the characteristics being visualized. The possibility of such a visual representation of abstract scenes is well known in sign languages. This is one more reason for us to choose sign language expression.

6 A few words about sign languages

To capture a sentence formulated in a sign language, we have to deal with three characteristics of that kind of expression [5, 6, 9].

6.1 Lexical signs: conventional but not arbitrary

The lexical signs are those you can find in a dictionary. A lexical sign can be described by its five components which are the configuration of the hands, their orientation, their position, their movement, and the mimic of the "speaker". It plays the same part as the word in linear languages. Following Vygotsky's theory, at a given stage of development it can be linked to an adult concept, at an earlier stage it is linked to a complexe.

6.2 Classifiers: a mean for representing the participants and their salient features

Classifiers are gestures that give information about some characteristic of the entity being described. They are also used to place the entities on the scene. For instance, with your two hands you can say which is the size of a box, or you can put two cars on a virtual road, one overtaking the other.

6.3 Syntax: a mean for drawing a situation in the space

Although different sign languages may use different lexical signs for the same notions, they all use the same syntax. The main rule is to put the background first, then to situate the participants, and at last to represent the interactions. Each participant is first named with a lexical sign and put on the spatial scene, on front of the speaker, then its characteristics are given using classifiers. When all the participants have been placed, the predicative form is expressed, using the same order. Of course, this decomposition is not so clear in everyday expression in deaf community. But our aim is not to simulate any sign language expression, so we shall make these simplifying hypotheses as long as they are not restraining for our objective.

7 The reconstruction of a situation

7.1 The capture of the gestures

The stage of capture of the gestural sentence is to be proceeded through a data glove device and a 3D localization device. This part of the work, carried out by Annelies Braffort, is presented elsewhere in the present workshop [2].

7.2 The detection of the entities involved in the situation

A sign language sentence being given, our objective is to recognize which entities are involved, and which are their interactions. The detection of an entity will be done through the recognition of its lexical sign, its place on the scene will be calculated from the orientation of the pointing gesture which is supposed to be expressed afterwards.

7.3 The detection of the predicate

The entities having been placed on the scene, the action will be expressed by a lexical sign and one or several pointing signs indicating which participants are concerned. All these informations are calculated, using the output data produced by the capturing devices.

8 The different kinds of knowledge

But separating signs, recognizing their type (lexical, classifiers, etc) is not always possible through the only analysis of the output signal from the recognition system. This is the reason why we include it in the MoHA system, as part of the developmental process of learning. The recognition system gains from the other kinds of knowledge already present in the learning model. For instance, the previous knowledge may suggest the choice of a meaning when a sign keeps ambiguous after the recognition stage. The exploration of memorized situations may give an indication about the verb being expressed in the sentence, or about the possible evolution of the situation being presently described.

Considering the integration of the recognition system in MoHA, we are able to list the different types of knowledge which participate at the building of the new situation

8.1 The sign sentence

This is the succession of signs, as it comes from the recognition system.

8.2 The lexical base

It covers two kinds of information about the signs. Firstly, physical information about the descriptive characteristics of the sign, what we could call "kinetic" information. Secondly, information about the signification of the sign, what could be called the "kinemic" information. One brings together the different measures coming from the capturing devices, the other permits the connection of the sign to all the previous situations where it has been used, to all the concepts it refers to, and to the words which can be considered as the different possible translations of the sign.

8.3 The semantic base

It roughly fits the semantic level of MoHA. Anyone familiar with classical approach to semantics may consider that it is the semantic network of the system, although it is of central importance for us not to consider a concept only like a node in a net. On the contrary, following Vygotsky, we assume that a concept is a structure, always changing, depending on the objective of the task in which it is invoked.

8.4 The previous experience (the situations base)

The situations base is the set of situations already present in MoHA at a given time. The complexes built around a given word are subsets of that set.

9 Conclusion

The general work is not achieved, although several parts of the model are now well specified.

The work described in the preceding sections more precisely reports to the lower level of the model. Its objective is to allow the double coding of knowledge (discrete and analogical) that psychologists such as Pavio suggest [7]. It necessitate to formulate the hypothesis of a perception which is already an interpretation, what we call a "cognitive perception". The analogical representation which we propose makes obvious the existence of morphological archetypes such as those described by R. Thom [11, 12]. The links between the situations in their analogical representation and the words which designate the entities and interactions occurring in them should allow, when numerous enough, the possibility of modelling the qualitative switch which brings the individual to the abstract level of adult concepts. This is the way we plan to model the central part Vygotsky gives to the word in the acquisition of thought and language.

References

[1] F. Bordeaux, F. Forest, and B. Grau. MoHA, a hybrid learning model: a model based on the perception of the environment by an individual. In B. Bouchon-Meunier, L. Valverde, and R. R. Yager, editors, *IPMU '92 – Advanced methods in artificial intelligence*, number 682 in Lecture Notes in Computer Science. Springer-Verlag, 1993.

[2] A. Braffort. ARGo: An architecture for sign language recognition and interpretation. In *this book*, 1996.

[3] G. Calbris and J. Montredon. *Des gestes et des mots pour le dire*. CLE International, 1986.

[4] J. Cosnier and Brossard. Communication non-verbale, co-texte et contexte. In *Textes de base en psychologie*, pages 10–26. Delachaux et Niestlé, Paris, 1984.

[5] C. Cuxac. *Le langage des sourds*. Payot, Paris, 1983.

[6] C. Cuxac. L'icônicité dans la langue des signes. In *VENACO*, 1993.

[7] M. Denis. *Image et cognition*. PUF, Paris, 1989.

[8] Lambert and Rondal. *Le mongolisme*. Pierre Mardaga, Brussels, 1979.

[9] B. Moody. *La langue des signes*. Ellipses, Paris, 1983.

[10] J.-A. Rondal. *L'interaction adulte-enfant et la construction du langage*. Pierre Mardaga, Brussels, 1983.

[11] R. Thom. *Stabilité structurelle et morphogénèse*. Interéditions, Paris, 2nd edition, 1977.

[12] R. Thom. *Esquisse d'une sémiophysique*. Interéditions, Paris, 1991.

[13] A. van der Straten. *Premiers gestes, premiers mots*. Bayard Presse, Paris, 1991.

[14] L. S. Vygotsky. *Thought and language*. MIT Press, Cambridge, 1962.

The Development of a Glove-based Input System as part of the Sign PS Project

J. Cracknell, C. Ramsay, A. Cairns, P. Gregor and I. Ricketts

The MicroCentre, University of Dundee, Dundee, UK

E-mail: jcrackne@mic.dundee.ac.uk
Telephone: +44 1382 344146 Fax: +44 1382 345509

Abstract

This paper will describe the techniques used by a glove-based sign input system for the extraction of sign parameters such as handshape, location, orientation and movement. The hardware used consists of a pair of Virtual Technology Cyber-Gloves, coupled with a Polhemus position monitoring system.

This research forms part of the Sign PS project, which is a European project funded under TIDE (The Technology Initiative for the Disabled and Elderly). The consortium consists of 5 partners; 3 based in the Netherlands, one in Germany and Dundee University in the UK. The work focuses on the development of a printing system, which will allow users to write documents using signs as input. There are several components to the system; a font to allow the 2-dimensional representation of signs; an editor to allow users to create and edit documents written in signs; a glove-based input system; a video-based input system; and also a sign prediction system to improve the accuracy and efficiency of the overall package.

1 Sign PS description

The Sign Recognition work described in this paper and accompanying poster forms part of a collaborative venture between five European partners: the SignPS project. SignPS is a Research and Development project funded by the European Community as part of the TIDE programme. The project consortium consists of:

- **IRV**, the Netherlands, Research Institute, Project Co-ordinator
- **LTI**, Aachen University of Technology, Germany, Research
- **MicroCentre**, University of Dundee, Scotland, Research Institute
- **RNR**, the Netherlands, Commercial Partner
- **Handicom**, the Netherlands, Commercial Partner.

The objective of the project is the development of a Printing System for Sign languages.

Sign languages form the first (and sometimes only) language for deaf people all over the world. Most deaf people also learn to read and write - but only in the language of the hearing community. It is comparable to having English as your mother tongue, yet using German for reading and writing. For many reasons, deaf and hearing sign language users may want to read their own language also.

To this end SignPS is investigating the recognition, prediction and representation of signed information. The system components are:

- A Sign Font which will enable signs to be represented graphically, e.g. a collection of small pictures of handshapes, facial expressions, and arrows to indicate movement.

- A Sign Editor which will allow the user of the system to create a representation of any sign they require by selecting and grouping the various elements of the Font to their liking and storing it in a database.

- A Document Editor which will allow the user to create documents full of sign pictures, optionally combined with textual information, in various formats. Standard word processing options will be available, e.g. cut and paste, and modify/edit signs (using the Sign Editor).

- Various input devices are being investigated to allow the user of the system to enter sign language information whilst creating a document and/or editing signs. These are an on-screen device which uses keyboard and mouse and more specialised devices which will present more natural signing methods: a video-based system and a glove recognition system.

- A Prediction and Completion System which employs knowledge of the usage and structure of signs to aid the specialised input devices in recognising sign information and which will also reduce user effort by predicting signs based on incomplete input parameters

This paper focuses on the glove recognition system. The hardware used for the glove recognition system consists of a pair of Virtual Technology CyberGloves (18 sensors), coupled with a 3Space Polhemus position monitoring system. These are connected to a 486 PC running Windows NT. A sample rate of 30–40 Hz was used.

1.1 Parameters

The parameter set used by the Sign PS system is shown below (Tables 1 and 2). This system is used by the SignPS modules to describe the manual elements of any sign. The static parameters shown below relate only to a single hand, whereas the dynamic parameters refer to the sign as a whole rather than a particular hand.

The parameters can broadly be separated into static and dynamic parameters. It is generally true that the value of the static parameters will be calculated directly from the data supplied by the hardware, whereas the dynamic parameter values will be calculated from the values of a sequence of static parameter values. For example, the

	Handshape	Palm Or.	Finger Or.	Location Body Part	Side	Distance
Starting	✓	✓	✓	✓	✓	✓
Ending	✓	✓	✓	✓	✓	✓

Table 1: Static parameters.

Repeat Handshape	Repeat Orientation	Contact Marker
Repeat Location	Path	Contact
Joint	Manner	Non-Dominant Hand Action

Table 2: Dynamic parameters.

value of *Non-dominant hand action* is calculated by comparing the parameters for the dominant and non-dominant hands.

2 System design

The design of the parameter extraction modules is shown in Figure 1. This process is split into three sequential phases: static parameter extraction; dynamic parameter extraction; and a final phase of parameter extraction. Each of the first two stages contains a number of concurrent units.

2.1 Static parameter extraction

The raw data provided by the gloves is processed by the extraction modules into a stream of corresponding parameter values. For example for handshape, a stream of parameter values would be produced incorporating not only the initial and final handshape values, but also all of the intermediate values as well. This stream of handshape parameter values is then passed to the dynamic handshape extraction module.

2.2 Dynamic parameter extraction

A dynamic extraction unit will attempt to establish a pattern within the stream of parameter values passed to it by the corresponding static parameter extraction module. For example given the stream of static handshape parameter values described above, the dynamic handshape extraction unit would try to establish the initial and final handshapes from this data, and also if there were any repetitions of this change within this stream, and if so, how many.

The output from the dynamic parameter extraction stage is a set of parameter values, which are passed to the packaging unit (see below).

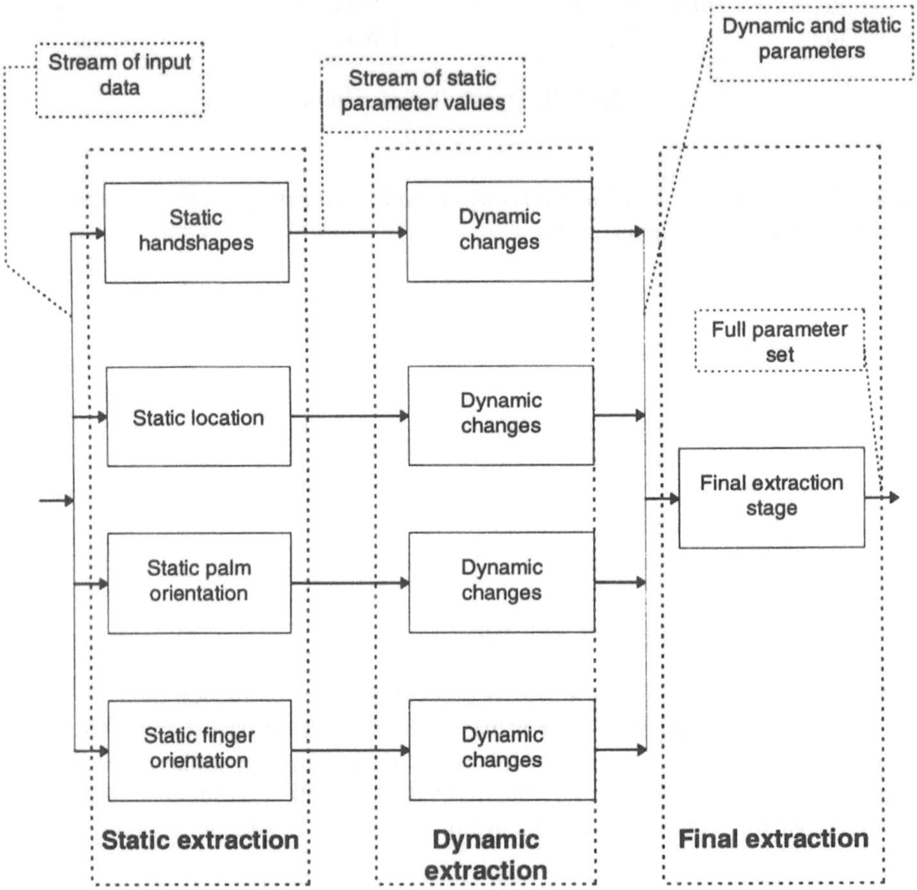

Figure 1: Internal components of the recognition module.

2.3 Final parameter extraction

Some of the parameters can only be calculated knowing the values of several other parameters. For example 'contact' would require knowledge of not only the location of the hands, but also their orientation and handshape. Thus a final stage of processing is required, which can incorporate the values of other parameters as part of the input data. The input for this stage is the parameter values calculated by the previous extraction units. The output (a subset of the full set of parameters) is passed to the packaging unit for onward transmission.

3 Static Parameter Extraction

This paper focuses on the techniques employed for static parameter extraction, namely handshape, location and orientation.

3.1 Handshape

Handshape is extracted using a rule-based approach developed jointly with LTI. The basic rules were designed to represent all of the handshapes in the three sign languages pertinent to the project (British Sign Language, German Sign Language and Sign Language of the Netherlands), using a number of low-level features.

Each institute then adapted the rules so that they fitted the characteristics of the respective hardware. For example, LTI are developing a video based system so rules relating to the visibility of parts of the hand were included. These were obviously not applicable to the glove system so rules relating to the capabilities of the glove system were added.

The process of extracting sign parameters consists of two stages. Initially the pre-calibrated data is converted into a set of qualitative features, using fuzzy logic. Each of these features can take one of a pre-defined set of values. For example, each finger joint has a feature relating to its crookedness. This can take one of the following values; straight, bent or crooked.

Once all of the features have been extracted, the rule-base is applied. This categorises all of the handshapes in BSL, GSL and SLN. Some example rules are shown in Figure 2.

3.2 Orientation (palm and finger)

Although palm and finger orientation are separate parameters a method was developed which calculated both concurrently. The data concerning orientation is supplied by the Polhemus sensor attached to the wrist of the CyberGlove. To calculate the finger and palm orientations additional data concerning the yaw and pitch of the wrist is required. This data is supplied by the CyberGlove itself. The values supplied each represent an angle of rotation about a specific axis.

The extraction method developed uses 3-dimensional geometry to calculate the position of a unit cube, of fixed origin as shown in Figure 3, after five sequential rotations have been applied to it. The final position of the cube is then used to calculate the

```
if((forefpos_mpj == STRETCHED || forefpos_mpj == BENT)
   &&(middpos_mpj == STRETCHED || middpos_mpj == BENT)
   && (ringpos_mpj == STRETCHED|| ringpos_mpj == BENT
         || ringpos_mpj == CROOKED)
   && (pinkiepos_mpj == STRETCHED || pinkiepos_mpj == BENT))
{
   if(dist_thumb_toforef == SMALL)
   {
      if(contact_allfing == ADDUCTED)
      {
         if(thumb_ij == BENT || thumb_ij== CROOKED)
         {
            *hand_type = 72;
            if(thumb_ij == STRETCHED)
               *hand_type = 73;
          }
          else
          if(contact_allfing == ABDUCTED)
              *hand_type = 76;
      }
      else
      if(dist_thumb_toforef == LARGE)
      {
         if(contact_allfing == ADDUCTED)
          {
              if(thumb == EXTENDED)
               *hand_type = 74;
         }
       }
   }
}
```

Figure 2: Example rules.

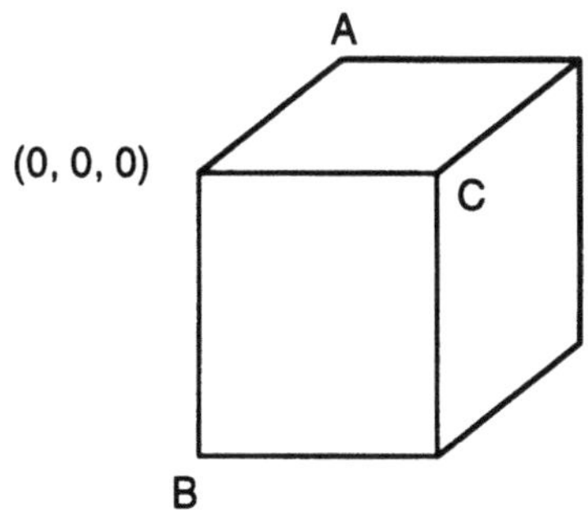

Figure 3: Orientation unit cube.

orientation values. The first three rotations use the data supplied by the Polhemus to calculate the orientation of sensor, and then the wrist flex values are used to calculate the final orientation of the hand itself.

The vectors OA and OB represent the finger and palm orientations respectively. Vector OC is analogous to a line running through the wrist. Initially the cube is as shown above, with the fingers pointing forwards and the palm facing straight down. It is then rotated in the following manner

- **Azimuth** This refers to a rotation of the hand about axis OB.
- **Elevation** This refers to a rotation of the hand about axis OC.
- **Roll** This refers to a rotation of the hand about axis OA.

Following these rotations the cube represents the position of the Polhemus sensor. To modify this to accurately represent the position of the hand the following rotations are applied.

- **Wrist Yaw** This refers to a rotation of the hand about the axis OB.
- **Wrist Pitch** This refers to a rotation of the hand about the axis OC.

The following equation was used to calculate the position of the cube following each rotation (Equation 1).

$$\begin{bmatrix} x_1 \\ x_2 \\ x_3 \end{bmatrix} = \begin{bmatrix} (1-2b^2)-2c^2 & 2ab-2sc & 2ac+2sb \\ 2ab+2sc & (1-2a^2)-2c^2 & 2bc-2sa \\ 2ac-2sb & 2bc+2sa & (1-2a^2)-2b^2 \end{bmatrix} = \begin{bmatrix} x'_1 \\ x'_2 \\ x'_3 \end{bmatrix} \qquad (1)$$

where (x'_1, y'_1, z'_1) is the result of rotating the point (x_1, y_1, z_1) by ϕr radians about the axis OA. In the rotation matrix above $s = \cos\frac{\phi}{2}$, $a = x_2 \sin\frac{\phi}{2}$, $b = y_2 \sin\frac{\phi}{2}$, $c = z_2 \sin\frac{\phi}{2}$ and A is the point (x_2, y_2, z_2).

Having calculated the final position of the unit cube, the last task is to turn the locations of A and B into the relevant orientation values. To do this a simple filtering process is used. The Sign PS parameter values consist of a combination of Up, Right and Forward components. For example, with the hand held forward inorder to shake someone else's hand, one would say that the *finger orientation* was Forward only, while the *palm orientation* had a negative Right component only. The filtering process consists of defining the regions of a sphere that contain all possible combinations of the parameter values, and then simply determining which regions the points A and B lie in.

3.3 Location

Hand location is specified using a combination of 3 parameters: body-part, side and distance. These refer to the body part that the hand is nearest to, which side of that body part the hand is on, and how far from the body part the hand is. For example, for the BSL sign '**what**': body part = torso, side = none, distance = middle, whereas for ' '**know**': body part = forehead, side = dominant, distance = close/touching.

To calculate location two calibrations are needed. The first is a calibration of the user, developing a 'body map'. This is performed once and involves a record being made of the user's dimensions. The other calibration is required at every session and is used to determine the position of the user with respect to the Polhemus source. Because the sensor positions are supplied by the Polhemus with respect to the source, this information is needed to ascertain how these relate to the user. Such a technique requires that the user stay reasonably still during each session.

To develop the body map, measurements are taken of the distance of various body parts from a central point. The central point is taken to be the point midway between the elbows when the arms are held by the user's side. This usually lies somewhere around the navel area. Using this point as the origin the three-dimensional positions of locations such as the crown of the head, the shoulders, armpits, throat and so on are taken. These values are then used to divide the body into a number of different regions which correspond to the parameter values required.

One feature of a location parameter set such as the one used in the Sign PS system is that user's perception of distance varies depending on which part of the body the hand is closest to. There are 4 values that the distance parameter can take: *touching*, *near*, *middle* and *far*. When the hand is around the head the boundaries between these areas are closer than when the hand is around the body. For example, if the hand were 30cm from the face this could be considered *middle*, whereas if the hand were 30 cm from the body it may be considered *near*.

In addition to this, the resolution of the body part parameter changes depending on the distance of the hand from the body. For example, if the hand were 'far' from the head, the *body part* parameter value would simply be 'head'. If the hand lay in the 'middle' region it would be necessary to specify whether the hand was related to the 'upper head' or 'lower head'. As the hand enters the 'near' region it could be related to say the 'dominant eye' or the 'mouth', and as it touches the face this reduces further to 'upper lip' or 'lower lip'.

This means that the process of calculating location can be expressed as shown below. This interdependence of parameters is not ideal, but cannot be avoided with such a parameter coding system.

1. **Does the hand relate to the head, body or other hand?**
2. **Calculate the distance parameter based on the answer of 1.**
3. **Calculate the body part based on the combination of 1 and 2.**
4. **Calculate side parameter.**

4 Future plans

The techniques for static parameter extraction described above are currently being tested, and results are expected in the near future. Initial indications are promising, with the handshape recognition module correctly identifying 71 out of the 86 total handshapes. The failures were due to an inability to distinguish between contact and non-contact forms of the same handshape (10 handshapes), and also because some of the handshapes (5 handshapes) are dynamic and can therefore not be recognised by a system designed for static parameter extraction only.

Future work will focus on techniques for extracting the dynamic parameters from the streams of static parameters. It is expected that a technique such as Hidden Markov models, or Recurrent Neural Networks will be used. In addition experiments with mounting the Polhemus source on the user's body by means of a harness may be investigated.

Synthesis of Hand-Arm Gestures

T. Lebourque and S. Gibet
LIMSI-CNRS, BP 133, 91405 ORSAY Cedex, France

E-mail: {lebourqu, gibet}@limsi.fr
Telephone: +44 1382 344146 Fax: +44 1382 345509

Abstract

This paper presents a model that generates natural hand-arm movements. A simple command, specified in terms of successive target end-points is translated through the control model into a complete movement trajectory. This high-level command provides an easy way to describe and manipulate sequences of gestures. Moreover, by its nature, the command tends to a symbolic gesture specification that can be extended to obtain a qualitative description of gestures.

1 Introduction

Human gesture production with communication purpose is a new active research field. A traditional approach uses pre-calculated gesture sequences that are played when needed [7].

Our aim is to generate communication gestures using an inverse kinematics method, but without heavy calculation and fastidious specifications usually used in classical approaches [3, 2, 4, 10]. We keep a strong link between natural gestures analysis and synthesis that allows us to validate our results, and provide information about human gesture in communication context.

Our approach is based on a self-organised system that generate motion of a human arm from a high-level command specification. Generated motions have emergent properties corresponding to those of human natural gestures. Users can then focus more on the motion itself than on its kinematics aspects. The model command is composed of a set of spatial positions (key positions that we call targets) that the arm end point has to reach or come close to, depending on a precision parameter. The command can be specified interactively, but we are working on an automatic targets extraction method from natural samplings.

Using this model, we work on a higher level gesture specification leading to a gesture specification computer language. For the moment, we can specify sequences of targets with their properties. We could compose these sequences together by specifying the way they are modified (translated, rotated or resized, for example) or linked to create gestures sequences. Then, we will be able to produce sign language gestures automatically by the way of an interpreter and production rules.

2 The model

The basic model has been designed for the motion control of articulated bodies, and has been adapted for the hand-arm gestures. Inside this model, we can distinguish two control levels by the nature of the signals transiting in each of them:

- a continuous level where we can find data involved in the arm control, updating the arm's state vector to produce planned movements,
- a discrete level composed of a set of goals evolving in time and space which will provide the command for the arm.

The first level is internal and automatic, the second one is the command level and is given to the system.

2.1 The sensori-motor model

This is a self-organized model [9, 11], and it is composed of three parts:

- The hand-arm system represented by a skeleton. It is modelled as an articulated geometrical system with several segments (Figure 1).

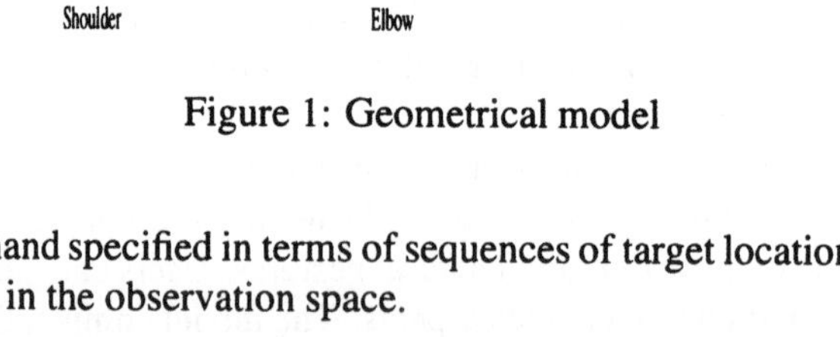

Figure 1: Geometrical model

- The command specified in terms of sequences of target location or angle configuration a_T in the observation space.
- The control system whose input is a quadratic function E of the error between the desired a_T and the actual a arm location, and the output is the joint angles state coordinates q (Figure 2).

The hand-arm system is modelled with a nonlinear function expressing the transformation law between the joint angles q and the position of the extremity of the arm a. In the proposed simulation, we considered a three-segments arm with seven degrees-of-freedom. The last segment is associated to the hand and has two degrees-of-freedom

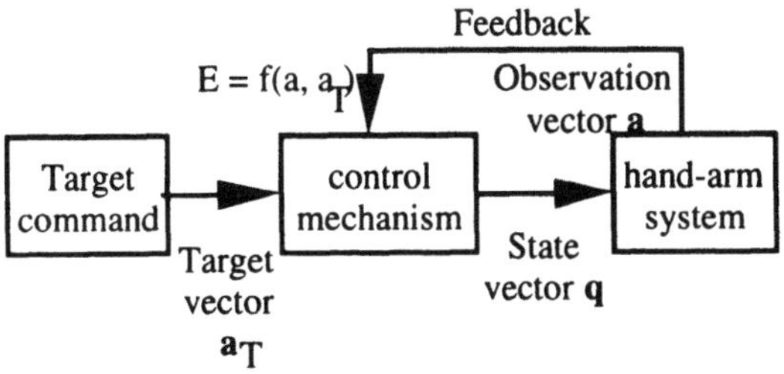

Figure 2: Control model

relatively to the wrist. Furthermore, each finger is modelled with three segments and is associated with four degrees-of-freedom.

This closed-loop model uses feedback from the observation space (Cartesian coordinates) to adaptively update the joint angles of the geometrical hand-arm system. It solves the inverse kinematics problem of finding the joint angle trajectories to achieve a desired end-point position. The proposed solution does not try to calculate the inverse transformation analytically. Instead, the method used is based on a principle of minimal effort, which corresponds to the minimization of a potential function. From an initial equilibrium state, a new target is specified and the dynamic system evolves toward a new stable equilibrium state, which minimizes the error between the current end-point position and the target position. The originality of our approach, compared to the ones used in Robotics, lies in the addition, into the control loop, of a nonlinear "sigmoïd" function. This sigmoïd function has two main influences:

- it increases the convergence of the algorithm in the vicinity of the minimum,
- it gives rise to natural behaviours of the whole system [5].

In the case of angular control, targets are specified in terms of angular configurations, and the error is computed between the current configuration and the desired one. The previous minimisation process is then applied.

Finally, the model is very efficient, since the same kind of sensori-motor loop is used to animate the arm system and each finger of the hand. Therefore, it can be used in real-time applications.

2.2 The target notion

As we explained before, a gesture is specified with a sequence of targets. A target is either spatial position that the arm's end point has to reach more or less precisely, or an angular configuration giving the arm's "shape", also with a precision parameter.

Moreover, we need additional data to control temporal or synchronisation parameters. Temporal information (when a does target become active) can be automatically computed using Fitts' law [8], but it is possible to specify it explicitly if necessary.

As the geometrical system is composed of an arm and a hand, we will need to control movements of two articulated bodies. These movements can occur simultaneously (like the fingers movements) or sequentially. For the moment, we focus on the

Figure 3: The French Sign Language that means "scarf"

movement of the hand relatively to the arm: when does the hand movement begin in relation to the arm movement?

Take, for example, the sign that means "scarf" in French Sign Language (Figure 3). At the beginning of the movement, the hand is in a closed configuration, and is open at the end of the movement. The opening of the hand occurs in the middle of the arm's movement.

This synchronisation problem is currently solved by the addition of a synchronisation primitive attached to the targets. The arm is used as synchronisation "master", that is to say that the hand's movement occurs relatively to the arm's one. In the previous gesture (Figure 3), three targets are needed to reproduce the arm's movement, and the synchronisation parameter is attached to the second target.

2.3 Generated gestures

We will present here two kinds of generated gestures : simple pointing gestures and cyclical movements. Psychomotor results are used to show that the model defined above satisfies natural rules of the movement.

For simple goal-directed movements, we consider the Fitts' law which expresses a general relationship between time and space [8]. In addition, we use the fact that the velocity profiles are approximately bell-shaped [5, 14], and present an asymmetry which depends on the speed of the movement.

The results for simulated data are shown on the Figures 4 and 5.

For cyclical movements, we use a cinematic law [5, 14] expressing a relationship between the tangential velocity and the radius of curvature of the movement: $V(t) = KR(t)^{\frac{1}{3}}$.

This rule has been verified for our model with cinematic data extracted from the simulation of a five cycles movement, as shown on the Figure 6.

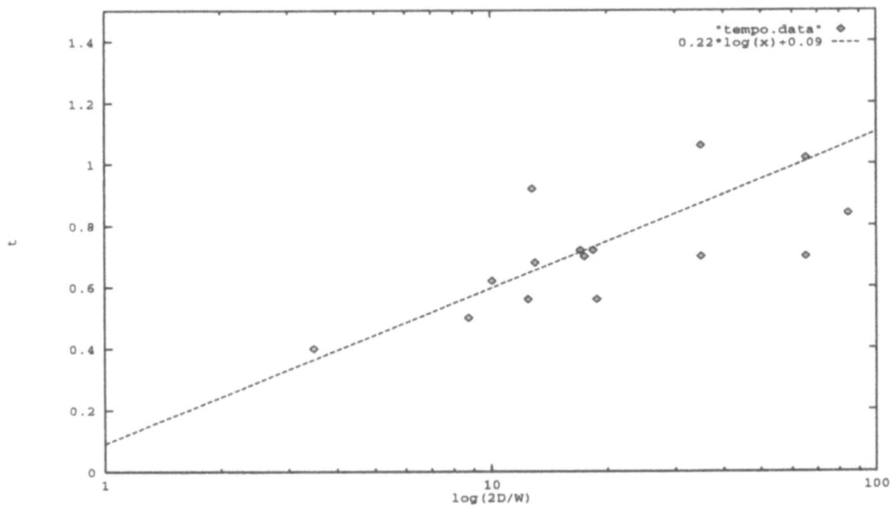

Figure 4: Fitts' law $T = a + b\log_2(2D/W)$, where T is the movement duration, D the distance between end-point location and the target, and W is the target width (equivalent to an accuracy).

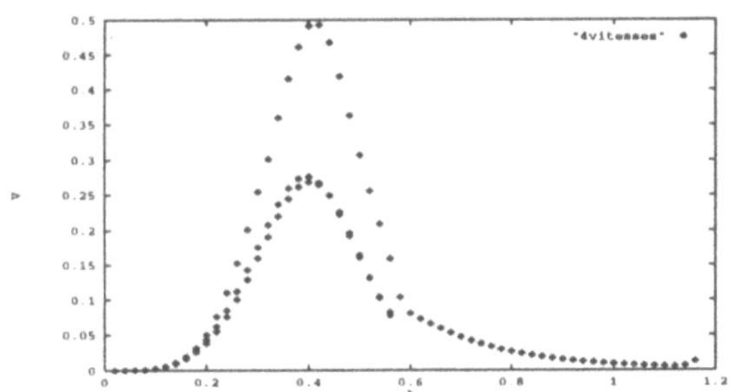

Figure 5: Shape of velocity profiles

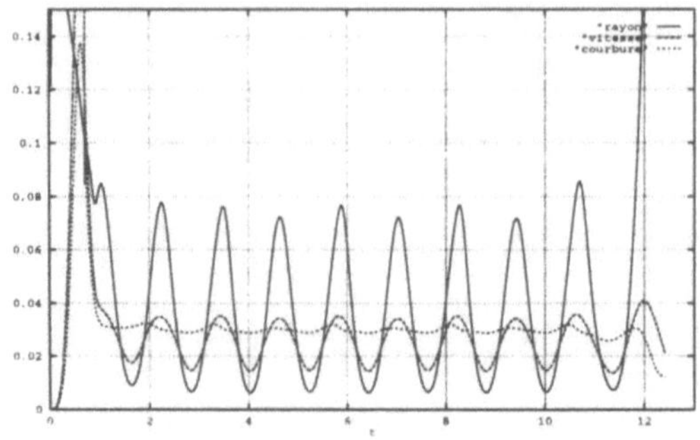

Figure 6: Relationship between the tangential velocity and the radius of curvature. The nearly straight curve represents the K coefficient.

3 Toward high level specification of gestures

For the moment, one of the main difficulties of an articulated body's movement specification arises from the command nature. Movement is given in terms of angular variations in the case of a geometrical model, and in terms of force and torque in the case of a dynamic model. It is hard to handle directly this kind of data because they are not in the same representation space than the movement itself. Another method consists in providing the whole trajectory with cinematic informations, angular or torque command being computed by approximation methods [1, 6]. But, in this case, the amount of information to handle becomes great.

3.1 Interactive edition

We have developed an interactive tool for the command specification. It allows to position spatial targets and to manage their parameters through a graphical editor. The tool is composed of a part dealing with the targets position, and a set of functions dedicated to the edition of parameters like timing or synchronisation. The interaction is mainly realised with the mouse and the classical three views (front view, side view, above view). The command can be tested at any moment via the movement execution unit. One can then easily create a gesture by repeating the process of edition/execution until the desired gestures is obtained.

3.2 Automatic target extraction from natural gestures samplings

The edition can be entirely in charge of the user, but it is also possible to work from real gestures. We are currently working on a software which will automatically extracts targets from human gestures samplings.

This software will place targets in space using kinematics criteria (detection of singularities in trajectories). The targets will be, if necessary, re-edited to adjust parameters. It will be possible to reproduce gestures or portions of gestures from natural gestures samplings.

3.3 Command specification

Whatever the way they are produced, command files respect a particular syntax which allows us to describe all the parameters necessary for the generation system's command. These parameters are:

- the target type (angular or spatial),
- target value (coordinates or angular values),
- precision,
- timing (if the default timing value is not acceptable),
- and the synchronisation parameter (target number).

At this point, we can specify targets. A gesture specification is a sequence of targets, described with the previous language. This sequence gives the shape of the gesture to execute. Using some geometrical operators (such as rotation, translation) or "structural" operators (such as concatenation of targets sequences), the language can be extended to lean toward a gesture specification language. This language would allow us to avoid quantitative description of the movement, and use a more qualitative one. This work starts from the study of Sign Language notation systems like HAMNOSYS [13].

4 Sign language gestures

Sign language gestures can be entirely characterised by five parameters: the hand shape, the hand orientations, the location, the movement and the other body information [12]. The proposed model is relevant for taking into account these different features of gestures.

Basic *hand shape form* (fist, flat hand, separated fingers, thumb combination) are realised by specifying an angular target or each finger at the command level. Bending, flattening, rounding or sharp bending are thus obtained through the specification of target vectors. In the same way, the *orientation* of the hand, which is conveyed by the wrist, the direction of the extended fingers and palm orientation, is carried out through the specification two wrist-angles and one elbow-angle in the arm model. The *locations*, which refer to areas on the body, correspond to spatial domains in the Cartesian space around the person. Finally, the *movement* is carried out automatically through the succession of targets in space and time.

The model, for the moment, does not take into account other body information such as head, lips or eyes movements, or facial expressions.

5 Conclusion and perspectives

This method provides a solution to the problem of natural gesture animation, which proves to be computationally very efficient. The proposed model has several interesting features which might help us to understand quantitatively how the hand-arm system achieves numerous flexible movements with simple goal-directed strategies.

With such a model, sign language gestures can be easily described as sequences of targets in time and space. In addition, the movements produced keep some interesting properties of human gestures, leading to a realistic and expressive gesture animation.

However, a complete model of sign language generation requires the extension of the model to the modelling of body and head movements, and facial expressions.

This model can be used in various implementations. Among these, two are of particular interest, for assisting the deaf:

- An interactive computer lexicon of sign language. Each gesture might be created, modified, and represented through a computer animation. At the moment, lexicons in sign language are documents that are not exhaustive, and gesture is represented by small drawings. The addition of new vocabulary seems rather difficult. The model proposed above is particularly adapted to the gesture edition through its command structure in terms of spatial specifications.

- A tool for learning sign language from text in natural language and/or learning natural language from sign language specifications.

Both of these applications require the development of a higher command level which would be able to deal with the gestural semantics.

References

[1] N. I. Badler and C. B. Phillips. Interactive behaviors for bipedal articulated figures. *Computer Graphics*, 25:359–362, 1991.

[2] R. Boulic et al. Goal-oriented design and correction of articulated figure motion with the track system. *Computer Graphics*, 18:443–452, 1994.

[3] R. Boulic and D. Thalmann. TRACK: a kinematic goal-oriented animation system for coordinated editing of joint-space based motions. Technical report, Cambridge, England, 1992.

[4] A. Bruderlin et al. Procedural movement for articulated figure animation. *Computer Graphics*, 18:453–461, 1994.

[5] D. Bullock and S. Grossberg. Neural dynamics of planned-arm movements: emergent invariants and speed accuracy properties during trajectory formation. In S. Grossberg, editor, *Neural Networks and Natural Intelligence*. MIT Press, 1988.

[6] T. W. Calvert and A. Bruderlin. Goal-directed, dynamic animation of human walking. *Computer Graphics*, 23:233–242, 1989.

[7] J. Cassell et al. Animated conversation: Rule-based generation of facial expression, gesture and spoken intonation for multiple conversational agents. In *SIGGRAPH '94*, 1994.

[8] P. M. Fitts. The information capacity of the human motor system in controlling the amplitude of movement. *Journal of Experimental Psychology*, 47(6):381–391, 1954.

[9] S. Gibet and P.-F. Marteau. A self-organized model for the control, planning and learning of nonlinear multi-dimensional systems using a sensory feedback. *Applied Intelligence: The International Journal of Artificial Intelligence, Neural Network and Complex-Solving Technologies*, 4:337–349, 1994.

[10] M. Girard. Animal movement in computer animation. In *Making them move*, pages 209–232. Morgan Kaufmann, 1991.

[11] T. Lebourque. Synthèse de gestes en langue des signes. Technical report, LIMSI-CNRS, France, 1994.

[12] B. Moody. *La langue des signes. Histoire et Grammaire*. Ellipses, Paris, 1983.

[13] S. Prillwitz and R. Leven. *HAMNOSYS Version 2.0*. Signum Press, 1989.

[14] P. Viviani and M. Cenzato. Segmentation and coupling in complex movements. *Journal of Experimental Psychology*, 11:828–845, 1985.

Gesture Orientation and Trajectory Deformation in Three Dimensional Space

M. Ghafouri and F. Lestienne
Laboratoire de Biologie et Physiologie du Comportement,
Université Henri Poincaré, Vandoeuvre-Les-Nancy, France.

E-mail: lestienn@scbiol.u-nancy.fr
Telephone: +44 1382 344146 Fax: +44 1382 345509

Abstract

This work describes the sensorimotor performance of drawing simple geometrical figures (for example ellipses, squares and figures of eight) in the air using arm movements.

Right handed subjects were instructed to draw the figure with the tip of the index finger. These gestures were performed in standing position. Three conditions were examined: eye opened, eye closed and under visual guidance. The instruction given to the subjects was to execute the gesture in three different planes, sagittal, frontal and horizontal.

From our data it is evident that the figure is executed in a plane which is always rotated with respect to the requested reference plane. The figures also showed a clear deformation related to the distortion in its periodic components. The motor representation of the figure presents a minimal rotation and distortion in the sagittal plane, whereas the rotation and the distortion increase in the frontal and horizontal plane.

The nature of the distortion and the kinematic aspects of the gesture can be used as criterions for the gesture segmentation.

1 Introduction

The actual challenge in man-machine dialogue dedicated to the gestural command is to extend the sensorimotor capabilities of the human-computer interface to take into account the high degree of coordination involved in natural three dimensional gesture.

The conceptual framework which is on the basis of our present research arises from studies on postural activities [4, 3]. From our experiments it is possible to infer that the implementation of different postural tasks requires the knowledge of the state of many variables which cannot be directly signalled by specific receptors. These include the segment length, the sequence of the segment linkage, the position of the center of mass, the muscles torque and so on.

This paper describes research in progress on investigating the relation between figural and kinematic aspects of gesture involving arm movements performed in the three dimensional space [5]. These experiments were based on our previous studies concerning the performance of astronauts drawing ellipses in weightlessness with prescribed orientation [1].

In these "microgravity experiments" it was clear that the performances were similar to those obtained in the terrestrial condition. The form of the figures drawn was not actually elliptical. The ellipses were more or less distorted depending upon the plane of execution of the gesture. However we found that the tangential velocity of the arm movement covary with change of the radius of the curvature. Behaviorally, this relationship results in the so-called *Isogony Principle* [8]. which has been found for a large scope of drawing movements such as handwriting, scribbling and various simple geometrical forms mainly executed in a constrained working plane. More recently Soechting and Terzuolo [7] provided a kinematic analysis of human arm movement which underlie the production of continuous movements (such as drawing figures of eight and stars) in free space. They demonstrated that continuous movements are composed by unit segment and that tangential velocity was found to be inversely related to the curvature of the motion at the wrist.

In the first part of the paper, we will provide a more detailed description of the extend to which the figural aspect (curvature radius) is correlated with the kinematic property (tangential velocity). In the second part we will show the existence of:

- a deformation of the figure which is strongly related to the plane of execution of the figure and

- a rotation of the execution plane with respect to the reference plane.

2 Method

Twelve adult right-handed subjects (7 male and 5 female) volunteered for the experiments. They stood erect and were instructed to draw ellipses, squares and figures of eight in the air with the tip of the right index finger. The subjects were asked to maintain a stable posture and to draw the figures by using most of the possible range of arm motions which normally involved the shoulder, elbow and wrist articulations. The hand did not touch the trunk at any point. No restrictions were imposed on head and trunk movements. Theses figures were drawn in three planes: sagittal, frontal and horizontal (Figure 1).

Each subjects had to draw a series of 3 to 7 consecutive figures without interruption. The size of the figures was not strictly specified. However the length of the long axis of the ellipse was, on rule, 0.6–1 m, the ratio of long and short axis was about 2:1. The time of drawing one figure was 2–3 s. Three conditions were examined: eye opened, eye closed and under visual guidance. In this last condition, the elliptical movements were performed by following with the tip of the index finger the edge of a template. However the subjects were not allowed to touch the edge of the template.

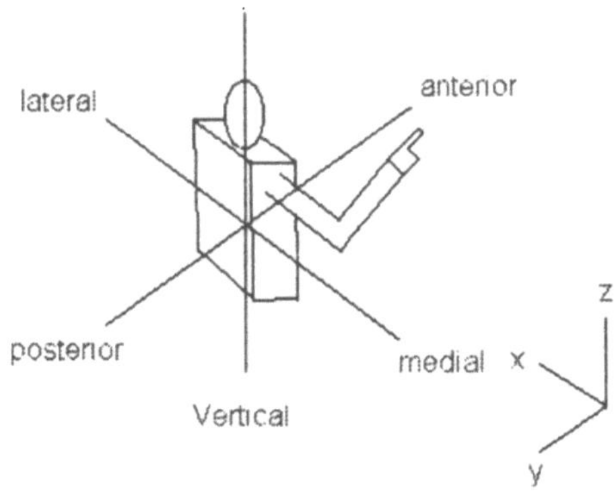

Figure 1: Orientation of the ellipses in relation with a cartesian coordinate system. Ellipses are drawn in the three different planes with long axis parallel or perpendicular to the longitudinal body axis (vertical axis). These planes are defined respectively by the vertical and latero-medial axis (frontal plane); the vertical and antero-posterior axis (sagittal plane); the antero-posterior and latero-medial axis (horizontal plane).

We recorded arm motion optoelectronically with the use of reflective markers 15×10^{-3} m in diameter placed over the shoulder, elbow, wrist. A special marker in the form of a thimble was put on the tip of the index finger. A set of three other markers was fixed on the chest along the midline of the body. A data station connected to a PC 486 DX2-66 synchronises a set of four 50–60 Hz CCD cameras with infrared stroboscopic light sources. The image of markers is digitized in real time by the data station. The location in the 3-D space of the centroid of each marker was computed with a spatial resolution of less than 10^{-3} m. After calibration of the optoelectronic system, we defined a cartesian X-Y-Z coordinate system aligned with laboratory referential. After recording, the three-dimensional trajectories were reconstructed by using Vicon software.

3 Results and discussion

3.1 Covariation of figural and kinematics parameters

3.1.1 General kinematic features

Figure 2 illustrates the basic finding with the help of one example: a square drawn in the frontal plane. On the left we plot the time course of the radius of curvature of the trajectory ($R(t)^{\frac{1}{3}}$) and the modulus of the tangential velocity ($V(t)$). On the right, numbers (from 1 to 7) are used to identify the relationship between the different components of the figure and the corresponding value of the time evolution of $R(t)$ and $V(t)$.

As in the case of free-hand gestures (handwriting, isolated letters, scribbles and so on) restricted to a working plane [8, 2], the relevant finding is the remarkable similarity between the time evolution of $R(t)$ and $V(t)$ observed during the free-arm gesture performed in three dimensional space.

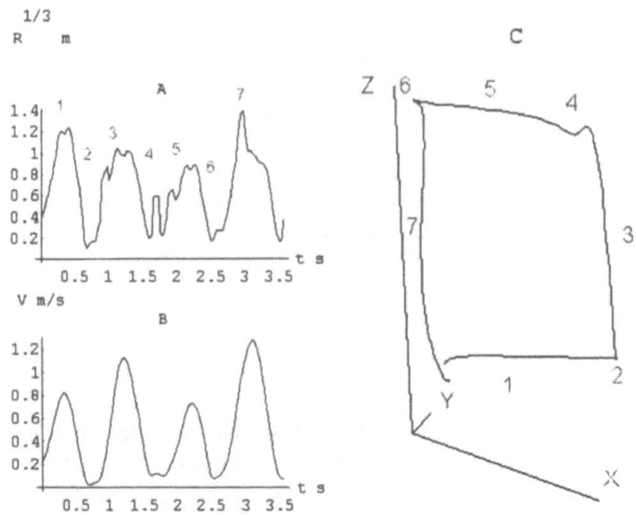

Figure 2: General kinematic and figural features of drawing square (Plots A, B, C) in a frontal plane.

3.1.2 Relation between figural and kinematic aspect of the movement

Figure 3 presents results from one subject who drew the ellipses in the three different planes with long axis parallel to the longitudinal, and latero-medial body axis (see Figure 1).

It is clear that a constraining principle exists whereby the figural and kinematic aspects of the gesture are reciprocally related. The relation between $R(t)$ and $V(t)$ can be expressed as a one-third power law of the curvature

$$V(t) = kR(t)^{\frac{1}{3}}$$

with $t_1 \leq t \leq t_2$, where we admit that the proportionality constant k may depend on the interval (t_1, t_2).

This covariation between figural and kinematic parameters of continuous gesture demonstrates the segmentation of the movement into well definited units of action [8, 6].

The relation between $R(t)$ and $V(t)$ is robust in the sense its holds even when the arm gesture is involved in the execution of a task of pointing to target in three dimensional space. In Figure 4 we show the trajectory of arm movement and the corresponding relation between $R(t)$ and $V(t)$ during a pointing task.

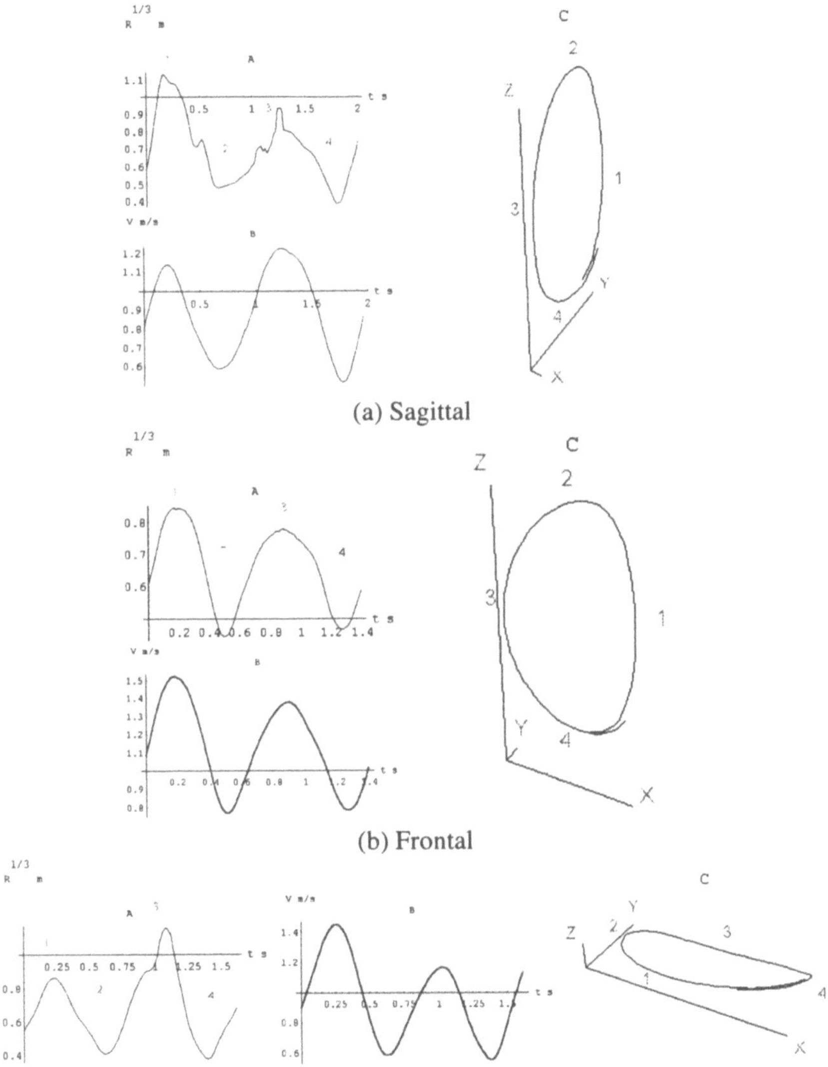

(a) Sagittal

(b) Frontal

(c) Horizontal

Figure 3: Plots of the time course of the radius of curvature of the trajectory $(R(t)^{\frac{1}{3}}$ and the tangential velocity $V(t))$ for one subject, drawing ellipses in different planes with long axis parallel to the latero-medial body axis.

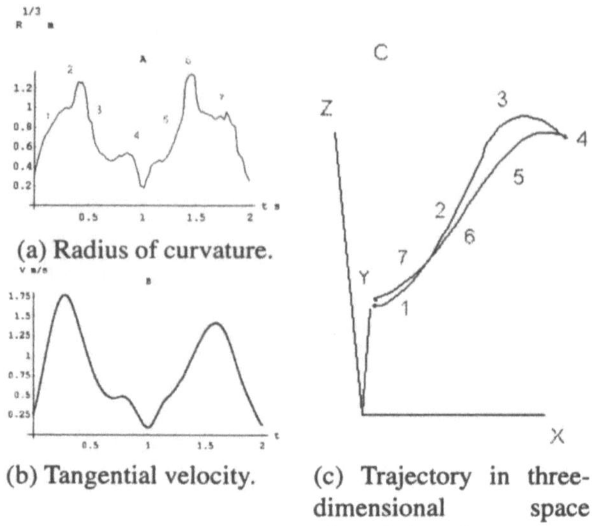

(a) Radius of curvature.

(b) Tangential velocity.

(c) Trajectory in three-dimensional space viewed from front.

Figure 4: Trajectory of arm movement during a pointing task. Numbers (from 1 to 7) indicate action units. The location of the target in cartesian coordinate system was $x = -0.286$ m (mediolateral axis), $y = +0.445$ m (anteroposterior axis) and $z = -0.012$ m (vertical axis). Lateral, anterior and upward directions are positive.

3.2 Figural aspect of the gesture: plane of motion and deformation

3.2.1 Plane of motion

Our data show that the figures are executed in a plane which is always rotated with respect to the requested reference plane: sagittal, frontal and horizontal planes. A dedicated algorithm, based on the best fit planar motion trajectory in least-square sense and adapted from [7], was used to determine how accurately the requested plane of motion of the trajectory of the figure was reproduced. We have chosen the planar elevation α and its azimuth β. Note that α and β are both zero when the motion of the index finger lies in the frontal plane, as in drawing on a black-board.

The rotation of the motion plane of the figures executed by the subjects relatively to the requested reference plane can be appreciated in Figure 3. For the sagittal plane (Figure 3a) : $\alpha = 0.6°$ and $\beta = 4°$, for the frontal plane (Figure 3b) : $\alpha = 0.7°$ and $\beta = 9°$ and for the horizontal plane (Figure 3c) : $\alpha = -78°$.

From this typical recording displayed on the above figure, it is possible, to propose a general rule concerning the rotation of the figures: the rotation is minimal for figures drawn in the sagittal plane and increases in the frontal and horizontal planes.

Why does the rotation of plane of the figures occur? This question will be taken in a further paper in which we stress that

- gravitational vertical plays a crucial role in elaborating a spatial reference and

- the worst performance of elderly population trained to produce elliptical figures was found when this population has to draw ellipses in the horizontal plane, the angles of rotation of the figure were increased by at least 40% relatively to the standard population.

3.2.2 Deformation

From our data it is evident that the figures drawn were often quite different from strictly geometrically-defined ellipses, squares and figures of eight. Concerning this first category of deformation, we will not go into the details in this paper. However, this deformation is much more important for the figures drawn in the sagittal plane comparatively to those drawn in the horizontal and frontal planes. The second category of deformation is in relation with the distortion of the figures. It is clear that the figures are not flat. For example the longitudinal ellipse has a little convexity (the apexes are shifted slightly forward in relation with the middle), and the tops can be displaced with respect to the bottom (ellipses slightly inclined forward or backward) (see Figure 3b). Considering that the deformations are related to distortion in periodic components of the trajectory, we have quantitively shown that the deformation is lower for the figures drawn in the sagittal plane than those produced in the two other planes. Finally, if we consider the distance D between the trajectory and the calculated plane of motion (see Section 3.2.1), Figure 5 reveals the similarity between the time evolution of $D(t)$ and $R(t)$.

4 Conclusion

From our results it is important to stress the existence of a more general constraining principle whereby the figural $R(t)$, the kinematic $V(t)$ parameters and the deformation represented by $D(t)$ are reciprocally related. These relationships could be an interesting support for proposing an extension of the segmentation concept of the movement into well definited units of action. This segmentation should be defined as a successive set of trajectory portions characterized by a covariation between $R(t), V(t)$ and $D(t)$ (Figure 5).

Acknowledgement

Supported by Institut National de Recherche et de Sécurité grant INRS 5961211 and by Centre National d'Etude Spatiale grant DAR 96/CNES/0225.

References

[1] V. Gurfinkel, F. Lestienne, Y. Levik, K. V. Popov, and L. Lefort. Egocentric references and human spatial orientation in microgravity. *Exp. Brain Res.*, 95(2):343–348, 1993.

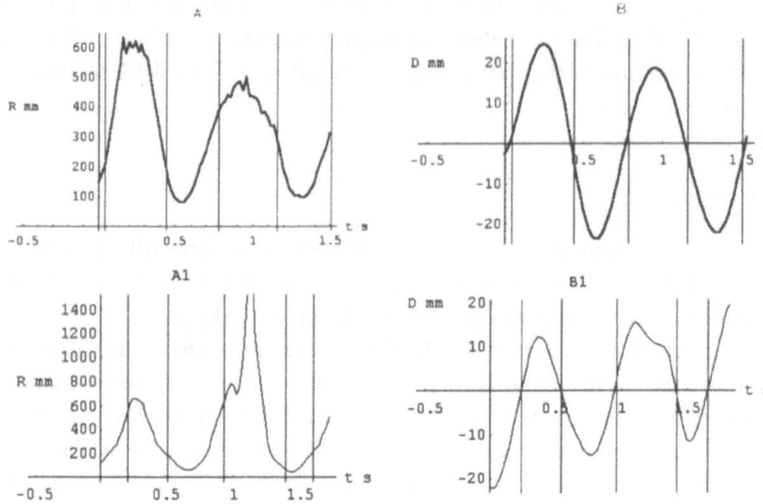

Figure 5: Segmentation of motion during the drawing of ellipses in the frontal (Plots A, B) and horizontal planes (Plots A1, B1), grid lines define segments bounds, *R* curvature radius, *D* trajectory distance to the calculated plane of motion.

[2] F. Lacquaniti, C. Terzuolo, and P. Viviani. The law relating the kinematics and figural aspects of drawing movements. *Acta Psychol.*, 54:115–130, 1983.

[3] F. Lestienne, M. Ghafouri, and F. Thullier. What does body configuration in microgravity tell us about the contribution of intra and extrapersonal frames? *Behav. Brain Res.*, 18(4):766–767, 1995.

[4] F. Lestienne and V. Gurfinkel. Postural activity in weightlessness: a dual process underlying adaptation to an unusual environment. *Trends in Neurosci.*, 11:359–363, 1988.

[5] F. Lestienne, V. S. Gurfinkel, C. Jeandel, and G. Ghafouri, M. andand Vançon. Production du geste graphique dans l'espace tri-dimensionnel: influence du vieillissement physiologique. In *Résumé des Communications, 2ème colloque de la société des neurosciences*, page H108, Lyon, 1995.

[6] A. B. Schwartz. Direct cortical representation of drawing. *Science*, 265:540–542, 1994.

[7] J. F. Soechting and C. Terzuolo. Organization of arm movements in three-dimensional space. *Neurosci.*, 23:53–61, 1987.

[8] P. Viviani and C. Terzuolo. Trajectory determines movement dynamics. *Neurosci.*, 7:431–437, 1982.

A Mathematical Model for Hand-Shape Analysis

R. J. Millar and G. F. Crawford

School of Computing and Mathematics, University of Ulster,
Jordanstown, Co. Antrim, Northern Ireland

E-mail: {rj.millar, gf.crawford}@ulst.ac.uk
Telephone: +44 1232 368155 Fax: +44 1232 366859

Abstract

A mathematical model of the human hand is presented. It models both the physical form and kinematic constraints of the fingers. An algorithm that takes as input six 3-dimensional coordinates, corresponding to the wrist and fingertip positions, and produces a geometric model of the hand is discussed. This algorithm uses the previously mentioned mathematical model. Results from an implementation of this algorithm are presented and discussed. The results show that fairly accurate geometric models of various hand-shapes can be produced very quickly using this algorithm. Critical analysis of the model and algorithm is undertaken and improvements suggested.

1 Introduction

Gestures and body language play an important role in human communication. Virtual reality and human-computer interaction researchers have also recognised the importance of this ability with regard to natural interfaces [5]. This has lead to the development and wide spread use of virtual reality gloves as a means of interacting with applications and virtual worlds. Many researchers have also used glove based approachs to interpret hand gestures [9, 3, 10, 7]. However virtual reality gloves are cumbersome, they restrict movement and their ability to recognise gestures accurately is directly related to their cost. These disadvantages have lead to recent interest in camera based systems. These systems removed the encumbrance factor and the hardware required is relatively cheap, however they introduce some interesting problems of their own. The most significant problem is the computational requirements placed on the system by the image processing tasks that must be undertaken to recognise hand gestures directly [8, 2, 1, 4, 11].

The human hand has twenty-one joints and fingertips (including the wrist), these joints/points must be located in 3-dimensional space in order to produce an accurate geometric model of the hand. This means that forty-two points must be located in a stereo image pair to produce an unambiguous model. A model can be constructed using one camera; this only requires the locating of twenty-one points (the length of the segments between joints must be known in this case), but the model must be iteratively fitted to the image because of the loss of the 3-dimensional data [2].

This paper presents a simple mathematical model of the hand and an algorithm that produces a geometric model of the hand from only six 3-dimensional points. The model is constructed from points and line segments and resembles a simple skeletal hand. The algorithm uses the position of the wrist, fingertips and thumb-tip as parameters and calculates the positions of the remaining fifteen joints. Locating the six points in space requires the locations of twelve points in a stereo image pair to be found, hence a large reduction in the image processing requirements of the system is realised. The system also has the advantage that the model gesture (i.e. the remaining fifteen points) can be found directly using the algorithm, no iterative fitting process is necessary. Lee and Kunii [6] present a hand model and algorithm which uses seven 3-dimensional points, however their algorithm requires an iterative process to fit the hand model. The inverse kinematics used in their model combined with the iterative process place a huge burden on processor time. The algorithm presented here has been designed with speed in mind and is computationally efficient.

2 The mathematical model

In order to produce an accurate geometric model, from limited data, a complex hand model must be used. If speed and efficiency are of importance then a simple model is preferable. Therefore, a balance must be reached between model complexity and speed required. The aim of this algorithm is to produce reasonable hand-shapes quickly, for this reason the model is simple but the complexity is still sufficient to produce recognisable hand shapes.

The model is presented in two parts. The first describes the physical aspects of the model (how it fits together), with little reference to movement constraints. The second part describes the kinematic (movement) aspects of the model.

2.1 Physical aspects

The mathematical model uses a simple skeletal model to represent the hand, see Figure 1. The hand is assumed to be constructed in a very simple manner. The main assumptions are:

1. Each finger is anchored at the wrist.

2. Each finger is constructed from four line segments.

3. All four segments lie on the same plane (they are co-planar).

4. The thumb originates at the wrist.

5. The thumb's first joint is anchored at a fixed point relative to the forefinger.

6. The thumb's last three line segments lie on the same plane.

7. The plane of the thumb segments is oriented such that it passes through the knuckle of the little finger.

8. The segment of each finger from the wrist to knuckle (referred to as palm segments) are co-planar.

9. The length of each line segment used to construct the hand is known.

10. The plane of each finger is perpendicular to the plane of the palm segments. See Figure 1.

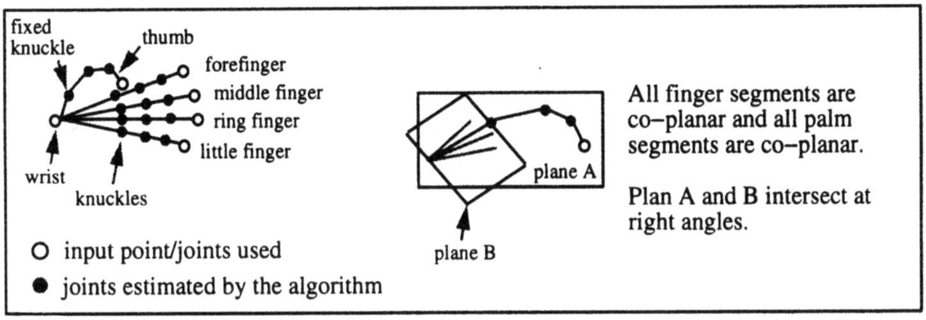

Figure 1: Physical aspects of the hand model

2.2 Kinematic aspects

The mathematical model also incorporates the kinematic aspects of the fingers in various ways. The following assumptions describe these aspects of the model.

1. The planes of the four fingers are evenly spaced, with an angle of approximately ten degrees between adjacent planes. This enables the orientation of the fingertip points with reference to the palm.

2. When a fingertip is required to be a particular distance from the wrist, there are corresponding maximum and minimum palm segment angles that define the range within which the finger will be able to reach this point, see Figure 2.

3. The middle and end joint movements of each finger are related. The angle produced by the end joint is approximately $\frac{2}{3}$ the angle produced by the finger's middle joint.

4. The middle and end joint movements of the thumb are related. The angle produced by the end joint and the thumb's middle joint are equal.

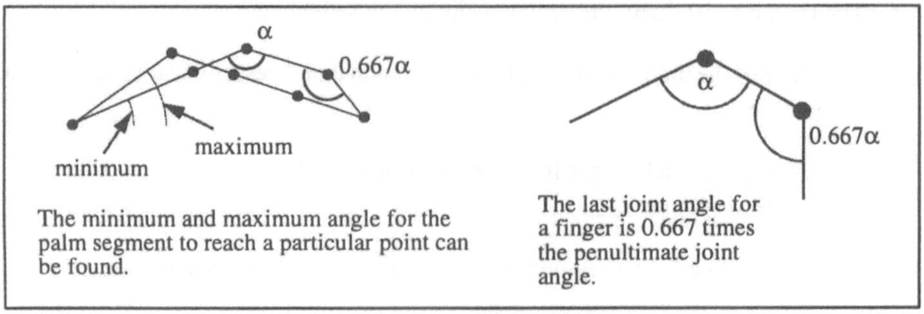

Figure 2: Movement constraints of model

The main disadvantage of this simple model with regard to its physical aspects is the offset location of the knuckles when certain hand-shapes are constructed. If we consider the location of the knuckle of the little finger when the fingers are straight and tight together we see the problem clearly. Figure 3 shows the hand-shape we are considering. Note that the knuckle position of the little finger varies greatly between the actual and that calculated by the model. This problem is unavoidable with this simple model construction, however changes to the model structure (a rigid minimum distance between knuckles) will greatly reduce the difference observed between the actual and calculated. The actual look of the output geometric hand is still recognisable, so no model refinement will be considered in this paper.

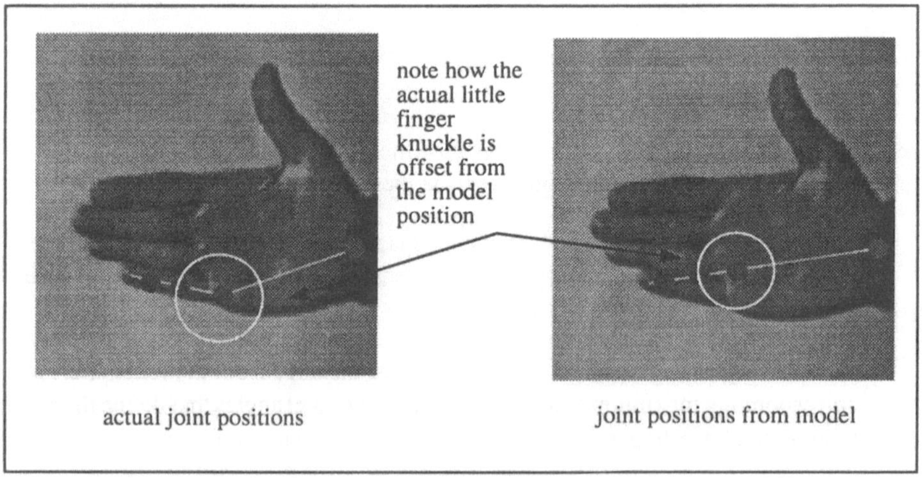

Figure 3: This shows the poor knuckle positioning with certain hand-shapes

A second problem associated with this simple model is that it does not consider the concave nature of the palm. The palm segment of the little finger produces most of this by subtending a lesser angle at the wrist than the other three finger palm segments. Future refinement of the model will consider this problem and attempt to redress it.

The model has the advantage that it is very simple. This enables the rapid analysis of hand gestures using a simple algorithm that does not resort to any form of iterative process to fit the model. This algorithm is discussed in detail in the next section.

3 The algorithm

The aim of the algorithm is to produce a geometric model of the hand, using the mathematical model discussed previously. The algorithm uses only six 3-dimensional coordinates (corresponding to the wrist position, the four fingertip positions and the thumbtip position). The use of this model means that the algorithm is very efficient, because no iterative fitting of the model is required.

The algorithm works in two stages. Let us define a pseudo data structure to hold the hand information, i.e. the joint and fingertip positions. Call this data structure *hand*, *hand* so that it can store all of the joint and fingertip positions. Now assume that the positions for the wrist and fingertips that are known (the parameters) have been assigned to hand. All joint positions that are not known are left unassigned. This means that initially *hand* will record the wrist and fingertip positions only.

3.1 Hand shape analysis algorithm

Firstly *hand* is translated and rotated so that the wrist is at the origin $(0,0,0)$ and the middle fingertip lies on the x axis. Now *hand* is rotated about the x axis until the fingertip positions are ideal for assumed palm orientation (it is assumed that the palm plane is oriented so that it intersects with the z axis). This is achieved by using a procedure associated with the first physical aspect of the model.

- The planes of the four fingers are evenly spaced, with an angle of approximately ten degrees between adjacent planes.

- In order to achieve this the following error measurement is minimised. Firstly the hand is translated so that the wrist is at the origin and the hand rotated until the middle finger lies on the x axis.

$$error_j = \sum_{i=1}^{4}(tan^{-1}(z_{i,j}/x_{i,j}) - ideal_i)^2$$

  $j = 0..360$, $z_{i,j}$ is the z ordinate of fingertip i at rotation j around x axis and $x_{i,j}$ is the x ordinate of fingertip i at rotation j around x axis. For the right hand $ideal_i$ is (-10,0,10,20) degrees. The value of j which produces the minimum $error_j$ is now assumed to be the angle through which the hand must be rotated so that the finger planes are perpendicular to the xz plane.

Now that the fingertips are positioned the maximum and minimum angles associated with each can be found. This is done by using a procedure associated with the second and third kinematic aspect of the model.

- When a fingertip is required to be a particular distance from the wrist, there are corresponding maximum and minimum palm segment angles that define the range within which the finger will be able to reach this point.

  The middle and end joint movements of each finger are related. The angle produced by the end joint is approximately $\frac{2}{3}$ the angle produced by the finger's middle joint.

- The second and third kinematic assumptions enable a palm segment angle range to be found. The following procedures are used to find the minimum and maximum angles for the palm segments.

  - *Maximum angle*
    The maximum angle can be calculated by finding the angle α (in degrees) that produces the required distance from wrist to fingertip. The following algorithm is used:

    $$\alpha_i = -1$$

    do

    $$\alpha_i = \alpha_i + 1$$

    $$x = palm\_length_i * cos(\alpha_i), y = palm\_length_i * sin(\alpha_i)$$

    $$check_{distance} = \sqrt{(fingertip\_distance_i - x)^2 + y^2)}$$

    while

    $$check_{distance} < finger\_length_i$$

    x, y, $check_{distance}$ are all variables, $palm\_length_i$ is the length of palm segment for the finger, $fingertip\_distance_i$ is the distance between wrist and fingertip i, $finger\_length_i$ is the length of finger i when straight.

    The value of i on exit from this loop provides the maximum value for the palm segment angle.

  - *Minimum angle*
    The minimum angle uses a very similar procedure.

    $$\alpha_i = -1$$

    do

    $$\alpha_i = \alpha_i + 1$$

    $$x = palm\_length_i + first\_finger\_segment_i$$
    $$+ second\_finger\_segment_i * cos(\alpha_i)$$
    $$+ third\_finger\_segment_i * cos(1.7 * \alpha_i)$$
    $$y = second\_finger\_segment_i * sin(\alpha_i)$$
    $$+ third\_finger\_segment_i * sin(1.7 * \alpha_i)$$
    $$check_{distance} = \sqrt{(x^2 + y^2)}$$

while

$$check_{distance} > finger\_distance_i$$

The value of i on exit from this loop provides the minimum value for the palm segment angle.

The maximum and minimum angles for each finger are now used to find an overall palm angle for the complete palm (remembering that the palm segments are co-planar and must have the same angle).

Now that the palm angle is known the knuckle positions can be found. This is achieved by simply rotating each palm segment through the palm angle and recording the final coordinates.

To calculate the angles of the finger joints the third kinematic aspect is used again.

The middle and end joint movements of each finger are related. The angle produced by the end joint is approximately $\frac{2}{3}$ the angle produced by the finger's middle joint.

The distance from knuckle to fingertip is calculated and the appropriate angle found using the following procedure.

$$\beta_i = -1$$

do

$$\beta_i = \beta_i + 1$$

$$x = first\_finger\_segment_i + second\_finger\_segment_i * cos(\beta_i)$$
$$+third\_finger\_segment_i * cos(1.7 * \beta_i)$$
$$y = second\_finger\_segment_i * sin(\beta_i)$$
$$+third\_finger\_segment_i * sin(1.7 * \beta_i)$$
$$check_{distance} = \sqrt{}(x^2 + y^2)$$

while

$$check_{distance} > knuckle\_fingertip\_distance_i$$

On exit from this loop β_i is the angle of the middle joint for finger i. The end joint is then $\frac{2\beta_i}{3}$.

The thumb angles are calculated by referring to the fifth aspect of the model's physical properties.

The thumb's first joint is anchored at a fixed point relative to the fore finger.

This enables the distance between the thumb's anchor knuckle and tip to be calculated. The angles required for the thumb to reach this position can then be found. A procedure similar to that above is used, but the relationship between the thumb's last and second joint is that defined by the fourth kinematic aspect.

The middle and end joint movements of the thumb are related. The angle produced by the end joint and the thumb's middle joint are equal.

Finally, all of the calculated joint angles are used to find the remaining joint positions in 3-dimensional space. The geometric hand model is now complete and can be displayed using a simple graphics program. The implementation discussed here, uses a simple graphics program which displays the hand model using line segments of different colours.

3.2 Advantages and disadvantages of the algorithm

The main disadvantages of the algorithm are due to the simplistic hand model used. The knuckle positions calculated by the algorithm may be offset, depending on the particular hand-shape being analysed, see Figure 3. The constraint that the fingertips lie on a plane which is perpendicular to the palm and which passes through the wrist, is not strictly accurate. The inaccuracies introduced by this assumption cause problems with the algorithm but again it is dependent on the hand-shape being analysed. These problems can be overcome by modifications to the mathematical model in both its physical and kinematic aspects. However the implementation demonstrates that this simple model, with all its failures, is sufficient to produce fairly good geometric representations of hand-shapes.

The algorithm has two main advantages. It requires only six 3-dimensional coordinates as parameters and so the actual image processing required is significantly less than most other camera based gesture recognition systems. It would seem reasonable, considering the work of Rehg and Kanade [8], that image processing algorithms will be able to extract these six points using an unadorned hand. It also requires very little processor time. The simplicity of the model's physical and kinematic assumptions mean that the missing joints are directly derivable, as described above. This process requires no iterative fitting procedure and so is very efficient.

3.3 Input

The system requires six points, corresponding to the wrist, four fingertips and thumb-tip position in 3-dimensional space. This data can be extracted from a stereo image pair. The points must be located in both images, requiring the locating of twelve points (six in each image). At present this is achieved by simply viewing the images and selecting the fingertip positions by eye. The twelve 2D points can then be used to calculate the six 3-dimensional points corresponding to the wrist, fingertips and thumb-tip position in space. Figure 4 shows a typical hand-shape and its corresponding 3-dimensional coordinates.

4 Results

The implementation produces a skeletal model of the hand using points and lines. This model is presented in three orientations, side elevation, top view and front elevation.

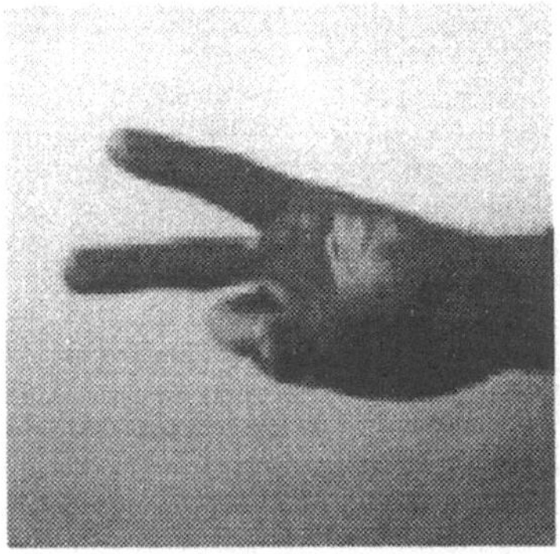

a typical hand–shape

	X	Y	Z
wrist :	0	0	0
thumb :	80	0	0
fore :	144	50	-37
mid :	157	60	0
ring :	82	10	13
little :	71	10	30

The above data shows the x,y,z coordinates extracted for this particular hand–shape.

Figure 4: A typical hand-shape and its corresponding coordinates

Each finger and thumb is colour coded, blue to cyan, to aid identification and the palm segments are shown in red.

In order to test the correctness of the algorithm in building geometric hand models, several test hand-shapes were used. Figure 5 shows six test hand-shapes along with the corresponding geometric model produced using the algorithm.

All results are recognisable as the input hand-shape. The problems caused by the incorrect positioning of the finger knuckles are very obvious in cases 2 and 6. In both cases the knuckle positions are closer together than is physically possible. Another consequence of this problem can be seen in case 1. The little finger of the input image is straight. However the output model has a bent little finger. This is also due to the offset knuckle problem. The distance from model knuckle to model fingertip is less than it should be, because the model knuckle is offset, and so the model must bend the little finger slightly in order to fit it between knuckle and fingertip location.

The knuckle offset problem seems to be the main cause of error in the algorithm. It should be possible to remove this by using a more realistic model of the hand. Future work will attempt to incorporate a more realistic model into the algorithm.

5 Conclusion

This paper has presented a simple mathematical model of the human hand. The physical aspects of the model are very simple. The model assumes that the fingers originate at the wrist and are constructed from four line segments which are co-planar. The kinematic aspects are more complex, it considers the relationship between finger joint angles (particularly the last and middle joint of each finger).

A simple algorithm, which uses the previously mentioned model, is also presented. Solutions to this model are sought with reference to only six parameters, the wrist, fin-

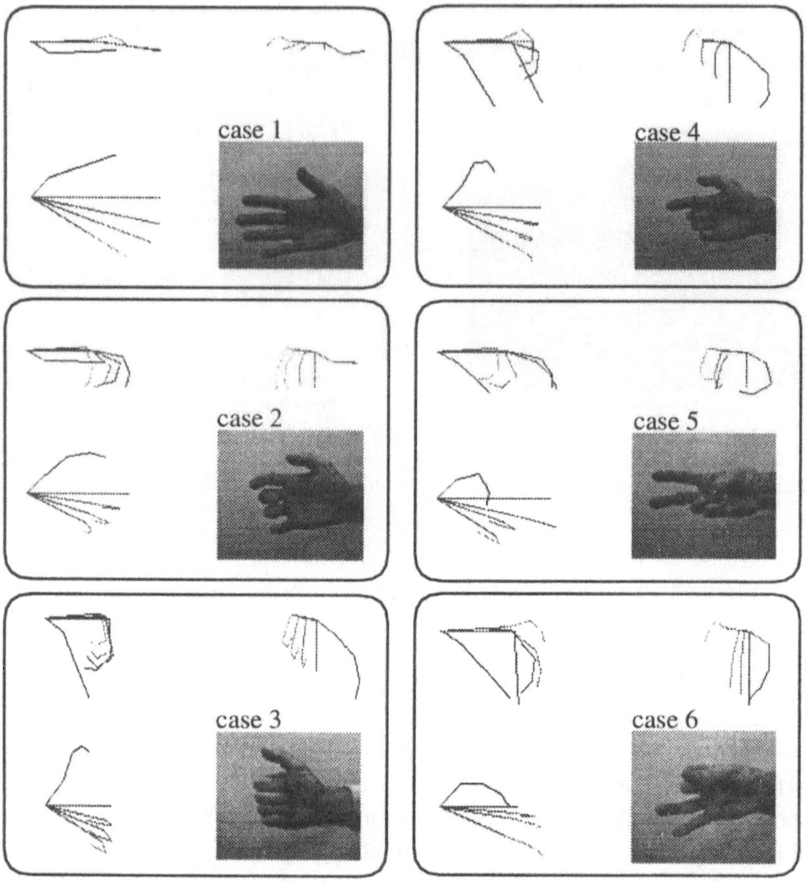

Figure 5: Results for the algorithm for six different hand-shapes

gertips and thumb tip position in 3-dimensional space. This small number of parameters means that image processing costs in a complete system are kept relatively small. The simplicity of the model means that the algorithm can be used to directly calculate the remaining model joint positions, without having to resort to an iterative fitting process. This helps to keep processor cost to a minimum.

The results obtained from an implementation of the algorithm are shown. These show that the algorithm produces reasonably accurate hand-shape representations, and that the processing time is very small.

Future work will incorporate a more complex physical model into the algorithm and refine the kinematic properties of the model to better match those of the hand. A better model rendering routine may also be added to the final algorithm to produce a more realistic hand.

The implication that a geometric model of a hand can be built with reference to only the wrist, fingertips and thumb-tip positions, is interesting. It implies that a hand-shape could be interpreted by examining these six points only. This may prove to be a very useful approach in gesture recognition algorithms.

References

[1] C. Charayaphan and A. Marble. Image processing system for interpreting motion in American Sign Language. *Journal of Biomedical Engineering*, 14:419–425, Sept. 1992.

[2] B. Dorner and E. Hagen. Towards an American Sign Language interface. *Artificial Intelligence Review*, 8:235–253, 1994.

[3] S. S. Fels. Building adaptive interfaces with neural networks: The Glove-Talk pilot study. Technical Report CRG-TR-90-1, University of Toronto, Toronto, Canada, 1990.

[4] C. Huang, C. Lien, and P. Lai. Chinese Sign Language interpretation through motion and shape analysis. In *ICIP '92 Proceedings*, pages 576–580, 1992.

[5] M. Lacy. Artificial laboratories. *AI Magazine*, 1989.

[6] J. Lee and T. Kunii. Model-based analysis of hand posture. *IEEE Computer Graphics and Applications*, pages 77–86, 1995.

[7] E. Ohira, H. Sagawa, T. Sakiyama, and M. Ohki. A segmentation method for sign language recognition. *IEICE Transactions on Informations and Systems*, E78-D(1):49–57, 1995.

[8] J. Rehg and T. Kanade. Digiteyes: Vision-based hand tracking for human-computer interaction. In *Proceedings of the IEEE workshop on Motion of Non-rigid Bodies*, pages 16–21, 1994.

[9] T. Takahashi and F. Kishino. Hand gesture coding based on experiments using a hand gesture interface device. *SIGCHI Bulletin*, 23:67–74, Apr. 1991.

[10] P. Vamplew and A. Adams. The SLARTI system: Applying artificial neural networks to sign language recognition. In *Proceedings of the 7th Artificial Neural Network conf. on technology for persons with disabilities*, pages 575–579, 1992.

[11] E. Wilson and G. Anspach. Neural networks for sign language translation. In *Proceedings of the SPIE – The International Society for Optical Engineering*, volume 1965, pages 589–599, 1993.

Discussion

The workshop had clearly demonstrated that progress was being made in the development of techniques for gesture recognition but an open question was what applications are particularly suited to gestural interaction. Is there a particular application or class of applications which will convince people that it is worth using gestural interaction?

One suggestion was that people with physical disabilities which prevent them from using conventional interfaces might be able to use gestures. Someone else suggested that he would like to be able to control his television by gesture.

A possible attraction of gestural interaction is that it is natural-language-independent and therefore might be used internationally without need for translation. However, the situation might not be that simple because cultural differences lead to different natural forms of gesture and hence might be said to not be universal.

Gestures have a part to play in high intensity applications which might encompass many different channels and use of different parts of the body, such as robot control.

Caution was advised with regard to attempting to apply gesture too widely. In particular, gesture seems inappropriate when small, precise movements are required. It is important to use the appropriate input device. For instance, the mouse is essentially a means for communicating the user's focus to the application and it is good at doing that, but if one tries to draw a circle with a mouse, for instance, it does not come out very circular.

A lot of discussion centred around the definition of gesture and in that light there was the suggestion that there already exist interfaces which use gestures in that mouse input is a form of gesture, that it is just a matter of how the gestures are captured.

The scope of the workshop and related work was questioned in that some deaf people would resent the suggestion that sign language is a form of gestural communication. Sign language is a natural language in its own right. It was agreed that it would be appropriate in future to refer to gestures and sign languages.

It was agreed that the term 'gesture' did cover quite a broad range, but that it was better to be inclusive, to encourage people with different perspectives on gesture to talk to each other and to share and swap ideas.

Perhaps gestures are part of something broader, just one of the non-verbal channels that can accompany speech. On the other hand, it was suggested that to try to separate gestures into those which are used subconsciously to accompany speech and those which are intentional – such as sign language – is naive.

Another definition which was proposed was that gestures encompass all the visual communication channels which accompany speech. The counter argument was this would exclude the use of sign languages by deaf-blind people - but then there is a suggestion that this is not gestural interation but something tactile.

A taxonomy has been developed in Grenoble, whereby gestures are categorized as:

- semiotic (e.g. pointing)
- echoic
- epistemic (e.g. fumbling for a light switch.)

It was also reported that David MacNeil in Chicago had developed a taxonomy of gestures used in accompaniment to speech.

A final question addressed was whether the workshop should be followed up, and if so how. There was universal agreement that there should be a similar event in the future. The topic should be kept as broad and indeed care should be taken to encourage the participation of sign linguists. Sponsorship might be sought and suggested sponsors were the IEE, the British Machine Vision Association and the British Computer Society. It was felt important not to rely on any one of the organizations so that the event would become biased to any one of them and their objectives.

Another form of collaboration which was suggested was the sharing of data. A database of output from as many devices as possible would allow different researchers to compare their algorithms without having to get hold of a variety of gloves. The data from the York Datawear could not be shared in this way because of a confidentiality agreement with the manufacturer, but apart from that Phil Harling said that the group could 'consider it done'. [1]

[1] This has now been achieved: `http://peipa.essex.ac.uk/gesture/`

Index

MIX
Papier aus verantwortungsvollen Quellen
Paper from responsible sources
FSC® C105338

If you have any concerns about our products,
you can contact us on
ProductSafety@springernature.com

In case Publisher is established outside the EU,
the EU authorized representative is:
Springer Nature Customer Service Center GmbH
Europaplatz 3, 69115 Heidelberg, Germany

Printed by Libri Plureos GmbH
in Hamburg, Germany